Contents

Contributors	v
Introduction: Broken Government? *Iwan Morgan*	1
1. 'Hail Gridlock'? Hamiltonian energy, Madisonian institutions and American dissensus *Andrew Rudalevige*	11
2. What's wrong with Congress and what should be done about it? *James A. Thurber*	33
3. Singularity, separation and sharing: Richard Neustadt's lessons for politicians and political scientists *Nigel Bowles*	59
4. Tenure reform and presidential power: the single six-year term proposal *Niall A. Palmer*	77
5. The politics of the US Budget: a metaphor for broken government *Iwan Morgan*	101
6. Losing voice, losing trust: the partisan dynamics of public evaluations of government in an era of polarisation *Brian F. Schaffner and John A. Clark*	123
7. Two years of achievement and strife: the Democrats and the Obama presidency, 2009–10 *Alex Waddan*	141
8. The rise of the Tea Party movement and American governance *Edward Ashbee*	163

Broken Government?
American Politics in the Obama Era

Edited by

Iwan Morgan and Philip John Davies

© Institute for the Study of the Americas, University of London, 2012

British Library Cataloguing-in-Publication Data
A catalogue record for this book is available from the British Library

ISBN 978-1-908857-02-6

Institute for the Study of the Americas
School of Advanced Study
University of London
Senate House
London WC1E 7HU

Telephone: 020 7862 8870
Fax: 020 7862 8886

Email: americas@sas.ac.uk
Web: www.americas.sas.ac.uk

Cover images: Piotr Krzeslak/Shutterstock.com, imagedj/Shutterstock.com, Tim Mainiero/Shutterstock.com

Contributors

Edward Ashbee is associate professor in the Centre for Business and Politics at Copenhagen Business School, Denmark. A specialist on socioeconomic issues, his publications include: *The Bush Administration, Sex and the Moral Agenda* (2007); *The Politics, Economics and Culture of Mexican-US Migration: Both Sides of the Border* (2007); and *The US Economy Today* (2010); and numerous articles in journals such as *Political Quarterly*, *Parliamentary Affairs* and *Society*.

Nigel Bowles is director of the Rothermere American Institute, Oxford University, and Honour Balfour Fellow in Politics at St Anne's College, Oxford. He has written widely on US politics, including: *The White House and Capitol Hill: The Politics of Presidential Persuasion* (1987); and *Nixon's Business: Authority and Power in Presidential Politics* (2005), which was awarded the American Politics Group's Richard E. Neustadt prize for 2006. He is also the author of a very popular text: *The Government and Politics of the United States* (1993, 1998).

John A. Clark is professor of political science and chair of the Political Science department at Western Michigan University. His research interests have focused on party politics, particularly with reference to the South. He is the co-editor of *Party Organization and Activism in the South* (1998), winner of the Southern Political Science Association's V.O. Key Prize for best book on Southern politics in 1999, and *Southern Political Party Activists* (2005). He has also authored or co-authored over 20 chapters and articles in scholarly journals, like the *American Political Science Review* and *Political Research Quarterly*.

Philip John Davies is professor of American Studies and director of the British Library's Eccles Centre for American Studies. He is the chair of the European Association of American Studies and former chair of both the American Politics Group and the British Association of American Studies. A specialist on US elections, on which he has written numerous books, he has also co-edited a number of studies with Iwan Morgan, including *America's Americans: Population Issues in US Politics and Society* (2007); *The Federal Nation: Perspectives on American Federalism* (2008); and *Assessing George W. Bush's Legacy: The Right Man?* (2010).

Iwan Morgan is professor of US Studies, head of US programmes and director of the United States Presidency Centre at the Institute of the Americas,

University College London. He is also chair of the executive committee of the Historians of the Twentieth Century United States. A specialist on budget policy, he has authored numerous studies on this topic, including: *Eisenhower versus 'the Spenders': The Eisenhower Administration, the Democrats and the Budget, 1953–60* (1990); *Deficit Government: Taxing and Spending in Modern America* (1995); and *The Age of Deficits: Presidents and Unbalanced Budgets from Jimmy Carter to George W. Bush* (University Press of Kansas, 2009), awarded the American Politics Group's Richard E. Neustadt prize in 2010.

Niall Palmer is lecturer in politics and history at Brunel University. He is the author of *The New Hampshire Primary and the Presidential Election Process* (1988); *The Twenties in America: Politics and History* (2006); and the *Dictionary of American Diplomacy* (2010), as well as scholarly articles in numerous journals, including *Presidential Studies Quarterly*. He holds a visiting fellowship at the New Hampshire Institute of Politics.

Andrew Rudalevige is professor of political science at Bowdoin College in Brunswick, Maine. He served as a visiting fellow in Princeton in 2004–05 and as visiting professor at the University of East Anglia in 2007–09, where he directed Dickinson College's study abroad programme in the United Kingdom. His authored and co-edited books include: *Managing the President's Program: Presidential Leadership and Legislative Policy Formulation* (2002), winner of the American Politics Association's Richard E. Neustadt Prize; *The New Imperial Presidency: Renewing Presidential Power after Watergate* (2005); *The George W. Bush Legacy* (2008); and *The Obama Presidency: First Appraisals* (2011). He also has practical experience of politics and government, having worked in state and local politics in his home state of Massachusetts.

Brian Schaffner is associate professor of political science at the University of Massachusetts, Amherst. His research focuses on public opinion, campaigns and elections, political parties, and legislative politics. In addition to being a regular contributor to the Pollster.com, he has published over 20 journal articles and is the author of *Politics, Parties, and Elections in America*, 7th ed. (2010).

James A. Thurber is university distinguished professor of government and director of the Center for Congressional and Presidential Studies (which he founded in 1979) at American University, Washington DC. He has written extensively on Congress — particularly on budgeting, ethics, institutional reform, congressional-presidential relations and congressional elections. He is a fellow of the National Academy of Public Administration. His many single-authored and co-authored publications include: *Campaign Warriors: Political Consultants in Elections* (2000); *Crowded Airwaves: Campaign Advertising in*

Elections (2000); *The Battle for Congress: Consultants, Candidates, and Voters* (2001); *Congress and the Internet* (2002); and *Rivals for Power: Presidential-Congressional Relations*, 4th ed. (2009). He was principal investigator of a campaign conduct study, financed by a seven-year grant from the Pew Charitable Trusts, and of a four-year study of lobbying and ethics for the Committee for Economic Development. He has also worked on four reorganisation efforts for the US House and US Senate since 1976. He also served as legislative assistant for Senator Hubert Humphrey (D-MN), Senator William Brock (R-TN), Senator Adlai Stevenson III (D-IL), and Representative David Obey (D-WI), and worked on ethics and lobbying reforms with Senator Barack Obama (D-IL).

Alex Waddan is senior lecturer in politics and American studies at the University of Leicester. He has published widely on American politics, including *The Politics of Social Welfare: The Collapse of the Centre and the Rise of the Right* (1997), *Clinton's Legacy: A New Democrat in Governance* (2001), and (with Daniel Beland), *The Politics of Policy Change: Welfare, Medicare, and Social Security Reform in the United States* (2011), and has published articles in numerous journals, including *Political Science Review*.

Abbreviations

ACA	Affordable Care Act
ANES	American National Election Study
ARRA	American Recovery and Reinvestment Programme
BoB	Bureau of the Budget
CBO	Congressional Budget Office
CBPP	Center on Budget Policy and Priorities
CREEP	Committee to Re-Elect the President
DOMA	Defense of Marriage Act
FY	Fiscal Year
GDP	Gross Domestic Product
GOP	Grand Old Party, i.e. the Republicans
HLOGA	Honest Leadership and Open Government Act
LDA	Legislative Disclosure Act
NCFRR	National Commission on Fiscal Responsibility
NRCC	National Republican Congressional Committee
NRSE	National Republican Senatorial Committee
PAC	Political Action Committee
PPACA	Patient Protection and Affordable Care Act
RNC	Republican National Committee
TARP	Troubled Assets Relief Program
TUTH	Tuesday to Thursday Club

Introduction
Broken Government?[1]

Iwan Morgan

Barack Obama's election as president in 2008 generated widespread hope that the United States was entering a new era whereby government, in an inversion of Ronald Reagan's famous inaugural address dictum, would be the solution to the nation's manifold problems amidst the worst economic downturn since the Great Depression. The Obama election slogan — *YES WE CAN* — had seemingly voiced a mood of hope that new leadership would put right what had gone wrong with America. Anticipating a new era of government activism, some commentators read the death rites on 'The Age of Reagan', the post-1980 rightward anti-statist trend of American politics. Within a short time, however, *YES WE CAN* gave way to *NO WE CAN'T* as America's government became enmeshed in gridlock and political polarisation.

Although the Democrats held substantial majorities in both houses of the 111th Congress, the many points of veto and obstruction in the legislative process allowed the Republican minority considerable traction in opposing what it labelled his socialist programme of big government. Despite early legislative success in enacting a $787 billion three-year economic stimulus to help lift the economy out of recession, the 44th president had to fight hard and make significant concessions to get other parts of his agenda onto the statute book. In particular, it took well over a year to secure passage of a comprehensive health-insurance plan, his banner campaign pledge. Initially hopeful of securing some bipartisan congressional support for his programme in the difficult economic times, Obama found himself wholly dependent on Democratic votes. Adding to his problems, Republican capture of the late Edward Kennedy's Senate seat in the Massachusetts special election of early 2010 denied his party the supermajority needed to limit filibuster in the upper chamber.

---

1 This volume is based on a conference held at the British Library in December 2010. The co-editors thank the BL's Eccles Centre for American Studies, the Institute for the Study of the Americas (ISA), the American Politics Group, the Political Studies Association and the United States Embassy for their financial assistance in making this venture possible. As ever, they are grateful to Kate Bateman and Jean Petrovic of the Eccles Centre and Olga Jimenez of ISA for their efficiency in the administration of the conference.

The intensification of political polarisation in Washington paralleled the growing partisan divide in the electorate. Giving the lie to the belief that the Age of Reagan was over, the emergence of the Tea Party movement proved that conservatism was alive and kicking at grassroots level, thereby stiffening Republican resolve to resist Obama. With its help, the GOP[2] made huge gains in the midterm elections of 2010, capturing 63 seats to take control of the House of Representatives, the largest advance by any party since 1938, and truncating the Democratic majority in the Senate through a net gain of six seats. As 2010 came to an end, polls showed that self-identified conservatives had overtaken moderates as the largest opinion bloc among the American public.

The first year of the 112th Congress in 2011 ranked among the most rancorous and divisive legislative sessions since the Civil War and Reconstruction era. With the Republican House and the Democratic Senate finding little scope for compromise, America experienced divided government in the fullest sense of the term. With his opponents openly declaring their intention to make him a one-term president, Obama had little success in deploying the resources of presidential leadership to break the deadlock. The normal give-and-take of politics gave way to a new brinkmanship in which the Democrats were usually the first to blink. Extensive wrangling over the budget nearly produced a government shutdown in April until the president and his party agreed to Republican demands for spending cutbacks. A repeat performance over a normally routine increase in the national debt ceiling nearly resulted in America defaulting on its interest payment obligations in August, an impasse only broken through another Democratic climbdown to accept GOP demands for substantial expenditure cuts. In a final re-run of the gridlock politics of 2011, disagreement over the one-year extension of stimulus measures deemed necessary by many analysts to keep the economic recovery on track produced only a two-month prolongation in December. On this occasion, however, the Democrats held fast against making concessions to obtain this. At year's end *The Economist* predicted more of the same in the next session: 'Mr. Obama will probably find Republicans no more disposed to compromise on taxes or anything else in 2012 than in 2011' (2011, p. 32).

In these circumstances the 'broken' descriptor became increasingly attached to American government. Some on the right-of-centre of the political spectrum employed it (Frum 2011; Fukuyama 2011). More commonly it was the adjective of choice for moderates such as former vice president Al Gore, current US Senator Jon Tester (D-Montana) and liberals like political commentator Jeffrey Sachs (Webster 2011; Flandro 2012; Sachs 2009, 2010). Debating whether American government was broken became a favourite topic not only for the

---

2 Republican Party (Grand Old Party is one of its nicknames).

media but also the academy. Cable news channel CNN, for example, ran a series of electronic op-eds on the question, 'Why is our government so broken?' *The Economist* had initially scoffed at such talk, preferring to put the blame for gridlock on the inadequacies of presidential leadership. 'It is not so much that America is ungovernable', one of this eminent journal's editorials proclaimed, 'as that Mr. Obama has done a lousy job of winning over Republicans and independents to the causes he favours' (2010). In the wake of the intensified gridlock of 2011, however, it launched an international debate among readers on the motion, 'This house believes that America's political system is broken.' The American people had seemingly made up its mind on this score already. Polls in the fall of 2011 showed huge majorities — more than four out of every five respondents, an all-time low — expressing distrust in US government to do what was right most of the time (Borger 2011; Gallup 2011).

This volume adds its voice to the debate on whether American government is broken and, if so, what can be done to fix it. The contributors have not approached the question with the pre-set idea that the answer to the first question is in the affirmative. They have borne in mind that the founders created a system of government with the deliberate intention of facilitating institutional competition and preventing single-branch domination. In the light of this, the gridlock of the Obama era might appear to be a fulfilment rather than a perversion of their aim. Moreover, if there is polarisation in Obama's America, this is hardly unprecedented in modern times. Labelled a period of new civil war by some historians, the 1960s witnessed considerable internal dissension over civil rights, the Vietnam War, and expansion of government programmes that occasioned not only peaceful mass protest but also violence and assassination (Isserman and Kazin 2000). Moreover, there was dissonance aplenty in the 1970s, 1980s and 1990s that should not be forgotten when implicitly viewing the Obama era as somehow uniquely discordant. Finally, the view of many right-wingers that American politics has not become dysfunctional simply because the Republicans are blocking the proposals of a Democratic president cannot be dismissed out of hand. In their opinion, the broken-government scenario is the nonsensical bleating of liberals who overlook how a Democratic House obstructed a Republican president in pursuit of his conservative agenda in the 1980s and a Democratic president thwarted a Republican Congress bent on fulfilling the conservative mandate gained from the 1994 midterm elections.

Andrew Rudalevige opens with an analysis of the contrasts between the expectations of one of the founding theorists of the Constitution and the present condition of American government. In '"Hail Gridlock"; Hamiltonian energy, Madisonian institutions, and American dissensus', he examines how Alexander Hamilton anticipated that the Madisonian system of separate institutions sharing power could achieve *energy* in governance to conduct its business with *dispatch, method and system*. In his assessment, the divisiveness of the Obama era is a worrying deviation from this vision rather than a healthy case of institutional check-and-balance. Instead of the Constitution abolishing factions by encouraging the pursuit *of the general welfare*, as Hamilton anticipated, recent developments show that under certain circumstances it empowers parties to become factions that are not representative of the broader nation. The solution, in Rudalevige's opinion, is likely to come, not from a single leader — even if a new FDR somehow emerged — or institutional reform, but from demographic change that will dilute present-day societal divisions. The challenge facing the US 'in the short-term will be to get to that long-term', a process that will depend on re-engaging the American people with politics as the pursuit of the common good rather than the benefit of particular interests.

The next section of the book examines the problems of governance within the American polity. It begins with an examination of the legislature, which constantly receives the lowest popular approval ratings — fewer than one in five respondents expressing satisfaction with its performance in 2011 polls — of any branch of national government. In 'What's wrong with Congress and what should be done about it?' **James Thurber** concludes that the public's dissatisfaction with Congress is well founded. In his assessment, most of the problems facing the way it works are directly linked to the lack of bipartisanship and the extreme polarisation of party politics. After reviewing how political divisiveness obstructs the policymaking channels that depend on co-operation for their lifeblood, he considers what can be done to put matters right. An academic with deep practical experience in congressional governance and past reform efforts, Thurber provides a civic charter for improving the early 21st-century legislature. His recommendations for enhancing congressional deliberation, representation, law-making and oversight and reducing polarisation merit serious engagement from all who look to rescue the reputation of arguably the world's most important legislature.

Two chapters then consider the problems of presidential leadership in a pluralistic system of government that lacks a dominant locus of authority. In 'Singularity, separation and sharing: Richard Neustadt's lessons for politicians and political scientists', **Nigel Bowles** considers what the mid-20th-century works of one of the giants of American political science can teach us about the problems of governance in the early 21st century. In his view, scholars and politicians alike have not fully recognised the heuristic value of Neustadt's understanding of the relationship between *authority*, derived from constitutional prescription, and *power*, which in essence constitutes influence. To demonstrate Neustadt's continued importance, Bowles examines: the practical relevance of his analysis of presidential power for presidents and those who work for them; the distinctiveness of his research methodology; the uniqueness of his over-the-president's-shoulder perspective; and his fundamental conceptualisation of the presidency as a weak office. In doing so, he presents a cogent argument that Neustadt needs to be read anew in the early 21st century because his work 'encapsulates priceless wisdom about the practical imperatives of *sharing* in the governing of a Madisonian system.'

In 'Tenure reform and presidential power: the single six-year term proposal', **Niall Palmer** considers whether a long-standing reform idea to enhance the presidency's capacity for creative leadership might be a solution for the institution's early 21st-century problems. He reviews the arguments that supporters of this change advance in favour of a single six-year presidential term to replace the current two four-year terms limitation. Firstly, it offers the opportunity to recalibrate some of the dynamics of executive power, bringing the office closer in concept to the original design of the founders while repairing the damage done to public esteem for the office by some of its recent occupants. Additionally, ending the president's preoccupation with re-election and diluting the impact of partisanship on decision-making would, it is claimed, remove two of the major systemic obstructions to bold and imaginative leadership. To critics of the reform, such notions are both unworkable and blatantly anti-democratic. A single, non-renewable term, they argue, would isolate the presidency by de-coupling it from the traditional sources of political legitimacy upon which it relies for its authority. It would also reduce the president's ability to engage on equal terms with other political institutions and actors and destabilise the traditional checks and balances of the constitutional system by removing the presidential re-election cycle while leaving the congressional cycle intact. Finally, critics contend, the reform idea is underpinned by a focus on presidential authority and independent initiative which moves the nation further away from, not closer to, the ideals of the founders. Palmer's evaluation of both cases results in a cogent insistence that a single term would add to rather than resolve the problems of contemporary governance.

In 'The politics of the US budget: a metaphor for broken government?' **Iwan Morgan** assesses the failure of American government to deal with the public debt problem that arguably constitutes the greatest medium-/long-term threat to America's power and prosperity. After a review of the 'old' mid-20th-century politics of budget policy, he explains why this policy domain became increasingly contentious in the late 20th century and generated new levels of partisan conflict as fiscal problems worsened in the early 21st century. This chapter also considers institutional reform proposals advanced to resolve the Obama-era budget deadlock that nearly resulted in a '*won't pay*' (rather than a

Greek-style '*can't pay*') US default on debt obligations. In Morgan's assessment such changes, if implemented, cannot resolve the fundamental problem of the budget process that neither party will compromise on the core value of low taxes (Republicans) or entitlement benefit preservation (Democrats), without which there can be no meaningful resolution of the growing public debt. If the root of the problem is politics, so is the solution, but there is no sign at time of writing that America's present-day leaders are close to setting aside their immediate political differences in the essential long-term interests of the nation.

The final section of the volume deals with the problems of partisanship and political values in American society. In 'Losing voice, losing trust: the partisan dynamics of public evaluations of government in an era of polarisation', **Brian Schaffner** and **John Clark** take issue with the conventional narrative of mass distrust and anger with government to offer a more nuanced view of popular dissatisfaction. Their analysis shows that anti-government opinion can largely be explained by partisan dynamics. In essence, their research finds that Democrats tend to trust government less and be more antipathetic to it when Republicans are in control, while GOP identifiers evince similar feelings when the opposition party is in charge. What shapes this pattern is not animosity to policies enacted by the party of government, but the loss of a voice in government. Thus, the anger towards government that found a voice with the Tea Party movement is best understood as an expression of the frustrations felt by conservatives shut out of government following the Democratic establishment of single-party control of national government in the 2008 elections. In line with this, mistrust of government declined among Republicans in general and Tea Party supporters in particular following the GOP take-over of the House of Representatives in the 2010 midterms. On the other hand, Schaffner and Clark find that partisan polarisation has intensified in recent years with the result that political animosity has increased and the number of party identifiers willing to compromise has diminished. In consequence, the consensus building that Barack Obama aspired to undertake at the outset of his presidency foundered on the rocks of increasingly bitter partisanship.

In 'Two years of achievement and strife: the Democrats and the Obama presidency, 2009–10', **Alex Waddan** reviews why Democratic success in the elections of 2008 was seen by some as a transformational moment that could usher in a new American political order and why conservatism proved so resilient despite this setback. The existence of the worst economic crisis since the Great Depression suggested that 2008 could be a repeat of 1932 in terms of old-order repudiation and new-order affirmation in accordance with the 'recurrent authority' model of political scientist, Stephen Skowronek. In Waddan's assessment, the Obama administration succeeded in enacting a significant portion of its agenda in its first two years in office, albeit at the cost of concessions that watered down core measures, but this did not add up to political transformation. In contrast to the New Deal and Reagan transformations, Obama's initiatives — particularly the 2009 stimulus and the 2010 health care reform — enhanced rather than undermined opposition resistance. It remains to be seen whether Obama's first-term achievements will eventually form part of a substantial political transformation in light of developments in 2012 and beyond. However, Waddan finds little prospect of the polarising politics of his presidency giving way to a different kind of politics even if he succeeds in winning re-election.

Finally, in 'The rise of the Tea Party movement and American government', **Edward Ashbee** argues that scholarly analysis of this phenomenon should go beyond ideational variables. In his view, it should consider the constituencies from which the Tea Party movement draws support (disproportionately composed of white men in the older age cohorts, many of whom can be considered independent or 'freewheeling' conservatives). In addition he focuses on the 'Janus-like character' of the institutional arrangements and rules that govern both the Republican Party and electoral processes. These encourage and facilitate collective mobilisation at grassroots level, notably through the primary process, while also incorporating structures and relationships that allow elite interests to maintain and sometimes bolster their position. The political friction that such institutional arrangements create contributes to the formation and growth of movements on the edges of the formal party system and thereby compounds broader problems of governance. Prior to the emergence of the Tea Party movement, it laid a basis for networks and organisations such as the 'new right', the Moral Majority, the Christian Coalition, and militia groupings. Whatever the short-term future of the Tea Party movement, Ashbee contends that independent conservatives are likely to remain a significant and potent constituency. Within the institutional contexts that shape US political processes, their anxieties will almost certainly give rise to further movements and protests on the edges of those processes and the political system.

Taken as a whole, the chapters in this volume offer a mixed assessment of the state of American governance in Barack Obama's first term. Although Alex Waddan rightly draws attention to the legislative achievements of the Obama presidency in 2009–10, all the chapters dealing with governance accept the 'broken government' thesis — or a variant of it — whether explicitly or implicitly. Andrew Rudalevige's trenchant analysis of the loss of Hamiltonian energy in the Madisonian system of government perfectly encapsulates this view. Some of the contributors consider what can be done to put things right. James Thurber and Nigel Bowles outline ways in which Congress and the presidency may be able to improve their performance, but Niall Palmer and Iwan Morgan are pessimistic about the value of the presidential reform and budget process reforms reviewed in their chapters. On the polarisation of the broader electorate, Rudalevige, Schaffner and Clark, and Ashbee caution against excessive pessimism about its fractured condition, while recognising the depth of divisions in the Obama era.

In essence, there is broad recognition throughout the volume that the solutions to America's current problems of government do not lie wholly within government itself. Rudalevige puts this best in his remark, 'We, the people, will have a lot to say about how our political system reacts to the present stalemate, in 2012 and beyond.' It remains to be seen, however, whether American voters can set aside political differences to accept the necessity of the short-term pain, particularly in the form of tax increases and entitlement reform, to resolve the nation's long-term problems.

In 2010, *New York Times* columnist Thomas Friedman, speaking on NBC's 'Meet the Press', fantasised tongue-in-cheek fashion about the beneficial consequences of the US becoming China for a day. 'We could authorise the right solutions … on everything from the economy to the environment', he declared, 'I don't want to be China for a second, OK, I want my democracy to work with the same authority, focus and stick-to-itiveness. But right now we have a system that can only produce suboptimal solutions' (frumforum). Of course, political democracy cannot work in this way because it encompasses debate, disagreement, and competing interests. Moreover, the fruits of 'authority, focus and stick-to-itiveness' may not be to the taste of all if American government could deliver them. In early 2012, political analysts Thomas Mann and Norman Ornstein predicted that the fastest way out of the Obama era political impasse would be a Republican sweep of the presidency and Congress in 2012. They warned, however, that GOP control, when the party was far more conservative than at any time in its history, would likely produce a massive assault on the New Deal/Great Society state beyond anything envisaged by Ronald Reagan in the 1980s and the Contract with America in the 1990s (2012).

The contributors to this volume have as far as possible kept their lens focused on Obama's first term and assessed future prospects with caution. Nevertheless, there is an implicit expectation running through their analysis that the US will overcome the problems of broken government. This is a nation that has shown immense capacity for renewal throughout its history. As such, it is worth ending this introduction with the assessment of Bill Clinton. In the former president's view, the deal-making that made American government work in the past no longer works because ideology, which claims to have all the answers in advance without consideration of the evidence, has trumped the greater flexibility of philosophy in the approach to national problems. As befits the man from Hope, he remains optimistic that the co-operative culture that provides the glue holding American government together will eventually revive, albeit without providing a formula for this restoration. Nevertheless, Clinton rightly concludes: 'People have been betting against the United States for 200 years and they all wound up losing money' (Schama 2011).

References

G. Borger (2011) 'America's love/hate affair with government', 29 Sept., in 'Why is our government so broken?' CNN News, www.cnn.com.

Economist, The (2010) 'What's gone wrong in Washington?', 18 Feb., www.economist.com.

— (2011) 'Backfiring brinksmen', 31 Dec., p. 32.

C. Flandro (2012) 'Tester: U.S. government in gridlock, but that will change', *Bozeman Daily Chronicle*, 13 Jan., www.bozemandailychronicle.com.

D. Frum (2011) 'Why our government is broken', CNN News, 26 Sept., http://edition.cnn.com/2011/09/26/opinion/frum-broken-government/index.html?iref=allsearch.

Frumforum (2010) 'Friedman: America should be "China for a Day" to fix its problem of politics and government', 25 May, www.frumforum.com.

F. Fukuyama (2011) 'America's political dysfunction', *The American Interest*, Nov./Dec., pp. 125–7.

M. Isserman and M. Kazin (2000) *America Divided: The Civil War of the 1960s* (New York: Oxford University Press).

T.E. Mann and N.J. Ornstein (2012) 'Congress: the good news is, no more gridlock...', *Washington Monthly*, Jan./Feb., www.washingtonmonthly.com/magazine/features/.

L. Saad (2011) 'Americans express historic negativity towards U.S. government', Gallup, 26 Sept., www.gallup.com/poll/149678/americans-express-historic-negativity-toward-government.aspx.

J. Sachs (2009) 'America's broken politics', *The Guardian*, 23 Nov., www.guardian.co.uk.

— (2010) 'Fixing the broken government policy process', *Scientific American*, 4 Feb., www.scientificamerican.com.

S. Schama (2011) 'Bill Clinton talks to Simon Schama', *FT [Financial Times] Magazine*, 14 Oct., www.ft.com.

S. Webster (2011) 'Gore: US suffering from a "broken system" of government', *RawReplay*, 2 Aug., www.rawstory.com.

1
'Hail Gridlock'?
Hamiltonian energy, Madisonian institutions and American dissensus

Andrew Rudalevige

'Standstill nation'[1]

> *The American voters sent us a message two Tuesdays ago. That message is that they want us to deliver. They want us to work together.*
>
> Senate Majority Leader Harry Reid (Nevada)
> (quoted in *The New York Times*, 16 November 2010)

> [The Republican] *plan ... was written for the Tea Party and not the American people. Democrats will not vote for it. Democrats will not vote for it. Democrats will not vote for it.*
>
> Senate Majority Leader Harry Reid
> (quoted in *The New York Times*, 27 July 2011)

Again there were tears in Grant Park, Chicago. In the summer of 1968, they flowed from the sting of police batons and wafting gas felt by anti-Vietnam War protesters in the infamous battle of Chicago at the time of the Democratic National Convention. But four decades later, as the lakefront park again filled with chanting crowds, they welled up not from divisiveness and anger, but from joy, mingled with no little disbelief. On 4 November 2008, Barack Hussein Obama — half white, half black, all outsider — with a background that stretched from the Kansas heartland to the Hawaiian islands, from Indonesia to Chicago — had been elected president of the United States.

The process had hardly been foreordained, no matter that evening's rose-coloured glow. Yet finally, it seemed, America had broken decisively with its embattled past. It had lived up to Obama's own words in Iowa, nearly a year earlier, as 'the moment when the improbable beat what Washington always said

---

1 This headline accompanied an article in *The New York Times*, 19 June 2011, about differences of opinion between the Democrats and Republicans in Washington.

was inevitable.'² Obama had carried 28 states in the Electoral College, won a higher percentage of the two-party vote than any candidate for two decades, and the highest popular-vote share of any Democratic candidate since passage of the Voting Rights Act in 1965. In Congress, Democrats netted 21 new seats in the House to add to their 2006 gains; their majority now stood at 257 seats (out of 435). In the Senate eight additional Democrats were elected, making that caucus 60-strong.³ As it polled in late 2008, the Gallup Corporation found only four states it could rate as 'solid Republican' and one more leaning that way.⁴ Surely the age of Reagan had ended, and the age of Obama begun (Wilentz 2008; White 2009).

Just two years later, however, the Republican Party swept to widespread congressional, gubernatorial and state legislative victories, flipping the American electoral map from solid blue to deep red. The GOP netted 63 House districts — the largest midterm swing since 1938 and enough for a 49-vote majority in that chamber — and cut the Democratic Party down to 53 seats in the Senate. If war and economic crisis had seemed to spur a new opportunity for the Democrats to promote sweeping change, two years later continued pessimism about the economy and loud doubts about Democratic policies had seemingly stalemated those hopes.

Certainly, six months into the new Congress, stalemate seemed the new normal. At the end of June 2011, Gallup found the country nearly exactly divided: Obama's public approval in tracking polls stood at 46 per cent, with 46 per cent disapproving. More troubling, despite the urgent problems facing the nation — lacklustre economic growth, budget deficits of unprecedented peacetime scope and a looming debt limit, troops embroiled on three fronts abroad — not much had changed on the policy side either. The 112th House had devoted itself to attempting to undo much of the legislation passed in the previous two years and to making increasingly fervent declarations in favour of lower taxes (no matter the actual topic at hand). The Senate was less fervent but did even less, perhaps in line with the admission of Republican minority leader Mitch McConnell (Kentucky) that 'the single most important thing we want to achieve is for President Obama to be a one-term president' (quoted in Miller 2010). And Obama, for his part, despite some aggressive moves abroad, had gained little traction over the policy agenda at home. He was reduced to

2   3 January 2008, quoted in Wolffe (2010), p. 102. For a useful discussion of just how far from inevitable the Obama victory was, see Wolffe, ch. 4.

3   That figure was not official until July 2009, when an extended recount process confirmed the victory of Al Franken over incumbent Norm Coleman in Minnesota, and lasted only until January 2010, when Republican Scott Brown won a special election to replace Senator Edward Kennedy, the legendary Massachusetts Democrat who had died in August 2009.

4   The states so identified were Idaho, Utah, Wyoming, and Alaska, with Nebraska 'leaning Republican.' Twenty-nine states were rated as 'solid Democratic' and six as leaning Democratic, leaving ten as competitive. See Gallup 2009.

scolding Congress for its lack of work ethic and his opponents for their stalwart unwillingness to compromise. As the US debt approached its statutory limit in August 2011, negotiations were marked mostly by sequential stormings-out of various well-appointed rooms, to the point where the full faith and credit of American national debt came to the brink of default. More petty, but as telling, was an incident in September. In the week leading up to the tenth anniversary of the unifying September 11th attacks, House Speaker John Boehner (Ohio) refused to allow the President to address a joint session of Congress to discuss the economy because it would have conflicted with a debate among Republican presidential candidates.

In short, divided government was back; the unity of 2008 had vanished; and paralysis seemed the order of the day. Surveying the state of American politics, *The New York Times* (Baker 2011) summed it up in two words: 'Standstill nation'.

'Hail Gridlock'?

Not everyone was unhappy about this state of affairs. 'Hail Gridlock!' read one sign held by a Tea Party activist, protesting against any attempts at legislative productivity after the 2010 election (Hulse 2010). Obama's opponents argued Big Government was doing far too much, not too little; at the same time the president showed limited interest in renouncing the tools of executive unilateralism aggressively asserted by his predecessor. 'The fact is that Barack Obama views the Constitution as an impediment to his Marxist agenda', frothed the website TeaParty.org (Carson 2011). Equally distraught, the other side of the political spectrum expounded at book length on 'the decline and fall of the American republic' brought on by the growth of executive authority (Ackerman 2010).

Further, the structure of government created by the American Constitution certainly anticipates and even encourages gridlock: stability was a major aim of its framers. *Federalist* #73 defended the presidential veto power by arguing that we should 'consider every institution calculated to restrain the excess of lawmaking, and to keep things in the same state in which they happen to be at any given period, as much more likely to do good than harm.'[5] Jefferson likewise famously observed that 'I am not a friend to very energetic government; it is always oppressive' (quoted in Flaumenhaft 1992, p. 79).

Nonetheless, it is hard to escape the conclusion that American governance has gone broadly astray from the vision of the Constitution's authors and original implementers. And for all the loud denigration of governmental action justified by rhetorical reverence for the 'founding fathers' and the 'plain text' of the Constitution, the divergence from the *Federalist Papers*' famous defence of

---

5   All cites to the *Federalist Papers* are to their online edition at the Library of Congress, http://thomas.loc.gov/home/histdox/fedpapers.html.

constitutional theory and practice goes largely in the other direction. Alexander Hamilton, and James Madison, too, distrusted 'mutability' — but they hated incompetence. They favoured stability but knew the need for 'energy', even activism, when it was called for. In short, they understood theory, but knew that reality must take priority. Hamilton, for instance, argued in *Federalist* #22 (in words unheard today in the Senate chamber) that however appealing a supermajority approval process might seem on paper, 'its real operation is to … destroy the energy of government.' It would impose 'tedious delays; continual negotiation and intrigue; contemptible compromises of the public good.' And such a situation, he warned, 'must always savor of weakness, sometimes border upon anarchy.'

Crucially, in the final analysis, it was anarchy, not government, that posed the greatest threat to individual rights and freedoms for the *Federalist* authors. The 'energy' of government was therefore something worth protecting. The new constitutional system of 1787 was supposed to provide the strength needed to solve difficult problems. Even Jefferson, when he became president, decided that his office was sufficiently energetic to complete the Louisiana Purchase of 1804 and implement the Embargo Act of 1807. This is not to argue for a 'unitary executive', especially not in the sense of that phrase used by apologists for unconstrained presidential power. Rather, Hamilton's political prescription, in the *Federalist Papers* and elsewhere, centres on administrative competence and — crucially — on the capacity of the system to make hard choices for the long term.

And here, I suggest, the United States is indeed on worrying ground. Its separate but power-sharing institutions require consensus, or at least consensual compromise, to move forward towards the general interest. But, as currently constituted, those institutions channel factional interests towards dissensus instead, echoing Hamilton's prescient words: 'the only enemy which Republicanism has to fear in this country is in the spirit of faction and anarchy. If this will not permit the ends of government to be attained under it, if it engenders disorders in the community, all regular and orderly minds will wish for a change, and the demagogues who have produced the disorder will make it for their own aggrandizement. This is the old story.'[6] The national mood is raw and very polarised; the outcome is a system in default, and not just in fiscal terms. It is particularly ironic, perhaps, that the national debt — one of Hamilton's greatest policy achievements — should have been at the forefront of the current stalemate.[7] But the old story is new again.

---

6   Hamilton letter to Colonel Edward Carrington, 26 May 1792. Unless noted otherwise, all cites to Hamilton's letters are to the online edition of the collection compiled by Lodge (1904).

7   It is perhaps worth quoting Hamilton's 1792 observation, attacking Jefferson: 'a certain description of men are for getting out of debt, yet are against all taxes for raising money to pay it off' (Chernow 2004, p. 407).

The remainder of this brief essay seeks to diagnose and discuss these developments: what ails American politics and the American polity? Can the system be re-set to reach the difficult decisions modern governance demands?

American energy: 'dispatch, method, and system'

Whatever people thought of him — and he had many enemies, political, personal or both — no one could accuse Alexander Hamilton of lacking energy. Through tireless effort spurred by astonishing ambition, this 'bastard brat of a Scotch pedlar', as John Adams famously tarred him, transcended his orphaned upbringing in the West Indies to come to the American colonies aged 15. Once there, he graduated from what is now Columbia University; impressed himself upon General George Washington and became Washington's one indispensable aide during the American Revolution; attended the Constitutional convention and secured the ratification of its work, not least through his explication of it in the *Federalist Papers*; and served as Secretary of the Treasury during Washington's presidency (Chernow 2004, p. 538). Afterwards Hamilton remained a key figure in the Federalist Party and a thorn in the side both to putative allies (President John Adams) and full-blown opponents (President Thomas Jefferson) until, aged 49, he was killed in a duel by Vice President Aaron Burr on 11 July 1804.

It is Hamilton's role as founding thinker that is most relevant to the present discussion, and in particular his idea of 'energy' as a positive quality of governance. The term arises frequently in Hamilton's political thought — it is used in fully a dozen of his contributions to the *Federalist Papers* and appears in his collected writings as early as 1780, when he was only 25.[8]

Those first thoughts targeted the Articles of Confederation government (which created a 'perpetual union' between the states, perpetuity turning out to last about eight years).[9] Recall that the Articles dictated that each state would receive one vote and that nine — or often a unanimous 13 — votes would be required for most decisions. There was no separate executive branch; rather, officers and offices were appointed by Congress. Then, as later, Hamilton saw the diffusion of responsibility this permitted as problematic, even paralytic. As he wrote to a prominent New York politician, James Duane, reforms were needed to 'give new life and *energy* to the operations of government.' Once properly constituted, 'business would be conducted with dispatch, method, and system.'[10]

---

8   And even earlier, in 1777, he complained of the 'want of vigor' of the executive branch proposed in a draft of the New York state constitution. See his letter to Robert Livingstone of 19 May 1777, in Morris (1957, p. 102).

9   The Articles were approved by Congress in 1777, but not ratified until 1781; the present US Constitution took effect in 1789.

10 Letter of 3 September 1780.

Dispatch, method, and system — this is what Hamilton craved for government. Government must be able to reach decisions, with some alacrity when needed; and it must have mechanisms for carrying out those decisions effectively and efficiently, without going back on its word. That implied certain institutional arrangements. In his letter to Duane (later expanded as part of a series of papers called, with tellingly high hopes, *The Continentalist*), Hamilton's worry was the 'want of method and *energy* in the administration.' That was caused in part by legislators having 'meddled too much with details of every sort. Congress is, properly, a deliberative corps, and it forgets itself when it attempts to play the executive. It is impossible such a body, numerous as it is, and constantly fluctuating, can ever act with sufficient decision or with system.'

One answer was to place single appointees, rather than boards or Congress as a whole, in charge of executive functions. Later, defending the separate executive branch headed by a single president established by the new Constitution, Hamilton would return to this point, stressing 'unity' as the key element of energy in that executive, which in turn was 'a leading character in the definition of good government' (*Federalist* #70).[11] An independent executive, unhampered by the divisions and collective action problems of the legislative process, would be key to resisting factional legislative behaviour, not only reflecting unity but positively providing it. 'We are attempting by this Constitution to abolish factions and to unite all parties for the general welfare', Hamilton noted in the 1788 ratification debate in New York (quoted in Morris 1957, p. 110).

The word 'energy', which came into English from the Greek, means (as per the *Oxford English Dictionary*) 'force or vigour of expression', but Hamilton did not have rhetoric in mind: 'When Hamilton spoke of "energy", what he had in mind was not display', writes one of his leading explicators, Harvey Flaumenhaft (1992, p. 72). Instead, 'the rejection of classical politics culminates in the politics of administration', of the role of administrative efficacy. Hamilton famously argued that 'the true test of a good government is its aptitude and tendency to produce a good administration' (*Federalist* #68). For, he added, 'a government ill executed, whatever it may be in theory, must be, in practice, a bad government' (*Federalist* #70).[12]

It is well known that Hamilton wanted an even stronger presidency than that sketched in the Constitution. But the notion of 'energy' — and of unity, too — goes beyond the presidency, and the 'decision, activity ... and dispatch' that office would provide. A series of a dozen or so of his essays in the *Federalist*

11 *Federalist* #70. Other elements of an energetic executive were duration (in office, i.e. a fixed term), adequate support (e.g. salary) and 'competent powers'.

12 As a result, he claimed that 'all men of sense will agree in the necessity of an energetic executive.' See on this point Stourzh 1970, p. 83.

Papers, culminating in #36, provide a summary of what it meant for a national government to possess that quality: basically, the ability to behave as a singular actor to effect national functions. Its laws must be supreme to state law and deal with individuals directly, not through a state-level filter, and those laws must be equally enforced across the states (thus necessitating an independent judiciary). Further, it must have the powers of national defence and the ability to regulate interstate commerce. And, most importantly, it must have authority to raise and levy taxes. Though some years later the power to tax would be termed the 'power to destroy',[13] for Hamilton, taxation was about creation and growth.[14] He chided those who would handicap the potential of the new nation. 'Nothing ... can be more fallacious than to infer the extent of any power proper to be lodged in the federal government from an estimate of its immediate necessities', he argued. 'There ought to be a capacity to provide for future contingencies as they may happen; and as these are illimitable in their nature, so it is impossible safely to limit that capacity' (*Federalist* #34).

That kind of talk usually made James Madison nervous. Still, the notion of 'energy' — and even the word — are echoed in Madison's contributions to the *Federalist* as well. In *Federalist* #37, Madison argued that 'energy in government is essential to that security against external and internal danger, and to that prompt and salutary execution of the laws, which enter into the very definition of good government.' The key, Madison notes, was to balance that energy against the concurrent need for stability: 'we must perceive at once the difficulty of mingling them together in their due proportions.' It was the young republic's good fortune, he suggested, that the genius of those attending the Constitutional convention was sufficient to the task.

The idea of this sort of calibrated 'mingling' comes quickly to the notion of competence. 'It may be laid down as a general rule that [the people's] confidence in and obedience to a government will commonly be proportioned to the goodness or badness of its administration', Hamilton argued (*Federalist* #27). Yet this was tricky, because what people said they wanted in the short term might have poor long-term consequences. Thus the very point of having an energetic government order was to be able to act for the long-term benefit of the people, exactly because of the structural ability to withstand their short-term disdain. As early as 1782, Hamilton worried that 'the situation of the State with respect to its internal government' was afflicted with 'the general disease which infects all our constitutions — an excess of popularity. There is no *order* that has a will of its own. The inquiry constantly is what will *please,* not what will *benefit* the people. In such a government there can be nothing but

13 By the US Supreme Court, in *McCulloch v. Maryland,* 17 US 316 (1819).
14 Indeed, rather startlingly (especially to Tea Party ears), Hamilton wrote in *Federalist* #34 that 'the objects that will require a federal provision in respect to revenue ... are altogether unlimited.'

temporary expenditure, fickleness, and folly.'[15] This formulation squares the circle between conservative desires for stability and the need for energy: long term, you need the latter to achieve the former.

In sum, the framers wanted 'to secure energetic administrative machinery that would operate reliably throughout an extended territory during a protracted time to produce one general interest from many most common interests' (Flaumenhaft 1992, p. 81). Decisions should be based on broader community interests, not on factional views. And this would work because 'the mischiefs of faction', in Madison's famous phrase in *Federalist* #10, would be mitigated by two structural elements of the new United States. The first was its status — not as a democracy, in the pure sense of ancient Athens (or, more proximately, 18th-century New England). Instead, it was a representative democracy — a democratic republic — with large and diverse constituencies. Each elected official would thus have to cater to many different and even contradictory interests — Hamilton, in *Federalist* #27, borrowed this idea to stress that 'on account of the extent of the country from which those, to whose direction they will be committed, will be drawn, they will be less apt to be tainted by the spirit of faction.'

The second structural protection against faction was the size of the new nation itself. There might be extremists scattered across the country, but they would be isolated — the crazies of New Hampshire would be unlikely to encounter their South Carolina peers and would thus be unable to combine their desires in ways that would gain political traction. Minority factions were to be expected, Madison argued, but that was fine: the natural course of legislative majority rule would subsume to the common good the detrimental desires of those minorities. A majority faction (recall that for Madison a 'faction' was any group of any size that seeks its own interest and not the common good) could therefore be a real problem. But a majority faction would not be able to form. Better yet, that outcome did not require the suppression of liberty but only the proper structuring of the expression of the popular will.

In the past, therefore, philosophers had argued that a small, homogenous, population could govern itself democratically. Madison turned this on its head. American government would work, he argued, precisely *because* of its divisions and size. As a result, it could attain unity — and unity, in turn, enabled energy.

The energy crisis

How does the current crisis match with this vision? At present, one of the kindest words applied to American politics is that it is 'dysfunctional' (see, for example, Binder and Mann 2011). Likewise, one of the operating assumptions of the conference that prompted this volume runs that 'the US government has

---

15   Letter to Robert Morris, 13 August 1782.

not performed with its habitual energy in the face of crisis during the present economic slump.'

To be sure, as suggested above, this received wisdom needs some refinement. Indeed, we must reconcile the idea that the government is 'out of energy' with the fervent belief — indeed, the simple certainty — of so many Americans, not all of them linked to the Tea Party movement, that the government is in fact not out of energy but out of control, embarked on a quest to devour liberty and impose socialism. A quick search on the Amazon website turns up book titles that reference 'Obama's plan to subvert the Constitution', Obama's 'war against America', 'How the Obama administration threatens our national security', and the like.[16] Indeed, the campaign literature of one candidate running for *state* representative in one rural Pennsylvania district claimed that President Obama's agenda was 'unraveling the fabric of our society' (quoted in Scott 2010). Surely you cannot unravel the fabric of American society without at least some energy being expended.

Such opinions reflect a series of governmental actions aimed at addressing the economic downturn. There were tax rebates in February 2008. There was the massive Troubled Assets Relief Program (TARP) passed — with rather less enthusiasm — after autumn's banking meltdown. The law provided $700 billion in funds, not only for troubled financial institutions and their toxic debt, but ultimately for massive loans to American car manufacturers as well, temporarily transforming General Motors into Government Motors. There was the stimulus bill (the American Recovery and Reinvestment Act) in early 2009, providing another $787 billion for pump-priming, mostly through tax reductions and aid to state and local governments. In mid-2010 came the Dodd-Frank Wall Street Reform and Consumer Protection Act.[17] Even after the 2010 midterm, Congress held a 'lame duck' session that resulted in a new stimulus package, some $850 billion worth of tax cuts and continued unemployment benefits. This list must also include the passage in March 2010 of the Patient Protection and Affordable Care Act (PL 111-148), a broad federal commitment towards the aim of universal health care. Vice President Joe Biden announced at the time that this was a 'big [expletive] deal', and he was right (quoted in Weiner 2010).

It is true that even the 111th Congress (2009–10) passed somewhat fewer public laws than most of its recent predecessors — a total of 383, compared

---

16 By, respectively, Ken Blackwell and Ken Klukowski; John Bolton; and Victor Davis Hanson.
17 Respectively, Public Law (PL) 110–185; PL 110–343; PL 111–5; PL 111–203. Further, starting in December 2008, the Federal Reserve Bank lowered its interest rates basically to zero, while propping up the market for commercial paper to an astonishing extent. The Fed. made some 21,000 loans providing close to $3 trillion in market liquidity, bought up $1.25 trillion in mortgage-backed securities, and created $2.3 trillion through the euphemistic joys of 'quantitative easing' from 2008 to June 2011 (see Chan and McGinty 2010).

to 460 in the 110th Congress (2007–08) and 482 in the 109th (2005–06). And tellingly, in the 112th Congress the gears of the law-making engine have seized up completely: the new House and Senate, over the first quarter of their tenure — January to June 2011 — managed to approve a stunningly low total of 23 laws. If that pace continues, legislators will produce just 92 enactments over two years.

Even so, this inventory suggests we cannot define 'energy' simply as a résumé of government *activity*. Nor can it be simplistically equated to Hamilton's most famous application of 'energy', that is to say, in the executive. After all, President Obama was as willing as his predecessor to leverage unilateral power in a variety of key areas ranging from war powers to criminal justice to environmental regulation.

So why did gridlock take hold? Why did energy seem to run dry? One obvious answer is that inaction was a natural response to the actions above. The most sanguine side of that reflects the notion raised earlier, that the status quo is privileged in the American political system, given the multiple institutions representing different constituencies that must come to consensus over an activist course. Better not to act, than to act rashly.

But that explanation, if necessary, seems far from sufficient. In general the backlash seemed grounded less in a desire for inaction than in a desire for salvation by faith, without work. The tears in Grant Park — and the million or more people who descended upon Washington DC for Obama's inauguration — represented a pent-up longing for change, to be sure, but in what sense? 'Yes, we can!' candidate Obama told the nation; but a specific predicate was rarely included in the claim. Indeed, what did voters actually want the president to do? The voice of the people may be the voice of god, but most prophets have come to realise that gods are sometimes hard to understand. The 2008 vote, like others, was a single, blunt act: did a given ballot represent an endorsement of national health care, or of shuttering Guantanamo Bay — or simply deepening disdain for George W. Bush? Politicians who win elections are left to look at the vote results and wonder exactly what the oracle meant to tell them. The president blamed bad communications, rather than bad policy, for his 2010 electoral reverses, but some suggest that Obama and his allies simply misread their mandate (see, for example, the Campbell and Edwards chapters in Rockman et al. 2012).

Much of Obama's original appeal, of course, flowed from his compelling calls for national unity — invoking (with shades of Hamilton) the power that unity could bring to bear on national problems. 'There's not a liberal America and a conservative America — there's the United States of America', he had told the Democratic National Convention in 2004, in the speech that brought him to national prominence. 'There is not a Black America and a White America and Latino America and Asian America — there's the United States of America. ... We are one people, all of us pledging allegiance to the stars and stripes, all of us defending the United States of America.' The Obama brand of governance was grounded in a sort of post-, or perhaps supra-, partisan competence. 'The key right now is to make sure that we keep politics to a minimum', the president told reporters during his first week in office, after meeting with the House Republican caucus (Obama 2009). The stimulus package being negotiated in early 2009 thus included a number of tax cuts long dear to the GOP. Obama invited Republican lawmakers to the White House to watch the Superbowl on television. Indeed, he even made them cookies (Zeleny 2009).

Yet if the cookies were eaten, they did not bring unity. Political polarisation had risen dramatically since pundits (for example, Broder 1972) declared in the 1970s that party discipline had declined to the point that 'the Party's over.' By the 2000s, the party had certainly re-started. And if unity is the fuel of 'energy', it was important that unity was suddenly being defined as intra-party, not cross-party, solidarity. Veteran law-maker Jim Cooper (D-Tennessee), puts it this way: 'now you are either an ally or a traitor' (quoted in Nocera 2011). Being an ally meant opposing anything the opposing party proposed, even it was something your party had previously supported, from the individual mandate in the health care plan to a payroll tax 'holiday' or infrastructure construction — apparently, as the novelist Arthur Phillips notes (2011, p. 103), 'philosophy is inclination dressed in a toga.' This made predicting the outcome of roll calls harder in one sense: past positions did not determine present votes. But it made it far easier in another: present party identification predicted all.

Various efforts to quantify partisan polarisation tend to converge on that same conclusion, demonstrating that the distance between the parties has grown and that the heterogeneity within each party has withered. Three examples will suffice. First, the *Congressional Quarterly* measures of party unity and support, published each year since the 1950s, showed that a majority of one party voted against a majority of the other on more than three-quarters of that body's total roll-call votes in 2010, a new record. Average party unity support — that is, the percentage of votes on which members vote with their own party — was almost 90 per cent, in both House and Senate. Further, of the 50 House members most inclined to cross party lines, 30 lost in the November 2010 election (Zeller 2011).

Likewise, the calculations of political scientists Keith Poole and Howard Rosenthal, measuring the preferences of members of Congress, showed that the divergence between the mean Republican and mean Democrat in House and Senate had grown steadily since the late 1970s (and, less consistently, from their low in the 1940s). By 2010 the gap between the parties was at its largest since not 1979, but 1879 (Poole and Rosenthal 2007; Krehbiel 1998).[18]

Adam Bonica's 'ideological cartography' project utilises these data to provide an animated graphic presentation showing the development of Senate polarisation, depicting state delegations of different parties fleeing from each other across the screen. Bonica also provides some useful detail about the makeup of the House, tracing a two-decade trend of increased polarisation as the average Democrat became more liberal and the average Republican more conservative. The median member, naturally, tracks that trend — and with the 2010 Republican gains, that median member is now the most conservative he/she has been in the 20-plus years Bonica measures.[19] Journalist Ron Brownstein termed the divisions tantamount to 'the second civil war' (Brownstein 2007; and see Abramowitz 2010, Jacobson in Rockman et al. 2012). It was small comfort to think that polarisation might have been higher in the years leading up to the *first* Civil War.

When the 2010 returns came in, then, they mostly reinforced the existing situation. Democrats had held 59 per cent of the Senate — yet 59 per cent of the votes were not 60, and 60 votes were now required for forward movement. Obama was a professed detractor of George W. Bush's legislative strategy, grounded as it was in narrow partisan margins emphasising short-term victories with diminishing returns. But soon he would learn that strategy had one important redeeming quality: it worked.

Partly because of these dynamics, the 'energy' of even the most substantial of the policies noted above was somewhat undercut by their reactive nature. While Obama preached long-term approaches to the structural problems facing the American economy, especially given the imminent ageing of a population fiercely attached to its entitlement programmes, the 111th and 112th Congresses found themselves lurching from one crisis to another. While Obama preached a Clintonian (even Blairite) third way, seeking 'what works', the bureaucratic edifices erected to provide services like universal health care whilst protecting the extant American health care industry seemed rather unlikely to work as planned.

Further, Obama effectively adopted Bush's tactics to win legislative roll calls. While still seeking nominal bipartisanship, his administration usually decided, given the choices on offer, that party-line votes to pass statutes were preferable to failing to pass them. But since Obama had pledged his 'brand' to a uniting vision of bipartisanship, the simple reality traced above — that well-honed

---

18 For the 1879–2010 time series see 'Party polarization 1879–2010', available at http://voteview.com/polarizedamerica.asp#POLITICALPOLARIZATION.

19 See http://ideologicalcartography.com/2010/08/03/a-visual-history-of-senate-polarization-from-1967-to-2010/ and http://ideologicalcartography.com/2010/11/05/introducing-the-112th-congress/.

party discipline is the key mechanism for legislative success — meant that even policy victories threatened to undercut the president's broadest appeal. Hence the 111th Congress held 'the odd distinction of being both historically busy and epically unpopular' (D. Fahrenthold et al. 2010).

Worse, as noted above, programmes passed in 2009 and 2010 that still needed time to germinate found themselves attacked in 2011 and 2012, either frontally (as with efforts to repeal health care reform) or more subtly (through the refusal, for example, to confirm any director of the new Consumer Financial Protection Bureau unless changes were made to undercut the power of that office). As Senate Republican leader Mitch McConnell put it in early 2011, 'We will see if [Obama] actually wants to work with us to accomplish things that we're already for.' Harry Reid's various pronouncements about cooperation were noted at the head of this chapter. These interactions were reminiscent of the Marx Brothers, without the virtue of being intentionally comedic.[20]

Public confidence in government plummeted during the pointless standoff over the debt limit in the summer of 2011, but not because the government had taken a stand with which people disagreed. Rather, once again, it had failed to do so.

What they didn't see coming

Why was this? Why could bipartisanship no longer gain traction on national decision-making? The answer could not simply be linked to personal animus among key decision-makers — many of the Framers bitterly disliked one another, after all.[21] Nor is there any inherent reason that divided government cannot produce legislation. In the abstract, it should encourage compromise (Mayhew 2005). To be sure, comity is not always a good in itself — consider the century-long gentlemen's agreement peaking in the 1950s that sought to elide civil rights from deliberation in Washington. But as Brownstein (2007, p. 79, and ch. 3 generally) points out, 'for all its defects th[at] system possessed one great virtue: It compelled political leaders who held contrasting views and represented differing constituencies to talk and listen to each other.'

Those processes bridged gaps; up to now bridges have been increasingly dismantled before they were built. Instead, American institutions have developed in a way that leads not to consensus, but dissensus. The 'age of bargaining' degraded for many reasons, but one was a shift in congressional culture that undermined norms and legislative procedures built for a different age. As travel back to constituencies became easier, and constituent service

---

20 In particular Groucho Marx, from the film *Horse Feathers*: 'Your proposition may be good, but let's have one thing understood: Whatever it is, I'm against it! And even when you've changed it or condensed it, I'm against it.' McConnell quoted in Winkler 2011. Thanks to David Hawkins at CQ Press for Marx quote reference.

21 For a catalogue of insults, see Chernow, *Alexander Hamilton*, pp. 405–7.

became a safer mechanism for representation than taking divisive issue stands, the 'Tuesday–Thursday' club of drop-in legislators replaced a residential ethos that made colleagues friends, through constant social interaction and not a little shared bourbon after hours.

More bourbon is not the whole answer, alas. In the House, enhancements to party leadership powers interacted with more unified caucuses to place restrictive controls on legislative participation and amendment. This made majority control more effective (if more resented) than in many years (Sinclair 2011). In the Senate the opposite problem prevailed: there, as noted above, majority rule proved increasingly elusive (Loomis 2011). It may be enough to observe that these trends coincided neatly in 2009–10, when 836 bills passed the House, but only 433 passed the Senate.

The ability of minority groupings, or even individuals, to prevent Senate action deserves special mention. In all the Senate sessions from the creation of cloture during the Wilson administration in 1917–18 through to 2006, the number of motions filed to schedule cloture votes — thus aiming to end ongoing or threatened filibusters — had never exceeded 80. In 2005–06, the last year of Republican majority rule in the George W. Bush administration, the figure was 68. But in 2007–08 and 2009–10, with the Republicans now in the Senate minority, that number more than doubled,[22] holding up everything from nominations to committee markups. Part of this behaviour sprang from polarisation and the zero sum interactions it encouraged. But this, too, was linked to the cultural shifts noted above. Gregory Koger argues, for instance (2010, p. 133), that it is the value of time that increases the incentive to filibuster: less time in session raises the leverage each member has when he threatens to stall any given session. Thus, as the Senate works less, it works less well.

These sorts of internal developments have been buttressed by larger ones. One intriguing argument comes from Morris Fiorina and Samuel Abrams in their book *Disconnect*. In the 1960s, they argue, the trend towards greater participation in politics backfired, since few people really care about politics. 'The unexpected conjunction of more open politics with a less trusting, less satisfied, and less involved citizenry is that the changes that occurred during the past generation had the unanticipated and perverse effect of making American politics *less* representative'. Elected representatives seeking to minimise common ground and undermine governmental competence, they argue, are acting perfectly rationally. An earlier generation's leaders were able to keep divisive social issues off the agenda; today, they not only can't, but don't want to, since the new political class is comprised of precisely those people who are activated

---

22 To 139 and 136, respectively. The tables may be found at the Senate historian's office website: www.senate.gov/pagelayout/reference/cloture_motions/clotureCounts.htm.

on the basis of such issues (2009, pp. 87–9). As Hamilton put it, 'it will rarely happen that the advancement of the public service will be the primary object either of party victories or of party negotiations' (*Federalist* #76).

This brings us back to the logic of *Federalist* #10. Recall that Madison made two main points on behalf of the new United States' ability to forestall factional influence. First, a representative democracy meant that constituencies would be diverse (and that legislators would have some autonomy in maneuvering across that diversity); second, a large nation meant that localised extremists would not be able to organise with their distant counterparts.

Yet, as with the shifts in Congress noted above, time and technology call both arguments into question. Each member of Congress now represents more than 710,000 people — far more than the 30,000 or so Madison defended as reasonable in the *Federalist*.[23] So far, so good, at least so far as diluting factions should go — except that a number of factors have made those members more, rather than less, predictable in their views and votes. One is that districts themselves have become more, not less, homogenous, even as they have grown. This is partly a result of geographical 'sorting', or self-segregation — the additive result of thousands of individual decisions as people finding a place to live seek out like-minded neighbours (Bishop and Cushing 2008; Brownstein 2007, ch. 6; Stolberg 2011). Partly, too, it results from more centralised decisions to *make* political districts like-minded: namely, from gerrymandering. The purposive redistricting of congressional seats to favour a given candidate is hardly new,[24] but it has gained greatly in efficacy over the past two decades, both because new computing technology allows for 'micro-targeting' likely voters and matching census tracts to them, and because state legislatures (who generally draw the districts) have also seen increased polarisation and thus greater incentives to aid their co-partisans. Constraining cross-party competition has the result of enhancing the importance of primary elections, meaning that candidates do not need to appeal to the median voter of the district as a whole but only to the median voter in their party. Indeed, since (as Fiorina and Abrams suggest) turnout in primary elections is disproportionately made up of party activists, the actual median voter in any given election may well be even more extreme. These larger districts, then, may be 'very narrow ponds', as Clinton aide Bruce Reed puts it. The result is that hardline members 'are accurately reflecting their constituencies by being more ideological than the country is as a whole' (quoted in Nelson and Riley 2011, p. 72).

---

23 See *Federalist* #55–6. After the 2010 census, the 'perfect' district should contain exactly 710,766 people, though this varies since some states' populations are lower than this figure.

24 The tactic is named after Elbridge Gerry, a member of the Constitutional convention — though, perhaps appropriately, he declined to sign the finished document.

Nor is the size of the nation still its own defence against conspiracy. It was perhaps never the case that no common ground would be found beyond an individual state — regional interests (not least slavery) existed from the start.[25] But even region has been supplanted by nation: local isolation has been undermined by interstate highways, jet travel, chainstore commerce and, of course, the stunning advances in communications technology. It was hard to foresee cell phones, a national satellite-transmitted media, or online social networking in 1787. But if distant factions found it hard to connect then, today a Facebook page is the work of a moment, and an email blast to a member of Congress the work of a few minutes more. To organise nationally is hardly different in kind than to organise at the neighbourhood level.

In itself, that does not create the majority factions that worried Madison. More lobbies than ever before now beat on the doors of official Washington (and Harrisburg, and Albany, and Sacramento), but while they are of many sizes it is safe to say that none by itself represents a majority of Americans. They are, rather, the organisational personifications of minority factions.

Their ubiquity, however, calls into doubt Madison's dismissal of the threat such factions might pose. Such organisations are very effective at advancing their particularistic interests and are particularly successful at preventing action they oppose from moving ahead. In that, of course, they take advantage of another Madisonian institution, the separation of powers. In Jonathan Rauch's (1994) punning metaphor, organised interests cause 'demosclerosis', clogging the arteries of government. The loudest voices politicians hear are the most extreme and the most self-interested.

Recall Hamilton's early hope that 'this Constitution' might 'abolish factions and … unite all parties for the general welfare'. Instead, under the right circumstances, it empowers those parties to become factions: their members are not representative of the larger whole. In this, it not only reflects polarisation but it also reinforces it. And in so doing it prevents majority rule — and produces a tyranny of the minorities.

Conclusion: 'The best good of the whole'

It will not do to end there. After all, the framers were realistic about the tasks that awaited the government they had created. They did not expect (as Hamilton observed in *Federalist* #30) 'to see realized in America the halcyon scenes of the poetic or fabulous age.' Madison added in *Federalist* #10 his famous caution that 'enlightened statesmen will not always be at the helm.' And Gordon Wood (2006, pp. 148, 164–5) details Madison's own frustrations with his early days in Congress: 'this was not what republican lawmaking was

---

25 Stourzh (1970, pp. 114–15) suggests Madison was 'either bookish or highly political' in avoiding the discussion of shared sectional interests.

supposed to be.' After the author of *Federalist* #10 joined the House in 1789, Wood adds, 'we do not hear any more talk about his notions of an extended Republic and the filtration of talent.'

Likewise, a description of a more recent president argues that 'he was trapped in a political and intellectual system that prized ideological consistency and partisan unity over flexibility, experimentation, and cooperation' (Brownstein 2007, p. 49). The subject is not Barack Obama, but Herbert Hoover.

That might raise hope. Can the system be re-set, as with the New Deal? Does Franklin Roosevelt wait in the wings? As noted at the outset, some thought that Obama was himself a 'president of reconstruction' (see Skowronek 1994), who could re-make the system in a new image. Another possibility is political reform, such as the recent California drive to move to 'top two' non-partisan primaries that might privilege more moderate candidates.

Most likely, though, the solution is longer term, grounded in demographic change (see Fiorina and Abrams 2009, ch. 8). There are key generational distinctions in American politics — indeed, age was an excellent predictor of the Obama-McCain vote in 2008. Young people on the whole are more tolerant along various dimensions, and certainly more libertarian on the social issues which have proved so insurmountable to their parents. Add high levels of continuing immigration (and the fact that second-generation Latino immigrants will be voters) and the continuing revolution in the role of women, and American politics are likely to look literally quite different in two decades than they do today. Thus diversity will (perhaps ironically) build unity — the fuel for 'energy'.

The challenge in the short term will be to get to that long term. As Hamilton reminds us, leaders must see popular government as distinct from governmental popularity (Flaumenhaft 1992, p. 78). His 1782 formulation still rings true: when 'the inquiry constantly is what will *please*, not what will *benefit* the people ... there can be nothing but temporary expenditure, fickleness, and folly.' At present the American system is configured in a way that reminds us uncomfortably of those words, channelling government not towards competence, but impotence; not towards consensus but towards dissensus. 'The great machine of government' has been set in motion, the *Gazette of the United States* proclaimed in 1790. Now the job was to adjust 'its various movements so as to produce the best good of the whole' (quoted in White 1956, p. 4). So it remains.

During the Cuban Missile Crisis, John F. Kennedy spoke to the Joint Chiefs of Staff, laying out some of the interlocking issues that made that crisis so difficult to solve by short-term force, however satisfying (May and Zelikow 1997, p. 113). The head of the air force, Curtis LeMay, responded, 'you're in a hell of a fix, Mr President', to which Kennedy properly replied, 'You're in it with me.'

There is some sort of unity in this, after all. We, the people, will have a lot to say about how our political system reacts to the present stalemate, in 2012 and beyond. But in the meantime, more tears — in Grant Park and elsewhere — seem likely.

References

A. Abramowitz (2010) *The Disappearing Center: Engaged Citizens, Polarization, and American Democracy* (New Haven, CT: Yale University Press).

B. Ackerman (2010) *The Decline and Fall of the American Republic* (Cambridge, MA: Harvard University Press).

P. Baker (2011) 'Standstill nation', *The New York Times*, 19 June.

S.A. Binder and T.E. Mann (2011) 'Constraints on leadership in Washington', *Issues in Governance Studies*, No. 41 (Washington, DC: Brookings Institution), 13 July.

B. Bishop with R.G. Cushing (2008) *The Big Sort* (Boston: Houghton Mifflin).

A. Bonica, 'Ideological cartography', http://ideologicalcartography.com.

D. Broder (1972) *The Party's Over* (New York: Harper & Row).

R. Brownstein (2007) *The Second Civil War: How Extreme Partisanship has Paralyzed Washington* (New York: Penguin).

B. Carson (2011) 'Obama will soon declare the Constitution – unconstitutional!', TeaParty.org, 26 Feb., http://teapartyorg.ning.com/forum/topics/obama-will-soon-declare-the?commentId=4301673%3ACommment%3A188622/.

S. Chan and J.C. McGinty (2010) 'Fed papers show breadth of emergency measures', *The New York Times*, 2 Dec.

R. Chernow (2004) *Alexander Hamilton* (New York: Penguin).

D. Fahrenthold et al. (2010) 'Stormy but highly productive 111th Congress adjourns', *Washington Post*, 23 Dec.

M.P. Fiorina with S.J. Abrams (2009) *Disconnect: The Breakdown of Representation in American Politics* (Norman, OK: University of Oklahoma Press).

H. Flaumenhaft (1992) *The Effective Republic: Administration and Constitution in the Thought of Alexander Hamilton* (Durham, NC: Duke University Press).

Gallup Corporation (2009) 'State of the states: political party affiliation', 28 Jan., www.gallup.com/poll/114016/state-states-political-party-affiliation.aspx.

C. Hulse (2010) 'With Tea Party in mind, Republicans have change of heart about earmarks', *The New York Times*, 16 Nov.

K. Krehbiel (1998) *Pivotal Politics* (Chicago: University of Chicago Press).

G. Koger (2010) *Filibustering: A Political History of Obstruction* (Chicago: University of Chicago Press).

H.C. Lodge (ed.) (1904) *Collected Writings of Alexander Hamilton*, 12 vols. (New York: G.P. Putnam's Sons), available online at http://oll.libertyfund.org/index.php?option=com_staticxt&staticfile=show.php%3Ftitle=1712&Itemid=28/.

B.A. Loomis (2011) *The U.S. Senate: From Deliberation to Dysfunction* (Washington, DC: CQ Press).

E.R. May and P.D. Zelikow (eds.) (1997) *The Kennedy Tapes* (Cambridge, MA: Harvard University Press).

D. Mayhew (2005) *Divided We Govern*, 2nd edn. (New Haven, CT: Yale University Press).

S.J. Miller (2010) 'Reid: McConnell comment a "road to nowhere"', *The Hill*, 3 Nov.

R.B. Morris (ed.) (1957) *The Basic Ideas of Alexander Hamilton* (New York: Pocket Books).

M. Nelson and R.L. Riley (eds.) (2011) *Governing at Home: The White House and Domestic Policymaking* (Lawrence, KS: University Press of Kansas).

J. Nocera (2011) 'The last moderate', *The New York Times*, 6 Sept.

B. Obama (2009) 'Remarks by the President after meeting with House Republican caucus', Office of the White House Press Secretary, 27 Jan., www.whitehouse.gov/the-press-office/remarks-president-after-meeting-with-house-republican-caucus-12709/.

A. Phillips (2011) *The Tragedy of Arthur* (New York: Random House).

K.T. Poole and H. Rosenthal (2007) *Ideology and Congress*, 2nd rev. edn. (New York: Transaction).

J. Rauch (1994) *Demosclerosis: The Silent Killer of American Government* (New York: Times Books).

B.A. Rockman, A. Rudalevige and C. Campbell (eds.) (2012) *The Obama Presidency: Appraisals and Prospects* (Washington, DC: CQ Press).

J. Scott (2010) 'Bloom, Baldwin meet in first debate', *The Sentinel*, 10 Oct., www.cumberlink.com/news/local/govt-and-politics/elections/article_cf989cac-d1be-11df-96f9-001cc4c03286.html.

B. Sinclair (2011) *Unorthodox Lawmaking: New Legislative Processes in the U.S. Congress*, 4th edn. (Washington, DC: CQ Press).

S. Skowronek (1994) *The Politics Presidents Make* (Cambridge, MA: Harvard University Press).

S.G. Stolberg (2011) 'You want compromise? Sure you do', *The New York Times*, 14 Aug.

G. Stourzh (1970) *Alexander Hamilton and the Idea of Republican Government* (Stanford, CA: Stanford University Press).

R. Weiner (2010) 'Biden to Obama: "A big [expletive] deal"', Washington Post.com, 23 March, http://voices.washingtonpost.com/44/2010/03/did-biden-tell-obama-signing-w.html.

J.K. White (2009) *Barack Obama's America: How New Conceptions of Race, Family, and Religion Ended the Reagan Era* (Ann Arbor, MI: University of Michigan Press).

L.D. White (1956) *The Federalists: A Study in Administrative History* (New York: Macmillan).

S. Wilentz (2008) *The Age of Reagan: A History, 1974–2008* (New York: Harper).

J. Winkler (2011) 'McConnell "skeptical" about Obama's centrist rhetoric ahead of State of the Union', *The Daily Caller*, 25 Jan.

R. Wolffe (2010) *Renegade: The Making of a President*, paperback edn. (New York: Three Rivers Press).

G.S. Wood (2006) *Revolutionary Characters: What Made the Founders Different* (New York: Penguin).

J. Zeleny (2009) 'Obama woos GOP with attention, and cookies', *The New York Times*, 4 Feb.

S. Zeller (2011) '2010 vote studies: party unity', *CQ Weekly*, 3 Jan., pp. 30–5.

2
What's wrong with Congress and what should be done about it?

James A. Thurber

Introduction

The United States Congress appears to be at one of the lowest ebbs in its history at the dawn of the second decade of the 21st century. The descriptors commonly applied to the national legislature in the media are deadlock and dysfunction. Procedural wrangling and partisan gridlock have tied the Congress in knots at a time when the nation needs a functioning government more than ever. Polarisation in the legislature, along both ideological and party lines, is a reflection of the American body politic itself, with both the House and Senate dominated by fierce, uncompromising partisanship. Leaders demand ideological purity and lockstep voting and routinely make use of strong-arm procedures to enforce partisan views and subsequent behaviour.

It is therefore unsurprising that popular satisfaction with Congress is at a historic low with just nine per cent of the public believing that it is doing its job. On the other hand, the view of Congress as broken and 'dysfunctional' is not wholly shared by scholars of Congress. Nevertheless, as important as the overall job performance rating is, how the American public evaluates the various functions of Congress more precisely illuminates the areas of prime dissatisfaction and, with that knowledge, a picture of whether the institution can be salvaged and how, can be drawn (see figure 1).

The Center for Congressional Studies 2010 survey of public attitudes about Congress found profound negative evaluations about the performance of the institution. The major result of the survey was that, on all questions where the public graded Congress, it was rated an underperforming institution: 'Dealing with key issues facing the country' – a D; 'Keeping excessive partisanship in check' – D-minus; 'Conducting its business in a careful, deliberate way' – D; 'Holding its members to high standards of ethical conduct' – D; 'Controlling the influence of special interest groups' – D-minus. In response to the question,

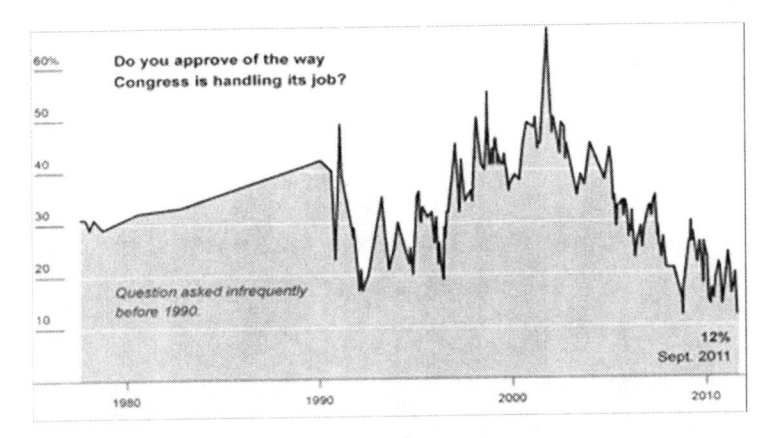

Figure 1: Public approval of Congressional job performance, 1980–2011
Source: Gallup Polls
Center for Congressional and Presidential Studies (www.american.edu/ccps/)

'Do members of Congress listen and care about what people like you think?', 33 per cent said 'no, not most of the time.' Another question asked 'What do you think is the main thing that influences what members of Congress do in office?' To this, 43 per cent answered 'special interests', and another 41 per cent specified 'personal self-interest'. On the broadest-gauge question — 'overall, do you approve or disapprove of the way Congress is handling its job?' — 84 per cent disapproved.

Delving further into the survey questions reveals bases for the general perception that Congress simply does not work for the public good. For example, in response to the question, 'Have you contacted your current member of Congress for any reason?', 61 per cent said they had but, of those, only 45 per cent said they were 'satisfied with the result of that contact.' This answer illustrates dissatisfaction at a very personal level. On representation, 71 per cent of people said that, when members of Congress vote, they have special interests in mind 'most of the time' or 'just about always'. Another common view widely held by the American public is that Congress is an excessively contentious place. When asked 'Do you believe that the delays in Congress are due to serious differences on the issues, or that members just like to bicker and score political points?', 66 per cent said Congress likes to bicker. Ironically, despite the low grades, personal feelings about the institution's characteristics and general negative attitudes about Congress, Americans still see Congress as an important institution in their system of government. The survey found that, when asked 'How much of an impact does the work of Congress have on your life?', a majority — 52 per cent — said 'a great deal' and another 36 per cent said 'some'. There is also a strong belief that Congress has a legitimate claim to share power with the president. In response to a question about which institution should take the lead — Congress or the president — in setting the national agenda, determining the federal budget, and deciding to go to war, very solid majorities said both the president and Congress should play a role. The conclusion is that Congress is important in the US system of government, but it is failing to do its job.

A 2010 survey of political scientists that asked the same questions as the public survey found that they gave the institution more positive reviews.[1] The experts gave Congress solid B grades on 'exercising its proper role in setting the legislative agenda' and for 'focusing on the key issues facing the country', and B-minus grades on 'generally fulfilling its national policy-making responsibilities' and 'protecting its powers from presidential encroachment.'

The survey found that the political scientists thought accessibility and openness were other areas of strength, with Congress earning a B-plus on being 'accessible to constituents', and B grades on being 'open to the public' and 'broadly reflecting constituents' interests'. Scholars gave Congress particularly weak grades on 'keeping excessive partisanship in check' — the House received a D-plus and the Senate only a slightly higher C-minus in that area. In response to whether the legislative process in each chamber 'involved a proper level of compromise and consensus', the Senate got a C-minus and the House a barely-better C. The political scientists also gave Congress C-minus grades on the questions: 'Does Congress keep the role of special interests within proper bounds?' and 'Does Congress consider the long-term implications of policy issues, not just short-term?' When scholars turned their attention to the voters, they gave them D grades for 'following what is going on in Congress on a regular basis' and for 'understanding the main features of Congress and how it works.' The political scientists gave the institution higher marks than the public, but gave the public flunking grades for their ability to understand and follow the workings of the institution. As knowledge of the institution goes down, the expectations of its performance seem to go up among the public who gave the national legislature very low grades.

The public has clearly given Congress poor grades while political scientists — with some significant exceptions (Mann and Ornstein 2006, 2009) — are much more satisfied with the institution. This chapter seeks to assess who is right. It reviews the most important failures with respect to the major functions of Congress: lawmaking (including the raising and spending of money for governmental purposes); oversight; deliberation; and representation. Thereafter, it considers what reforms can improve the workings of Congress.

---

1 See Appendix for survey results.

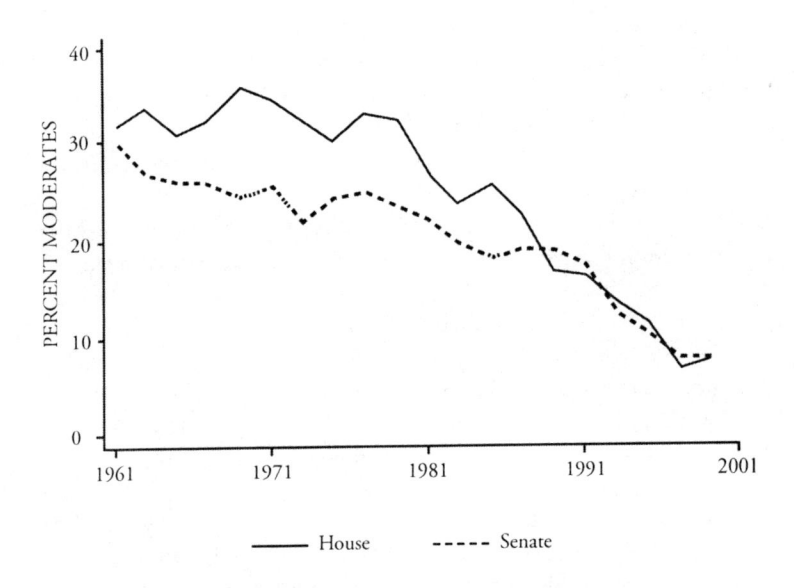

Figure 2: Decline of moderates as a percentage of House and Senate members 1961–2001

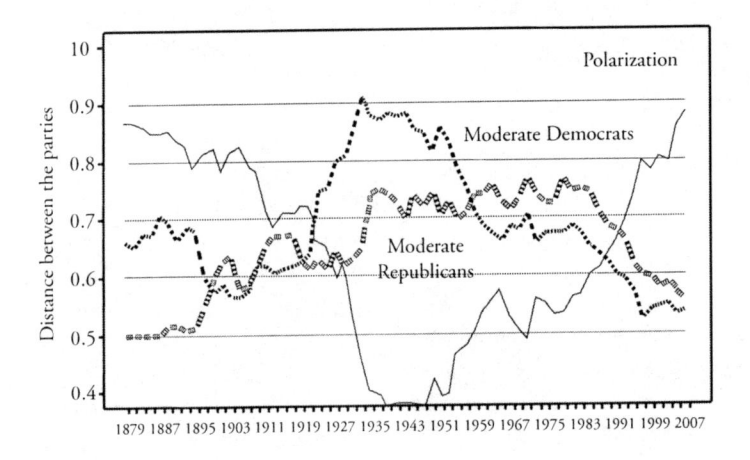

Figure 3: Trends in partisan polarization and moderate membership of the Senate 1879–2007

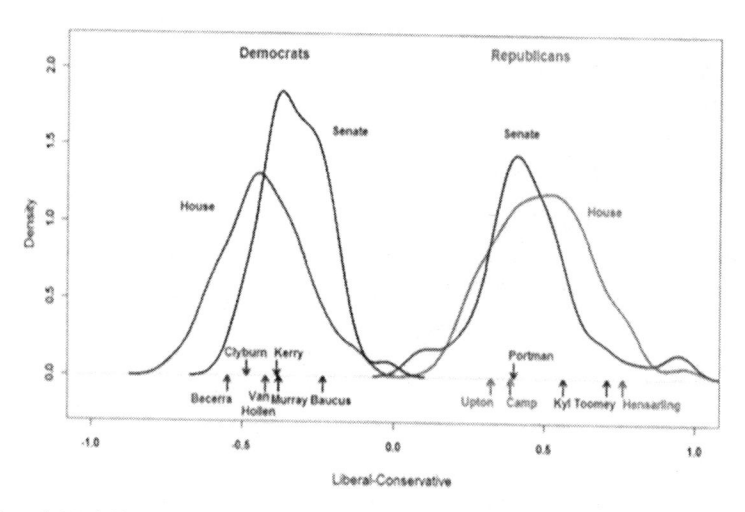

Figure 4: 112th House and Senate common ideological space scores, with Super Committee scores highlighted (Democrats dark, Republicans light)

The causes of congressional dysfunction

The missing middle

A fundamental reason for gridlock and dysfunctionality is the disappearance of the moderates or what some call the vital centre in Congress (Nivola and Brady 2008). There has been a steady decline in the number of moderates in Congress since 1960 (see figures 2, 3, and 4). Four decades ago there was a vigorous middle in Congress. Both parties spanned the ideological divide that exists today. Each party had a large liberal and conservative wing. On divisive issues such as civil rights, liberal Democrats and Northern moderate Republicans would join forces against the conservative wings of both parties. Getting the votes needed to stop a Senate filibuster required a bi-coalition. Paul G. Kirk, Jr., a former aide to the late Senator Ted Kennedy, who was appointed to fill his seat temporarily in 2009, explains, 'More commonly than not, the conservatives in the two parties would be together, the progressives in the two parties would be together, and then you'd kind of have a moderate center and find the 60. The breadth of political thought overlapped.' (Schatz 2010, p. 959). In contrast, the lack of common ground between the 12 members of the Joint Select Committee on Deficit Reduction (the Super Committee) demonstrates the ideological gap between the parties and why they failed to reach an agreement.

Related to the lack of the middle in the two parties is the movement of both to more extreme partisanship, which is another source of congressional dysfunction. In recent years over 80 per cent of roll-call votes have pitted a majority of Democrats against a majority of Republicans. This is the highest percentage of party unity votes since *Congressional Quarterly* began measuring voting patterns of Members of Congress in 1953. In the 1960s, the yearly average of such partisan votes was less than 50 per cent (Schatz 2010).

Re-districting abuse and the missing middle

Partisan gerrymandering occurs in most states, but the Supreme Court and Congress have ignored the problem. Rep. John Tanner (D-Tennessee) describes the negative consequences of partisan gerrymandering:

> When Members come here from these partisan districts that have been gerrymandered . . . they have little incentive to really work across party line in order to reach solutions. If one comes here wanting to work across the aisle, one has to watch one's back, because the highly charged partisans don't like it. (*Congressional Record*)

The House has been redistricted to safe seats (26 seats were competitive in 2004, 65 in 2006, 68 in 2008, and 85 in 2010, while 60 are predicted to be competitive in 2012 after the 2010 redistricting is completed (McDonald 2006). The creation of these safe House districts has led to the election of increasingly 'ideologically pure' representatives with a relatively harmonised constituency, little institutional loyalty, and an unprecedented degree of partisan homogeneity (high party unity scores mentioned above) within the two parties. In their case the party primary, which has a traditionally low turnout (18.8 per cent on nationwide average since 1986) and where activist organisers get out the ideological party vote, becomes the election that counts. Moderate voters are easily shut out of the process because appeals to the 'base' drown out serious debate on broad issues of national concern. This has increased the importance of ideology in legislating and lobbying activities — creating deadlock, a divided, partisan and mean-spirited House and a subsequent lack of comity and civility in the way decisions are made in Congress or more than likely not made. Political parties in the US are establishing electoral districts that effectively eliminate the right to vote of those who live in districts in which their candidates can never be elected. In effect, the Representatives choose their voters, hardly a democratic ideal.

The inability of Congress — in the absence of a vigorous, bipartisan centre — to address effectively such known and crucial issues as job creation programmes; tax reform; the rising accumulation of public debt; a looming Medicare and Social Security shortfall; immigration reform; a failing education system; and serious energy and environmental problems is a legitimate cause of public dissatisfaction. A Congress that cannot confront these visible challenges will surely lack the reserves of comity and trust to face any unknown and sudden —and perhaps even more dangerous — crisis.

President Obama and many Members of Congress talk publicly about the difficulty of finding bipartisan solutions to public problems based on common ideological ground. The partisan debate has become so rancorous that it prevents the resolution of America's most important public problems. There seems to be no prospect that Congress will deal with this crisis on its own. Most Americans believe it is time for legislators, even in an election year, to show that they are attempting to solve the very real problems of unemployment, debt and deficit facing the United States and not simply storing up points for the 2012 fall campaign. This has engendered some speculation as to whether there will be a non-partisan anti-incumbent wave in reaction to the current unpopularity of Congress.

Lawmaking and legislative procedural manoeuvres

Congressional procedural changes have undermined the normal legislative process in the past four decades. For the most part these entail misuse and overuse of long-standing legislative tools rather than structural reform, but the effect has been to undermine trust in the institution. Current concerns focus on today's majority congressional leadership, but the same tactics were practised in the past by the minority party leadership. A cycle of alleged past abuse and continuing retribution has infected the Congress. This process cannot therefore be blamed solely on one political party. Parties have increased their use of House rules to deny the minority a full debate or effective votes and to make significant alterations of legislation passed by the committees of jurisdiction.

An additional problem is the increasing use of filibusters, amendments and holds to clog the legislative work in the Senate. Figure 5 shows the dramatic rise of cloture motions to stop filibusters in the Senate since 1973. The term 'filibuster' is applied to many different actions in the Senate including: objections to unanimous consent requests; efforts to delay proceedings such as offering scores of amendments, raising points of order and demanding numerous and consecutive roll calls; and the anonymous 'holds'. The latter exemplify misuse of longstanding conventions that are unrecognised in Senate rules and precedents. They allow Senators to give notice to their respective party leader that certain measures or matters should not be brought up on the floor. Since party leaders usually honour such requests, they provide significant leverage to members who wish to delay action on nominations or legislation (Oleszek 2010). The mere threat of a filibuster prompts the majority leader to halt action on a bill, or to quickly move to cut off debate, meaning that the minority can block legislation without actually holding the floor and talking for hours on end, like in the 1939 Frank Capra movie, *Mr. Smith Goes to Washington*. There are too many holds and hostage-taking opportunities for narrow policy objectives and nomination stalling. Filibusters are currently

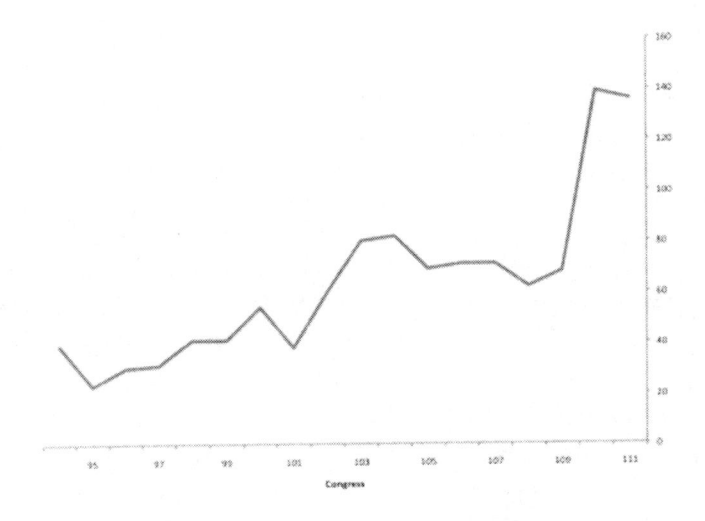

Figure 5: Cloture motions filed in US Senate, 1973–2011

rarely invoked — but often threatened — to gain political bargaining power and negotiating leverage.

Lawmaking and the shattered power of the purse

The Constitution gives the Congress the power of the purse by providing that, 'No money shall be drawn from the Treasury, but in Consequence of Appropriations made by Law' (Article I, Section 9). The entire government will shut down if appropriations are not enacted annually. However, the budget process is seriously broken and needs reform. There is overly frequent reliance on massive omnibus appropriations bills; 'minibus' appropriations; and riders and earmarks added to must-pass appropriation bills as a crutch for acting on significant policy issues. This is often late at night, out of the public view. A major criticism in the last three decades about Congress's performance has been that the legislature is not doing its budget and appropriations job. It is prone to crisis management and always late at every step.

There are too many continuing resolutions and omnibus spending bills. The former, a temporary stopgap funding measure whenever Congress cannot complete action on one or more of the 12 regular appropriations bills by the beginning of the fiscal year (1 October), is an especially egregious problem. In the past, these were only used for short periods (one or two months) but the practice has increased, a significant indication of congressional dysfunctionality. A record 21 continuing resolutions were needed in 2000 before the Republican Congress and President Bill Clinton compromised on their differences regarding the appropriations bills. Partisan deadlock over a continuing resolution in the spring of 2011 came within a few hours of shutting government, as happened in late 1995–early 1996.

There are also too many earmarks and an excess of back-door spending by authorisation committees. Congress keeps changing the rules when it cannot make tough budget decisions. The rules guiding the congressional budget process have been altered almost every year since the implementation of the Budget and Impoundment Control Act of 1974. As former US Representative Lee Hamilton (D-Indiana) concluded: 'When people call Congress dysfunctional, when they say it's not working well, the budget process is Exhibit A in that charge. It's a very serious problem. The world's greatest democracy cannot produce a budget' (2011). The concurrent budget resolutions have been passed on time only twice since 1976, with the federal government having been forced to run on continuing resolutions and supplemental appropriations.

'Backdoor' spending, namely spending not subject to the yearly appropriations process, is the usual way money is 'appropriated' for particularly significant expenditures, such as Social Security payments; veterans' benefits; Medicare and Medicaid (entitlements that together account for over 60 per cent of federal budget outlays). The backdoor funding provisions developed for these entitlement programmes by authorising committees clearly bypass the 'front door' of the two-step authorisation-appropriations sequence and decimate the power to control spending through the appropriations process. The laws that enable the authorising committees charge them with mandating expenditure of federal funds or direct spending on such areas as contract authority; borrowing authority; and entitlement programmes (the fastest growing type of backdoor spending). Backdoor spending subverts the ultimate power of the purse, which is with the appropriators. When the funds for these activities are removed from budget consideration, congressional appropriators find themselves in a poker game with very few chips.

The 2011 experience with multiple continuing resolutions and the debt limit negotiations, reveal a deadlocked Congress. As if that were not enough, the added failure of the Joint Committee on Deficit Reduction to reach any agreement confirms the judgement of dysfunction. Individuals and corporations who try to budget on the bases of brinkmanship, continuing resolutions and off-limit activities often find themselves in home foreclosure and bankruptcy, respectively. It is no wonder the public has lost collective patience with the Congress.

Lawmaking and earmarks

The ballooning of 'earmarks' in the actions of Congress — appropriations, authorisations and tax legislation — may be the most offensive legislative manipulation, and possibly the most egregious of all forms of misbehaviour by Members of Congress. Earmarks, named for the pinning of an ownership tag in the ear of a cow, are when committee members add special narrowly cast provisions in appropriations, tax and authorisation bills, usually for the benefit of their constituents. Typically, they are specific spending provisions inserted at the behest of particular Members and often to meet the particular needs of special interests. The Congressional Research Service identified some 3,000 earmarks worth $19.5 billion enacted in 1996. By 2005, the number of earmarks had grown to almost 13,000, valued at $64 billion. Reform in 2007 shrank the numbers to under 6,000, but they soon climbed back to 8,500 in fiscal year 2009 representing a total of $7.7 billion (Clarke 2009). In 2010, Congress passed a moratorium on appropriations earmarks, but legislators then found a way around the restrictions, especially for tax and authorisation legislation. There has been no enforcement of tax and authorisation earmarks since the 2007 reforms required more transparency and justification for the earmarks. There are instances, no doubt, in which Congress has legitimate reason to specify how money is spent. However, many recent earmarks appear to have been inserted into legislation without public debate, notice, or attribution, especially in must-pass defence and homeland security appropriations, which means the moratorium is not working.

Earmarks present ethical challenges for legislators. The 2005 criminal conviction of US Representative Randy 'Duke' Cunningham (R-California) was built on an exchange of earmarks for personal cash and in-kind payments. They have also been associated with, if not causally linked to, campaign contributions and the exercise of the power of incumbency. The earmarking of funds for a project in the Member's district, fully disclosed and debated, can be a legitimate part of the legislative process. However, project funding as a secret response to a lobbyist's request goes against open and fair budget deliberations. The ability of a single Member of Congress to direct funds to a lobbyist's clients must have further curbs. One way to accomplish this is to require Members of Congress to certify that they have neither sought nor received campaign contributions from an individual registered to lobby them for an earmark in the current Congress. Congress should create a single, searchable online database for all earmark requests (for appropriations, taxes and authorisations) and the amount approved by committee of jurisdiction. The sponsor of any earmark is now identified, but the following information should also be supplied: the department or agency involved; the state or district of the member who made the request; the name and address of the intended recipient; the type of organisation (public, private nonprofit, or for profit entity); and the project name, description and estimated completion date. Finally, a quarter of the House or Senate members present should be empowered to require a roll-call vote on any earmark.

Lawmaking and committees

There are too many committees and subcommittees — numbering 218 altogether as of 2011 — and resultant multiple Member assignments to these panels. Consequently, Congress cannot achieve a rational division of labour, enabling it to work either effectively or efficiently. The policy fragmentation of jurisdictional overlap and competition is excessive, causing delay and deadlock based on jurisdictional turf battles, rather than policy differences. This was clear to the American public in the battles over health care reform and climate-change legislation. The fight over turf has often become more important than policy. Examples of policy fragmentation are extensive: the number of committees and subcommittees with jurisdiction over homeland security is 108, for energy-environment 56, while all 218 panels potentially have some involvement in jobs/economic security.

There is also a problem of policy balance because too many committees are captured by specific interests that represent only one view of issues. This is typically the case with the agriculture and armed services committees, many of whose respective members reside in farm states and close to military bases or defence companies. They may give short shrift to views that represent national concerns, rather than local or parochial interests. When there is little policy equilibrium within committees in the deliberation of various competing policy positions, there is a perception of unfairness and unequal access for policy preferences.

Although there have been periodic attempts to reduce the number of committees, rationalise jurisdictions and decrease the number of committee assignments, potential reforms of the committee system in the House and Senate have all failed since the Senate committee system was overhauled in 1976. There have been 13 committee reform efforts since the Joint Committee on the Organization of Congress in 1946 established the present system of committees. It has been a sorry history of turf protection and defence of the status quo. The consequences of an antiquated congressional committee system are unequal workloads of committees and members, unnecessary duplication, delay and gridlock. Ultimately committees should be used to address and propose solutions for major public problems with the precision that can only result from study, hearings, and debate representing all views (Koempel et al. 2011). A bill should come to the floor with amendments considered in committees from both sides. The practice of not having real conference committees to reconcile differences in House and Senate versions of a bill has also become more common. Congress needs to return to a system that requires members of both the majority and minority to participate and to compromise with one another in order to reach final agreement on a bill that truly encompasses the votes of both chambers.

Oversight

Rigorous oversight of federal agency actions is essential to ensure Congress is aware of the president's policy initiatives and that the laws it has passed are properly implemented. Congress is often too timid on this score when there is unified party government and too aggressive with divided party government. Congress practises 'fire alarm' oversight, waiting until problems arise before reviewing in detail agency activities, rather than a 'police patrol' approach of regular, planned and active oversight. There has been long-term decline in the ability or even willingness of Congress to make thorough use of its oversight powers to keep the executive branch in check. Robust oversight could potentially have prevented or lessened the 2007–08 financial crisis, and the Gulf oil spill of 2010, and ascertained whether agencies were prepared for natural disasters like Hurricane Katrina in 2005. Members of Congress are typically not involved in laws after they are enacted. In some cases, there are too many friendly alliances between committees that authorise programmes, the interest groups that benefit from them and the agencies that administer them. In other instances, the Committee chooses to distance itself from the implementation, knowing the results will not please every constituent. Whatever the excuse, the committees are the guardians of the programmes under their purview. All laws have intended and unintended consequences and they need to be monitored carefully by Congress. As former congressman Lee Hamilton (D-Indiana) contended: 'If we want to make sure that federal agencies are doing their jobs appropriately, with the best interests of the American people constantly in mind, then Congress must do a better job of oversight, looking into every nook and cranny of their activities' (2010).

Deliberation

There is a difference between deliberation and dysfunction. The right to talk a bill to death, the filibuster, has been allowed by the Senate's rules since 1806, but at first it was used sparingly. Its use is on the rise, as shown in Figure 5. Senators these days feel very little compunction about stopping the work of the Senate. The collapse of comity is also a serious problem undermining deliberation. The influx of more partisan former House members into the Senate has undermined its capacity for bipartisan deliberation. There is a lack of true deliberation, comity and civility in House and Senate. There are fewer committee meetings and hearings; conference committees do not meet; laws are often written or substantially revised behind closed doors by the party leadership; and there has been a general demise of the regular order.

Representation and the role of money

The drive for re-election is a logical part of a representative democracy, though it continues to get more expensive. The growth of the 'permanent campaign', with its corollary of negative tactics for undermining the opposition, threatens to weaken severely or even destroy the institution. Its components have carried over into governing, aided by the incidence of wedge issues that help elect people rather than solve public problems.

Too much money in elections and the deregulation of campaign finance that obscures transparency about who is giving and for what have all led to problems of representation in Congress (Garrett 2007). The post-*Citizens United v. Federal Election Commission* (2010) avalanche of non-transparent campaign money from corporations and unions is a serious challenge to representative democracy in America.

Campaign spending has grown rapidly from $3.08 billion in 2000 to $5.29 billion in 2008 for presidential election years and from $1.62 billion in 1998 to $3.65 billion in 2010 in non-presidential election years. Too much money is being spent on elections and too little time is spent in Washington. Campaign costs have become so monumental that Members must spend most of their time raising money, leaving less time for legislating and working with their fellow legislators. There is intense pressure to constantly raise money and campaign. Moreover, congressional candidates — including incumbents — often run against the institution of Congress, thereby undermining trust in the institution even further.

The ease of jet travel allows many Members of Congress to stay with their families in their home district for much of the week and commute to 'work' as part of the infamous 'Tuesday-to-Thursday Club'. In 2011 the House of Representatives spent fewer than 100 days in actual session, the smallest number in 60 years. This is far too short a time to address the monumental challenges of unemployment, debt-deficit, war and the day-to-day issues requiring governance. It is also way too little time for Members of Congress to get to know each other, learn to work together, and find ways of compromise.

It is necessary to find a way of substantially reducing the role of the fundraising lobbyist. When lobbyists participate in campaign fundraising for the same Members of Congress whom they later lobby, there is a serious issue of conflict of interest, coercion and lobbyists getting unequal access to the Members of Congress.

Leadership Political Action Committees (PACs) are also a major part of the question of whether money is being raised and spent appropriately. A Leadership PAC is affiliated with a politician that is separate for his or her official campaign committee. High-level lawmakers have used leader PACs to collect money from their donors for redistribution to their parties' candidates in other districts and states currying favour with candidates who receive the money. Growing numbers of Members of Congress, not just leaders, have formed 'Leadership PACs' to accumulate more money than would otherwise be legally allowed to assist other campaigns and causes. A significant number of these PACs are managed by lobbyists who have direct business with the Members of Congress whose PACs they manage. It is alleged that the choice of a member to chair a committee may depend on his or her ability to raise significant funds in a leadership PAC. Fundraising quotas are often set by the top party leadership for committee chairs and subcommittee chairs. This is a growing problem because money is given by donors who have direct business with the chairs and ranking members of committees who have the quotas.

Campaign contributions closely linked to votes and to earmarks must be restricted. The post-*Citizens United* world of secret unlimited campaign contributions to organisations that may campaign for or against candidates at all levels of government is also a growing problem of conflict of interest and lack of transparency about who is giving and for what.

Representation and lobbying

President Barack Obama has argued that the major problems with Congress stem from interest groups and lobbyists. As presidential candidate in 2008, he made this promise:

> I intend to tell the corporate lobbyists that their days of setting the agenda in Washington are over, that they had not funded my campaigns, and from my first day as president, I will launch the most sweeping ethics reform in U.S. history. We will make government more open, more accountable and more responsive to the problems of the American people (quoted in Thurber 2010, p. 2).

Obama also addressed the destructive power of lobbyists in a town-hall meeting in Bristol, Virginia: 'We are going to change how Washington works. They will not run our party. They will not run our White House. They will not drown out the views of the American people' (quoted p. 2). He continued his tough attack on lobbyists and special-interest money on 8 August 2008: 'I suffer from the same original sin of all politicians, which is we've got to raise money. But my argument has been and will continue to be that the disproportionate influence of lobbyists and special interest is a problem in Washington and in state capitals' (quoted p. 2).

Lobbyists and the massive amount of money from special interests in campaigns are certainly part of the problem with Congress. In the light of President Obama's historic lobbying and ethics reforms in 2009, it is evident that lobbyists are not solely responsible for the problems of deadlock, extreme partisanship and the hostility the public sees in Congress today. Nevertheless, lobbying for local, partisan, and private special interests too often prevails over the national interest, and the real question is whether this stems from the need of each member to collect and spend vast amounts of campaign money or corrupt lobbyists. Lobbying is indelibly linked in its image to campaign finances. However, it can be an essential part of congressional policy-making, as when lobbyists provide expertise that would not be available to the members, but its influence on Congress gives rise to concerns about conflict of interest and whether the advent of massive lobbying campaigns wrinkles rather than levels the playing fields.

The number of registered lobbyists soared from 16,342 in 2000 to 34,785 in 2005, but dropped to around 13,000 in 2010 after the lobbying reforms in the Honest Leadership and Open Government Act of 2007. The drop in the number of lobbyists does not mean there is less lobbying in Washington. The decline in registered lobbyists is due at least in part to failure to register by sliding in under the requirements, in the letter but not the spirit of the reforms. In 1998, registered lobbyists reported spending $1.427 billion; in 2004, they spent at least $2.128 billion on reported activities; and in 2010 their outlays grew to $3.5 billion. However, probably three to four times more is spent in 'grassroots lobbying' and other unregulated efforts. Spending by registered lobbyists has grown by 62 per cent in the last five years. Astonishingly, this averages out to over $9.7 million in lobbying expenditures each day Congress was in session in 2008 or over $6.5 million per year for every Member of Congress. This does not include money spent for strategy; public relations; grassroots; coalition building; issue advertising on television and in the print media; and advocacy on the internet (Thurber 2011). We need new rules to achieve transparency on the access of lobbyists to Members of Congress. There needs to be a new threshold of what is considered lobbying since most advocacy in Washington is not covered by the Legislative Disclosure Act of 1995 (LDA) and the Honest Leadership and Open Government Act of 2007 (HLOGA). Moreover, the current legal definition of a lobbyist is much too narrow because it fails to capture most of the advocacy activity that takes place in Washington (American Bar Association).

Representation and ethical behaviour

Serious problems continue with the way Congress polices itself in respect to ethical behaviour (Straus 2009). There has been a collapse of ethical standards even after the 2007 reforms and the scandals that led to those reforms. In the light of campaign contributions for earmarks and campaign fundraising activities closely scheduled around important votes, there is need for more rigorous enforcement of ethics in Congress. The legislature should enforce existing ethical codes, ensure transparency concerning ethical problems, and impose additional restrictions and reporting requirements similar to those it has placed on lobbyists. In this regard the Senate would do well to follow the lead of the House and establish an independently managed Office of Congressional Ethics — more commonly called an Office of Public Integrity in state government (Straus 2011).

Conclusion: what is to be done?

Most of the problems facing the way Congress works are linked to the lack of true bipartisanship and extreme polarisation. The House and Senate are more partisan than at any time in more than half a century, there is little consensus about major policy problems and solutions, and it is harder than ever for the majority to get its way. However, as long as politics are so polarised in the US, and parties demand strict loyalty, procedural tinkering and minor reforms are unlikely to change how Congress works. We have concluded that Congress is indeed floundering, and in danger of sinking. Therefore, before we give up on the institution, what do we believe are the most important reforms that would improve lawmaking, lead to more consistent and careful oversight, encourage deliberation, and fulfil its constitutional mandate to represent the people? Here are some suggestions:

Reduce polarisation by increasing the number of moderates, a goal that would most likely be accomplished through redistricting by non-partisan commissions.

Improve lawmaking through legislative procedural reforms. Return to the regular order, limit restrictive rules and improve protection of the minority in the House. The Senate needs immediate filibuster reform (Davis et al. 2010). Making it easier to stop the almighty filibuster through invocation of cloture is essential, through a vote, say, of 60 on a first vote to 51 on the fourth vote (Beth 2005). Moreover, Senate filibuster rules must be changed to ensure that the content of filibuster floor speeches is relevant rather than frivolous obstructionism. Secretive and lengthy holds on bills and nominations must also be limited through rule changes.

Of particularly critical importance to the improvement of lawmaking is to require members of both chambers to spend more time on their jobs in Washington. The so-called Tuesday to Thursday Club (TUTH) needs to be stopped with an enforceable required schedule of work in the nation's capital. Members should be in Washington doing the work of committees, oversight, lawmaking, and educating themselves about problems and their solutions. Both parties have tried to stop the TUTH Club, but to no avail. It is time for the party leadership in both chambers to set rules of attendance that have consequences. There needs to be a new schedule for Congress in session, which includes not only the show time on the floor, but the work time in committees and their offices. Congress must also return to real post-enactment conference committees that are transparent to the public and fair to both parties.

Congress generally needs increased transparency in the way decisions are made. Reducing the number of committees and subcommittees, realigning jurisdictions, reducing the number of committee assignments and reducing the amount of policy fragmentation will go a long way to enabling the interested persons and even the public in general to understand the policies being considered. Major advancements in educating the public about the workings of the committee system have been made in the last 30 years, but much more transparency is needed. In particular, all committee and subcommittee hearings should be easily accessible on the internet as they are being held and easily searchable after they have occurred. All congressional documents should be easily accessible and searchable on the internet, including the results of mark-ups and oversight hearings, within a reasonable amount of time.

The ultimate in legislative procedural reforms must come with the congressional budget process. Enforce the calendar and stop the growth of continuing resolutions and omnibus spending bills. Establish a biennial appropriations process with one year for appropriations and the next year for oversight of government programmes. A two-year process is reasonable, as at present the budget is often passed right on the heels of the next year's budget talks. Establish a true Pay-As-You-Go (PAYGO) rule covering expenditures, taxes and authorisations. Abolish earmarks in both the House and Senate by requiring open access to, and discussion of, all narrowly cast appropriations. Stop all new 'backdoor spending' by authorisation committees and require all permanently authorised legislation to be reviewed on a regular basis.

Improve congressional oversight by enforcing oversight calendars set by all committees when getting their legislative branch appropriations. Improve the use of the Government Accountability Office reports and inspectors' general reports. Develop productive working relationships with agency heads and the Office of Management and Budget. Challenge the president on his expansion of power through signing statements, war powers and using secrecy to cover various executive branch decisions.

Improve congressional deliberation by taking advantage of the recommendations above to reduce excessive partisanship, restore the regular order of doing business, reject omnibus bills and other legislative short cuts as well as establishing a predictable work schedule in Washington, which would return fairness to the legislative process.

Improve congressional representation. Thomas Mann and Norman Ornstein argued in two works that a transformational election was needed to change the dynamics of Congress and begin to repair the 'broken branch' (2006, 2009). However, two elections have had a dramatic effect on the make-up of Congress since their initial study appeared, but neither led to significant reform. In fact, the election of 2010 has worsened partisanship and deadlock. Awaiting another transformational election does not therefore offer grounds for optimism that institutional change will surely follow on its heels. The reform agenda needs to be promoted right away rather than eventually.

A key part of representation in America is pluralism, the expression of interests, lobbying through organised groups. The 2007 lobbying and ethics reforms were a weak down payment on improving the regulation of lobbying. There needs to be better definition of lobbying and better enforcement of the Congressional rules and laws. Codes of ethics in both House and Senate are rarely enforced but, coupled with greater enforcement, the Senate should create an office of public integrity and the House should step up its investigations and public reporting of ethical violations. There should be an absolute ban on lobbyists raising money for those they lobby. Leadership political action committees have no role in good government and should be abolished. Fundraising quotas set for committee chairs and ranking members are an invitation to practise undue influence; the quotas benefit no one.

Campaign finance reforms to free legislators from the constant burden of fundraising and engagement in the permanent campaign should be a high priority. In considering the shape of the reforms, all ideas should be on the table, including: limits on money collected and spent; limits on the time money can be spent on campaigning; free television and radio coverage, or equal access at a reasonable price for candidates to help reduce campaign costs; and transparency concerning the source of campaign funds and how they are used. The Supreme Court's *Citizens United* ruling dealt campaign reform a huge blow and spurred the massive growth of money in politics. New reforms are needed to cut the cost and time of campaigning, including restricting or at least disclosing campaign contributions. The time to foster civic engagement and educate the public about how Congress works is now rather than some dimly perceived future.

Finally, democracy requires participation of the electorate and participation can increase by implementing easier early-voting procedures, establishing an Election Day holiday or even half-holiday, expansion of polling hours and lowering registration standards for voting.

We began this discussion with the results of two surveys: one of the public and the other of political scientists. We posed the question as to which group more accurately described the state of Congress today. In the light of the above analyses of problems with the institution today, one can only conclude that the academics inflated their grades and the public saw the problems more clearly. Nevertheless, the suggested reforms have the potential to raise the grades the public award to Congress from Ds to As, raise the assessments of the academics from Cs and Bs to As and, in doing so, provide us all with better, more representative and responsive government.

References

American Bar Association, Task Force on Federal Lobbying Laws, Section of Administrative Law and Regulatory Practice (2011) *Lobbying Law in the Spotlight: Challenges and Proposed Improvements* (Chicago: American Bar Association), 3 Jan.

R.S. Beth (2005) *Entrenchment of Senate Procedure and the 'Nuclear Option' for Change: Possible Proceedings and Their Implications* (Washington DC: Congressional Research Service), 25 March.

D. Clarke (2009) 'Earmarks: here to stay or facing extinction?', *CQ Weekly*, p. 613, 16 March.

Congressional Record (2008), 110th Congress, 2nd Session, H7285, 29 July.

C.M Davis, V. Heitshusen and B. Palmer (2010) *Proposals to Change the Operation of Cloture in the Senate* (Washington DC: Congressional Research Service), 27 July.

S.R Garrett (2011) *The State of Campaign Finance Policy: Recent Developments and Issues for Congress* (Washington DC: Congressional Research Service), 28 Jan.

L. Hamilton (2010) 'There is no substitute for robust oversight', The Center for Congressional Studies at Indiana University, 9 June, http://congress.indiana.edu.

— (2011) 'Assessing the budget breakdown in Congress', The Center for Congressional Studies at Indiana University, 28 Oct., http://congress.indiana.edu.

M.L. Koempel, J. Schneider and B.P.J. Tabit (2011) *Committee Rules in the House on Legislative Activities: Planning for the 112th Congress* (Washington DC: Congressional Research Service), 24 Jan.

M.P. McDonald (2006) 'Redistricting and competitive districts', in (eds.) M.P. McDonald and J. Samples, *The Marketplace of Democracy: Electoral Competition and American Politics* (Washington DC: Brookings Institution Press), pp. 222–44.

T.E. Mann and N.J. Ornstein (2006) *The Broken Branch: How Congress is Failing America and How to Get It Back on Track* (Washington DC: Brookings Institution Press).

— (2009) 'Is Congress still the broken branch?', in L.C. Dodd and B.L. Oppenheimer (eds.), *Congress Reconsidered* (Washington DC: CQ Press).

P.S. Nivola and D.W. Brady (eds.) (2008) *Consequences and Correction of America's Polarized Politics, Volume Two* (Washington DC: Brookings Institution Press).

W.J. Oleszek (2010) *Proposals to Reform 'Holds' in the Senate* (Washington DC: Congressional Research Service), 15 July.

K.T. Pool and H. Rosenthal (1985) 'A spatial model for legislative roll call analysis', *American Journal of Political Science* 29 (2), pp. 357–84.

J.J. Schatz (2010) 'Looking for room to maneuver: can the Senate be fixed?', *CQ Weekly*, pp. 952–62, 19 April.

J.R. Straus (2009) *Enforcement of Congressional Rules of Conduct: An Historical Overview* (Washington DC: Congressional Research Service), 18 Dec.

— (2011) *House Office of Congressional Ethics: History, Authority, and Procedures* (Washington DC: Congressional Research Service), 8 Feb.

J.A. Thurber (2010) 'President Obama, Congress and the battle with interest groups and lobbyists', paper for Conference on American Government, Politics and Policy at the American University at Sharjah, 25 Jan., www.american.edu/spa/ccps/upload/Thurber-Paper-for-AUS-Conference.pdf.

— (2011) 'Obama's battle with lobbyists', in Thurber (ed.), *Obama in Office* (Boulder CO: Paradigm), pp. 127–44.

Appendix

Survey of Political Scientists' Evaluation of Congress
The Center for Congressional Studies
Indiana University
December 2010

1. Does Congress protect its powers from presidential encroachment?
   A   7.5%
   B   47.5%
   C   37.5%
   D   7.5%
   F   0.0%

2. Does Congress carry out effective oversight of the president and executive branch?
   A   2.5%
   B   32.5%
   C   50.0%
   D   10.0%
   F   5.0%

3. Does Congress generally fulfil its national policy-making responsibilities?
   A   15.0%
   B   42.5%
   C   27.5%
   D   12.5%
   F   2.5%

4a) Does the HOUSE allow members in the minority to play a role?
   A   2.6%
   B   10.3%
   C   33.3%
   D   28.2%
   F   25.6%

4b) Does the SENATE allow members in the minority to play a role?
   A   39.5%
   B   39.5%
   C   13.2%
   D   7.9%
   F   0.0%

5a) Does the HOUSE follow good process in conducting its business?
   A   5.0%
   B   40.0%
   C   32.5%
   D   17.5%
   F   5.0%

5b) Does the SENATE follow good process in conducting its business?
A	2.5%
B	10.0%
C	22.5%
D	37.5%
F	27.5%

6a) How well is the HOUSE able to handle the balance between allowing careful deliberation while also being able to act?
A	2.5%
B	42.5%
C	42.5%
D	5.0%
F	7.5%

6b) How well is the SENATE able to handle the balance between allowing careful deliberation while also being able to act?
A	2.5%
B	7.5%
C	35.0%
D	32.5%
F	22.5%

7a) Does the HOUSE engage in productive discussion?
A	2.6%
B	17.9%
C	41.0%
D	33.3%
F	5.1%

7b) Does the SENATE engage in productive discussion?
A	2.5%
B	25.0%
C	40.0%
D	27.5%
F	5.0%

8a) Does the HOUSE allow multiple points of view on an issue to be heard?
A	10.3%
B	28.2%
C	28.2%
D	28.2%
F	5.1%

8b) Does the SENATE allow multiple points of view on an issue to be heard?
A	37.8%
B	48.6%
C	5.4%
D	8.1%
F	0.0%

9a) Does the legislative process in the HOUSE involve a proper level of compromise/consensus?
A	2.6%
B	36.8%
C	34.2%
D	21.1%
F	5.3%

9b) Does the legislative process in the SENATE involve a proper level of compromise/consensus?
A	5.1%
B	23.1%
C	25.6%
D	30.8%
F	15.4%

10a) Does the HOUSE keep excessive partisanship in check?
A	2.7%
B	5.4%
C	32.4%
D	40.5%
F	18.9%

WHAT'S WRONG WITH CONGRESS?

10b) Does the SENATE keep excessive partisanship in check?
A	2.6%
B	15.4%
C	25.6%
D	41.0%
F	15.4%

11a) Is the MAJORITY leadership in the HOUSE effective?
A	47.2%
B	44.4%
C	2.8%
D	2.8%
F	2.8%

11b) Is the MINORITY leadership in the HOUSE effective?
A	12.8%
B	48.7%
C	23.1%
D	10.3%
F	5.1%

11c) Is the MAJORITY leadership in the SENATE effective?
A	16.2%
B	40.5%
C	40.5%
D	0.0%
F	2.7%

11d) Is the MINORITY leadership in the SENATE effective?
A	30.8%
B	41.0%
C	23.1%
D	5.1%
F	0.0%

12) Does Congress hold members to high standards of ethical conduct?
A	5.3%
B	44.7%
C	31.6%
D	13.2%
F	5.3%

13) Does Congress focus on the key issues facing the country?
A	20.5%
B	48.7%
C	25.6%
D	2.6%
F	2.6%

14) Do members educate themselves well on the key issues facing the country?
A	5.1%
B	48.7%
C	33.3%
D	10.3%
F	2.6%

15. Does Congress consider the long-term implications of policy issues, not just short-term?
A	2.6%
B	15.4%
C	43.6%
D	30.8%
F	7.7%

16. Does conflict in Congress reflect substantive differences, rather than political game-playing?
A	7.7%
B	30.8%
C	41.0%
D	17.9%
F	2.6%

17. Does Congress exercise its proper role in the decision to go to war?

A	2.7%
B	13.5%
C	35.1%
D	32.4%
F	16.2%

18. Does Congress exercise its proper role in determining the federal budget?

A	5.4%
B	32.4%
C	35.1%
D	24.3%
F	2.7%

19. Does Congress exercise its proper role in setting the legislative agenda?

A	17.9%
B	59.0%
C	17.9%
D	2.6%
F	2.6%

20. Does Congress reflect our nation's diversity?

A	2.6%
B	33.3%
C	43.6%
D	10.3%
F	10.3%

21. Does Congress make its workings and activities open to the public?

A	23.1%
B	59.0%
C	15.4%
D	0.0%
F	2.6%

22. Do legislators broadly reflect the interests of their constituents?

A	25.6%
B	46.2%
C	23.1%
D	2.6%
F	2.6%

23. Do legislators make a good effort to educate their constituents about Congress?

A	7.7%
B	23.1%
C	41.0%
D	23.1%
F	5.1%

24. Do legislators make a good effort to be accessible to their constituents?

A	41.0%
B	51.3%
C	5.1%
D	0.0%
F	2.6%

25. Does Congress keep the role of special interests within proper bounds?

A	5.1%
B	10.3%
C	48.7%
D	25.6%
F	10.3%

26. Does Congress reform itself sufficiently to keep up with changing needs?

A	5.1%
B	7.7%
C	61.5%
D	20.5%
F	5.1%

27. All things considered, how well does Congress do in representing the interests of the American people?
A	2.5%
B	35.0%
C	47.5%
D	12.5%
F	2.5%

Grade of US Citizens

1. Contacting their members of Congress on issues that concern them.
A	5.0%
B	35.0%
C	45.0%
D	10.0%
F	5.0%

2. Following what is going on in Congress on a regular basis.
A	0.0%
B	2.5%
C	35.0%
D	45.0%
F	17.5%

3. Voting in congressional elections.
A	0.0%
B	5.0%
C	65.0%
D	30.0%
F	0.0%

4. Working through groups that share their interests to influence Congress.
A	2.5%
B	37.5%
C	55.0%
D	5.0%
F	0.0%

5. Understanding the main features of Congress and how it works.
A	0.0%
B	2.5%
C	25.0%
D	52.5%
F	20.0%

6. Having a reasonable understanding of what Congress can and should do.
A	2.5%
B	0.0%
C	32.5%
D	55.0%
F	10.0%

7. Understanding the role of compromise in Congress.
A	2.5%
B	5.0%
C	35.0%
D	50.0%
F	7.5%

8. Being able to get to the core facts of issues before Congress.
A	2.5%
B	2.5%
C	50.0%
D	42.5%
F	2.5%

3

Singularity, separation and sharing: Richard Neustadt's lessons for politicians and political scientists

Nigel Bowles

It is difficult, if not impossible, to imagine the state of scholarship on the American presidency without the work of Richard Neustadt (1960, 1990). He did what few scholars are capable of doing: he not only defined the field but structured it. His propositions are the point of our departure for study of the presidency. So decisive is the influence of Neustadt's intellectual framing that, in the last two decades and more, some critics of his work have urged the need to move beyond his legacy in order to answer new questions through use of new theoretical frameworks. In line with Neustadt's defenders, such as Charles Jones (2001), this study contends that scholars of the presidency have not yet fully recognised the heuristic value of Neustadt's approach and that politicians have not fully grasped the practical political value of his scholarly writing. In making that argument, it explores where the relevance of his intellectual contribution lies and raises other questions in the process of doing so.

> What was his legacy? What imprint did he leave on the office, its character, and public standing; where did he leave his party and the other party nationally; what remained by way of public policies adopted or in controversy; what remained as issues in American society, insofar as his own stance may have affected them; and what were the American positions in the world affected by his own diplomacy? (Neustadt 1990, p. 167)

These are the questions that Richard Neustadt invites us to ask about American presidents. Following his death in 2003, they also suggest questions to ask about him. What is Neustadt's legacy to his professional colleagues? What imprint did he leave upon the profession of political science, its character and public standing? Where did he leave study of the presidency nationally?

Neustadt was a rare political scientist because he transformed the understanding not only of his academic colleagues but also of politicians and general readers regarding what American government actually was and the implications of this, both for presidents and for understanding the office that they hold. He focused, and remained focused, upon the fact and significance of three conjoined realities: the presidency's singularity; that singularity's expression in and through a system of separated branches of government; and of powers being shared between separated and coordinate branches.

In the half-century and more following publication of *Presidential Power* (1960), Neustadt provided the point of intellectual departure for all political scientists and politicians endeavouring to understand what he sought to explain about the presidency. The attention professional scholars still accord to his work indicates that it continues to provide a point of departure through the intellectual appeal of examining the relationship between authority and power over time.

The book explained how American presidents might make the most of their weak office in a separated federal system of coordinate branches of government operating under judicial review. It did so by exploring the relationship between formal constitutional *authority* and *power*, understood as influence. In establishing a framework for analysing this facet of the presidency, Neustadt implicitly invited other scholars to view presidential power as he viewed it, comparing within and across presidencies.

Neustadt connected the academy to the Washington Community. His book caught the attention of politicians in that community because *Presidential Power* took the form of a briefing paper. Through his writing he communicated with his intended audience members in a mode that they recognised and a style they appreciated about the common problems they jointly confronted in making separated government work. As his own memoranda to presidents demonstrated, his private advice had a temper that echoed his public writings. Consistency was Richard Neustadt's watchword: he was nothing if not both authentic and a man of integrity.

One scholar has written that Neustadt's focus upon the relationship between presidential authority and power was 'a critical intellectual breakthrough that forced us to broaden and clarify our thinking and encouraged us to emphasise explanation and generalization in our research. This is the legacy of *Presidential Power* into the 21st century' (Edwards 2000, p. 14). So it was. But it is also more than that. Neustadt may have changed his mind about a number of aspects of presidential politics (and about presidents), but he found no good reason to alter his central contribution to presidential leadership. His signal formulation was to show that a president's power, his 'effective influence', derives from three related sources. The first comprises the presidency's bargaining advantages by which he seeks to persuade others in the Washington Community (members of both Congress chambers especially) that what he wants them to do is what they ought in any case to do for their own reasons. The second are the expectations of members of that Community about 'his ability and will to use the various advantages that they think he has' (1960, p. 179). And the third are the judgements of members of the Community about how voters regard the president, and of how they themselves might be regarded by those same voters if they were to do what the president wants.

Neustadt thereby presented a framework for understanding political leadership in Washington — and by no means just presidential leadership. In the estimation of Truman and Eisenhower, MacArthur and McCarthy were leaders, too. Had these adversaries not been leaders, the two presidents would not have faced such problems in dealing with them. Neustadt's perspective upon Washington is one of interactive perception in a separated and coordinate system. From that perspective, he revealed the differences that an individual president of unusual temperament, experience, confidence and clarity of political purpose can make in a system of government where any number of elected and unelected officials have powerful incentives to contest and resist his asserted leadership. As such, he illuminated what Isaiah Berlin (1957) had termed agency in politics and history.

American federal government provides an appropriate arena for the study of leadership using Neustadt's framework — not just in the White House, but also in Congress and in federal agencies because all participants in that government have to deal with partial and limited grants of authority distributed across coordinate, if rarely coordinated, institutions (Skowronek 2005).

Can Neustadt's framework be used to guide research in presidential politics and government? Despite the prominence of his work in his lifetime, few other scholars employed Neustadt's framework. Yet, as Charles Jones has shown, his work is plainly 'chock-full' of testable propositions (2002, p. 712). It is no less rich a source of wisdom for presidents — aspirant, elect and sitting. Neustadt's intellectual legacy has four decisive elements for them. The first is his *work's practical political relevance for presidents and those who work for them*; secondly, his *distinctive research methodology, especially his thinking in time*; thirdly, his *perspective from over the president's shoulder*; and fourthly, his *perspective upon the presidency as a weak office*.

1. Practical political relevance

Both a political scientist and a political actor, Neustadt facilitated contact between and among the two professional communities. He asked what students of the presidency would have to do to say things to presidents that might be relevant to them. It helped, of course, that he thought it possible for political scientists to say things that were helpful to presidents in their attempts to lead, anticipate and negotiate with Congress, federal agencies, centres of private and public power, American voters, allies and enemies at home and abroad. He was clear about his own answer to the rhetorical question that he posed:

he sought to help presidents see for themselves the possibilities, constraints and risks of leading, in other words of doing more than merely preside over a system of separated powers saturated with points of veto and hobbled by his own weakness in authority. He aimed, first, to convey effectively to presidents what he thought they needed to know; and second, to help them adjust to and surmount their own pessimistic inferences from the presidency's weakness of formal authority.

Quite how Neustadt managed to achieve what he did in bridging the academy and the White House is mostly beyond the scope of this study, but something must be said on the point. There are clues in Neustadt's past to his intellectual perspective and development. His practical political education began early with the compelling theatre of observing the New Deal spectacle of institutional disruption and transformation at close quarters in Washington. The excitement of conversations with his father about participation in the New Deal, and his exhilaration at government's seeming revival of purpose under the leadership of a galvanising president never left him. Nearly 70 years later, he told Charles Jones that: 'People do not believe me when I say that no one walked on the sidewalk in Washington in 1934; they floated six inches above it. At night you could stand in Lafayette Park and look over at the White House and see that halo' (2003, p. 3).

People were, of course, right not to believe the gentle tale that Neustadt told against himself. But his self-mocking narrative matters, for it reveals not just the profundity of his admiration for Franklin Roosevelt but his wider excitement about the possibilities of presidential leadership in the public interest. Neustadt understood perfectly well that the separated nature of the federal system left the United States with a system of coordinate institutions, not a presidential system. But he also held that the presidency offered no more than a possibility — only a possibility in such a system where the office's authority was thin and its domestic power required crafting rather than executing — of reasoned reflection, decision and action. Neustadt's awe at Roosevelt's consummate sense of power in a separated system never left him. He saw in FDR not merely a model but the archetype of how a president should conduct his public life in a Madisonian order. Neustadt's shrewd observation that Roosevelt's self-image was of himself in office and holding power finds an echo in Neustadt's ideal image of the presidency appearing to have been that of Franklin Roosevelt in the Oval Office.

Neustadt's excitement in working at the centre of institutional politics in government survived the freezing experience of war-time service with the US Navy in the Aleutian Islands. Its product was a hunger for a share in government within a separated system, an intellectual but mostly practical hunger. That was why he elected to remain in Washington and take a job with the Bureau of the Budget (BoB) rather than return to Harvard where he had worked before the war. Neustadt felt reassured to find that colleagues in Cambridge and Washington understood his motivation, not least because so many of his academic contemporaries shared and expressed his commitment to government and governing. What a different world that was! Political scientists and students of public administration between 1930 and 1960 were actually valued by politicians. And if the mutuality of the valuation was not general, it was nevertheless sufficient to validate political scientists playing fundamental roles in reconfiguring the executive branch for a new age and new demands upon government.

Neustadt thought that the BoB was the agency best placed to afford presidents the crucial benefit of institutional memory, a sense and knowledge of historical development, of continuities and discontinuities, sources and processes of change. That was a characteristically shrewd assessment of its pivotal significance to the political interactions between the White House, Congress and executive agencies. In his time at BoB during the Truman Administration, Neustadt found the satisfying combination of an important institution doing an indispensable job for a president wise enough to use it as it should be used and a lens through which, as a political bureaucrat and political scientist, he could himself observe the politics of presidential policy-making. The BoB that served the president's political needs therefore served Neustadt's intellectual ones.

Continuing to work on his Harvard doctorate while serving in the Truman administration, Neustadt obtained his PhD in 1951 and then wrote two seminal *American Political Science Review* papers on the legislative clearance function. With the advent of a Republican president, he returned to academia, first holding a post in Cornell and then in Columbia, where he worked from 1954 to 1964.

As he explained to fellow political scientist Charles Jones, Neustadt understood himself not as an academic but as a person active in government who went back to the academy that he had last experienced as a graduate student. In that vein, he brought to his teaching at Columbia, as he did later at Harvard, a perspective of academia from the Washington Community. In his professional life, observing the academy from government and government from the academy, Neustadt did what in *Presidential Power* he had urged presidents to do: to draw relevant lessons from experience for effectiveness. Neustadt was a mightily effective teacher, in part because he met the challenge of rethinking apparently familiar problems. Having read the literature on the presidency published since he had finished his courses at graduate school, he concluded that he wished to say something rather different about the presidency than other scholars had done. *Presidential Power*, aimed at the two target audiences of the academy and government, filled the gap between the academic literature on the presidency and his own experience of the office (Neustadt 1960; Jones 2003, pp. 1–2). Sceptical of its path-breaking approach, four publishers turned down the manuscript but it was finally taken up by John Wiley.

Moving from Columbia to Harvard, Neustadt became Associate Dean of the Kennedy School of Government and, a little later, the founding director of the Institute of Politics within the School, where he worked with Graham Allison and Don K. Price. The three infused the Kennedy School with extraordinary vitality. Neustadt's purpose was crystal clear:

> We did it because we wanted to train public servants, not political scientists. In fact we were not interested in political science per se. I remember saying to myself in the middle '60s, I don't want to have to think about 'whither political science' ever again. It was a boring subject as far as I was concerned. Here [we] were trying to train people to work in the world (Jones 2003, p. 6).

The Institute exemplified Richard Neustadt's commitment to linking political science and political service, worlds that — as former President Bill Clinton acknowledged in his statement of condolence upon Neustadt's death — he bridged more effectively than any political scientist since Charles Merriam himself.

2. *Bringing history back into politics*

Neustadt held to an understanding born of his own long experience, that practical political relevance required three qualities: institutional memory, knowledge and historical awareness. No one could be useful to a president without them. By contrast, a superfluity of adrenalin and hubris among the Nixon, Carter and Reagan staff had, he argued, produced heat rather than light (2000a). Neustadt's proposition on this point lay at the centre of all his writing about presidential politics: thinking about the nature of presidential power could not, he argued, usefully be done except as had been done historically, searching for clues from relevant experience and knowledge about political institutions within and beyond Washington.

Thinking about the nature of political power in this way prompts reflection about inherited values, commitments, ideas and institutions. American federal institutions are distinctive among democratic states in that most are created by acts of lawmaking rather than (as in France and the United Kingdom) by executive prerogative. Their foundation is, literally and symbolically, in public law. Accordingly, politics in America is in large part lawmaking. Indeed, political action in America depends, to an extent unusual among advanced democracies upon law, derived both from the Constitution and from statutes. It is an aspect of American exceptionalism that underlines the force of Neustadt's entreaty to politicians and political scientists alike to find clues in history because the roots of present policy lie in a law-based past. In his public writing and in his advice to presidents, Neustadt looked for such clues and enjoined presidents to do likewise from their own perspective for their own purposes. Among the clues from institutional history upon which presidents and their advisers need to draw are those contained in the institutions and programmes, established by statute, which comprise much of the political architecture of presidents' inheritance from past presidents, congresses, courts and public opinion.

Shortly before he died, Neustadt wrote that 'Social science was much less self-conscious when I went to the government in 1942 or when I came to Columbia in 1954 than it has since become.' This opinion hints at his own attitude to research methods when he was preparing to write *Presidential Power* in the late 1950s (Jones 2003, p. 100). Neustadt was a pioneer of participant observation in the study of presidential politics. It is a major legacy: his work on the BoB's Legislative Reference Division and on *Presidential Power* carry conviction not just because of their analytical depth but because they have the authenticity of an active participant and observer.

Neustadt spent more time in the White House and the Old Executive Office Building than any student of presidential politics save Woodrow Wilson himself. He supplied much of his historical evidence drawn from his own experiences of government. He thought intensely and wrote rigorously about the politics of choosing and the implications of aggregated choices over time. From the White House Office and the BoB, he looked out upon a separated system of government. He observed the weakness of the presidency from within and the temperature of those who saw it from without, and understood the implications of the latter for the former. He drew inferences about the qualities that a president needed to exercise power — which he defined as 'personal influence of an effective sort on governmental action' (1990, p. ix). As Neustadt himself recognised, the section of the analysis in the original edition of *Presidential Power* carrying least conviction is the one in which authenticity is missing — that of Neustadt's assessment of President Eisenhower's use of power, of his attempts to see his power stakes for himself. Eisenhower was the one president out of the three Neustadt studied for the book's first edition whom he either had not seen at second hand (as he had FDR), or had worked for (as he had Truman). His later assessments of Kennedy have the flavour of authenticity for a similar reason: Neustadt advised him, and so assessed him within the framework that he set out in *Presidential Power*.

Neustadt did not get Eisenhower right in 1960. He failed to see the political craft and subtlety in Eisenhower's fiscal and cultural conservatism; his scepticism not just about government but about imperfect markets; and his feel for power in successfully navigating partisan and ideological fissures within both parties. Neustadt's initial failure to get Eisenhower right was less because of the president's conservatisms (which were real) than because he appears at that time to have associated leadership primarily with decisions to act rather than with decisions whether and when to act or not. Neustadt characteristically admitted the error in his 1990 edition entitled *Presidential Power and the Modern Presidents*, Fred Greenstein and others having done close research on Eisenhower's presidential papers in Abilene by the time it was published. In *The Hidden-Hand Presidency*, Greenstein invited his readers to consider fresh evidence bearing upon Eisenhower's political craftsmanship, not least his fine calculations about the costs and benefits, now and prospectively, of acting and of not acting and of presenting those decisions appropriately to different audiences within Washington and beyond (Greenstein 1982). He demonstrated that Eisenhower's leadership had been more creative than the caricatures popular among some liberal critics. And he showed his personality to be more nuanced than was apparent in other portraits of Eisenhower, whose authors could not see beyond their distaste for what they took to be his values.

Neustadt uses the word 'prospectively' to emphasise the importance he attaches to presidents and their advisers' thinking in time when defining problems and clarifying options for choice-making: forward to the intended outcome, and backward from intended outcome to the steps required to attain it. He argues that the improvement of political judgement requires the drawing of appropriate lessons from relevant historical experience, and thereby reducing the risk of repeating grievous errors of commission and especially omission. Writing with Ernest May in *Thinking in Time*, he recommended listing what is known, what is unclear and what is presumed with the object of clarifying options amidst complexity and confusion. Thinking precisely and systematically about historical analogies (not least in being clear about what is analogous and what is not) where national security is at risk was essential, they argued (1988, p. 235). History supplies few answers through analogical reasoning, but does suggest questions both relevant and unsettling. That is history's (and historians') value to decision-makers. Combining these two disarmingly simple techniques would have helped President Carter in deciding how to deal with the supposed 'discovery' of the Soviet brigade in Cuba (Neustadt and May 1988, pp. 92–6). Presidents Johnson and Bush might have helped themselves, too — to think more clearly, in their cases, about the appropriateness, form, timing, and size of American armed intervention in Vietnam and Iraq respectively (Goldman and Berman 2000, p. 51). What Presidents Johnson and Bush did not know, but presumed about South-East Asian and Iraqi history and security, greatly outweighed what they knew, thought they knew, did not suppose important, or felt it inexpedient to enquire about.

Neustadt's concern for history has important implications for scholars of the presidency. Congress is an institution substantially open to scholars; the presidency, by comparison, is closed. Presidents Reagan and George W. Bush tightened that underlying condition by administrative actions that further restrict access to their papers in presidential libraries well beyond limits previously set. Neustadt, however, had the special access that all of his contemporaries lacked. Most scholars of the presidency have not worked and will not work for a president of the United States. Aware of that, Neustadt encouraged scholars to exploit the huge resources of presidential libraries, supplementing them where possible and appropriate with interviews. He did not, so far as I am aware, consider the importance of research in the private papers of US senators and congressmen or of sub-federal officials in order to understand the nature of presidential power as he defined and framed it. Neustadt's omission is surprising because, as he argued, a president's sources of power in those two spheres (professional Washington watchers on the one hand and voters on the other) are functions of the *perceptions* that others have of him and of what they think he might do.

In this respect, his work needs to be improved upon by other scholars. If American politics is to be considered as an interactive and purposeful activity, occurring within and between separated and coordinate institutions with both exclusive and shared spheres of authority, it is necessary to do work in congressional archives. It further requires knowing more about what members of Congress think in private conversations as well as in public speeches about operating in a system of separate institutions of government sharing power. And much more needs to be ascertained about what their constituents tell them. Neustadt's emphasis upon separated institutions *sharing* power implies that presidential authority and power cannot be understood without examining congressional authority and power. Neither can be done without knowing more about how congressmen and senators, past and present, interpret and assess a president's actions and options, capacities and intentions. Their perceptions of him, of what he is capable of doing, of what he might do, are crucial to that knowledge and understanding. From this, it follows that evidence bearing upon the formation and modification of such perceptions is also crucial.

Upon such perceptions, politicians and other members of the Washington Community act. Those perceptions are — as historians have always known and as game theorists have explored — interactive and iterated. The multiplication of interaction and iteration provides a universal framing and the federal system of separated institutions sharing and competing for powers supplies a peculiarly American constitutional engineering. Within the latter Neustadt shows how to evaluate presidents acting politically, and therefore prospectively, in a system that denies the president much by way of authority. The point is extended to (and for) *all* those with whom a president deals.

3. *His perspective from over the president's shoulder*

The third aspect of Neustadt's legacy is his perspective, in his words, *from over the president's shoulder*. From that perspective, Neustadt tried to understand two audiences, each engaging with the other: a 'Washington Community' judging the president's professional reputation and a popular audience judging his prestige. As revealed in his essay 'The presidency at mid-century', his book *Presidential Power*, and his memos to president-elect Kennedy in the winter of 1960–1, Neustadt was alive to the threats to the president's interests that others in his entourage — Cabinet officers certainly, but White House staff too — might pose. In *Presidential Power*, he shows that his staff will neither suffice nor substitute for the president's active looking ahead and thinking backwards. It is what the President sees and how he interprets what he sees that matters. Staff need to help him do his seeing and interpreting, but cannot substitute for his doing so. Their perspectives are not his, Neustadt insists, since 'of all the self-perceptions that can help a President, nothing helps so much as an awareness of his absolutely unique place ... he can count on no one else in Government to sense his interests in precisely his own terms' (1956, p. 642).

Neustadt therefore assesses presidents in regard to their self-awareness, alertness to the singularity of their own perceptions of government and the world, and the implications of that singularity for other people's perceptions of them and of their purposes. It is in this context of iterated anticipatory judgements of presidents by the Washington Community, and vice versa, that Neustadt poses questions about his key concept of 'professional reputation', one of the two foundations of his effective influence. Neustadt's questions are: 'What do members of the Washington Community make of the President? Are they convinced that he has the skill and will to use his advantages in a particular case? How do their judgements of him in a particular case shape his influence over them? What do they expect the President to do and why? What do they think he might dare to do?' The second foundation is his concept of 'popular prestige' as being not merely the president's popularity but congressional interpretations of that popularity which, he writes, is shaped by 'what the people outside Washington see happening to themselves' (1990, p. 83).

What Neustadt is not engaged in is an attempt to subvert the Madisonian system by manipulative means. Rather, he seeks to convey his understanding of how the Madisonian system might work. His perspective is *from* the President's desk, but the perspective is *of* other legitimate sources of authority and power in a system anything but presidential. And it is in this setting that Neustadt makes what he terms his 'crowning point', that it is politically wise for a president to make decisions and exercise judgements with a view to his *prospective* influence

(1990, p. xviii). That the president should do so matters, Neustadt wrote, for the president himself now and in the future, the other branches of the Madisonian system, and for American citizens:

> Not the President alone but everyone who cares about our government's performance has a stake in his concern for his own influence prospectively. A President serves others in the system as a customary source of the initiatives, the mediation and, on certain issues, final judgements that are needed by those others in the doing of *their* jobs. The better he does his, the better they can do theirs ... our Madisonian government is energized by productive tension among its working parts (1990, p. xviii).

4.   *His perspective upon the presidency as a weak office*

Neustadt identified the presidency's weakness of authority as being expressed in multiple constitutional and political constraints, and in the limitations of a system neither majoritarian nor unitary. Working for Truman and advising Kennedy had taught him that there existed a 'basic and dilemma-nurturing disparity between the Presidency's obligation to initiate and its capacity to achieve' (1956, p. 640). Reliance upon authority to frame and set agendas would not suffice for governing effectiveness. His many illustrations in *Presidential Power* (not least, the steel seizure case and the dismissal of MacArthur) strengthen his argument that in a separated system, a president's exercise of authority is but the starting point of leadership. Persuasion, cajoling, inducement and bargaining with coordinate authorities both elected and unelected had, he wrote, to precede and follow such exercise of authority.

Explaining institutional and policy change in American politics requires an account of presidential action and its bases in authority and power. Neustadt insisted that the distinction between 'powers' and 'power' was fundamental. Neustadt interpreted 'powers' (which he understood to be a synonym of 'authority') as being that which a president may lawfully do; and 'power' that which he has the resources, capacity and will actually to do. The distinction can be applied to any public official. The two concepts are different, and presidential politics lie at the heart both of the difference between them and their relationship in political practice. No analytical sense of the argument in *Presidential Power* and *Thinking in Time* can be made without holding on to the distinction. Neustadt felt sharply the frustration of his colleagues' failure to do so:

> The whole profession balked at that distinction. As far as I know, nobody applies it. Yet it's the essential piece of shorthand that I thought would keep the analysis on track. Well, if everybody ignores it, it sure as hell doesn't keep the analysis on track. What have I done wrong? There isn't a single political scientist who is meticulous about distinguishing personal influence from constituted authority (Jones 2003, pp. 10–11).

Quite why the analysis should have moved off-track is a question mostly beyond this chapter's scope. But the explanation might in part lie with the concept of authority having for a long time been remote from the concerns of political scientists. With the exceptions of Hannah Arendt and Joseph Raz, modern political theorists have had little more to say about it than do empirical political scientists or political historians (Raz 1990). That said, interest has grown palpably in the first decade of this century, not least among scholars of the presidency. Some political scientists, working on the foundations of constitutional scholars such as Edward Corwin, Louis Fisher and Richard Pious, argue that the sphere of presidential authority is extensive and highly consequential. Kenneth Mayer (2001), Philip Cooper (2002), William Howell (2003), Greg Robinson (2001) and Andrew Rudalevige (2005) have in different ways developed accounts of those initiatives (including executive orders, proclamations, signing statements and tightened control over the federal regulatory process). Presidents can use these creatively on their own account without need of *immediate* recourse to Congressional assent. Neustadt himself welcomed this intellectual development which, in one respect, marks a return to a distinguished tradition of constitutional law that, somewhat ironically, once formed a large part of the literature on the presidency against which Neustadt had himself reacted when he taught American government at Columbia (Howell 2003, p. 181).

More research into presidential authority is required for its own sake. But it is also needed in order to build on this fourth aspect of Neustadt's intellectual legacy. The key problem arising is the relationship between authority and power over time and between policy arenas. Fundamental though the analytical distinction between the two concepts is, they are in political practice temporally related. Among all public officials, only the president has the political and governing capacity to disrupt, destabilise and disturb the patterns of policy and politics across the multiple arenas of American public life. He has the huge advantage of being first mover in an arena of his choosing. But he is not the only necessary mover. To sustain his initiatives, Neustadt argued, the president in a separated system needs to base his action upon more than his own authority.

Has Neustadt's claim become more contestable since the early 1970s? President Nixon's decisions in August 1971, to control prices and wages by command, impose trade tariffs and abandon the Bretton Woods system, rank as three of the boldest uses of presidential authority in post-war American history. Bristling with confidence that a Republican president publicly set against such controls would lack either the imagination or the effrontery to embrace them as his own, a Democratic Congress had in 1970 given the president legal authority to impose price and wage controls. (Nixon's authority to impose trade tariffs, by contrast, sprang from his own expediently expansive conception of presidential authority under Article II.)

These instances of authority are very different, constitutionally and politically. But Nixon's initial political success in employing them, a success fundamental to his successful re-election in 1972, was common to both and appears to undercut the notion of the presidency's weakness in authority. He spent almost all of his foreshortened second term in failed attempts to deal with the consequences of his attempt to reduce the rate of inflation by commanding that it fall: between December 1972 and August 1974, short-term interest rates rose from 4.77 per cent to 8 per cent and the rate of consumer price inflation rose from 3.41 per cent to 10.95 per cent. Yet viewed over a period of three years rather than 18 months, Nixon plainly paid a high price for stretching his authority so far: his tactically creative use of authority to shore up his popularity before the 1972 elections proved a strategic failure.

Since the early 1980s, presidents have frequently enjoyed success not only in identifying opportunities to act unilaterally and recognising the advantages to them of doing so, but in often being able to act without significant congressional resistance. This is signified, for example, by President George W. Bush's sequential prosecutions of war and state-building in Iraq. Yet the case of Iraq is consistent with Neustadt's argument, not least because the occupation's outcome has been complex and contested and beyond the capacity of a president to cope with unilaterally. The use of authority and powers of command had, in the case of Iraq, to yield to the politics of interaction, bargaining, persuasion and argument, especially as congressional-presidential politics again became infused with cross-party distrust. In other words, the politics characteristic of the separation of powers reasserted themselves. The attractions of politics as the invoking of authority, so beguiling in the short-term, proved inadequate in the long-run as the complexities of policy implementation overwhelmed the deceptive clarity of command.

In the short-term, a president's use of authority has formidable potential to transform the subject of political debate, its terms of reference and the costs and benefits to others of participating in it. Employing authority as command may indeed induce both shock and awe in the observer (and the recipient). In the medium-term, however, authority does not suffice. Both the Nixon and Bush 43 presidencies illustrate some of the limits to its potential. By using authority on behalf of unachievable objectives, a president risks not just his policy objective but his professional reputation and standing in history.

Conclusion

The four aspects of Neustadt's legacy to students of presidential leadership matter, not least for continuing to offer the opportunity of shaping an agenda for research into America's singular public office within a separated system. Right up to the end of his long life, he remained optimistic about the vitality and possibilities of a separated system of government. The president and Congress, Neustadt observed, are 'at once so independent and so intertwined that neither can be said to govern save as both do.' On the rare occasions those two formally coordinate branches actually coordinate in government, they face 'other claimants to a share in governing: the courts, the states, the press, the private interests, all protected by our Constitution ... All these are separate institutions sharing each other's powers. To share is to limit; that is the heart of the matter, and everything in this book stems from it' (1990, p. x).

Responding to papers given at a conference at Columbia some 40 years after the writing of *Presidential Power*, Neustadt reflected upon two questions:

> Can what we do as students dealing with the presidency be relevant to sitting presidents? My answer is yes, sometimes, though with difficulty often and uncertainty always ... And how hard should we try? My answer is, harder than we do now (2000a, p. 459).

Neustadt thought there were five obstacles to success in striving for relevance (and in being recognised by presidents and other officials as relevant):

First, Neustadt adjured scholars of the presidency and presidents alike to think about relevant experience, but cautioned those advising inexperienced presidents (as presidents in their first year and beyond necessarily are) that a president may not know what he needs to know, but also may not know his inexperience prevents him from recognising the fact.

Second, Neustadt warned that presidents often fail to think temporally, not recognising that — given the organisation of the White House being typically sequential, arranged around decision-making, of choosing between options — it is essential not to suppose that matters once decided are closed or, worse, solved.

Third, Neustadt observed that presidents sometimes appear to conclude that the presidency is even weaker than most presidential scholars believe it to be. There are indications that this conclusion resides in the minds of most post-war presidents, Barack Obama not excluded.

Fourth, Neustadt regretted the low standing of the political science profession among politicians, which he thought a product of too little political science being written in accessible language and of many political scientists' ill-concealed distaste for politics. Politicians, he thought, find quixotic the pursuit of regularities in political behaviour with the aim of producing predictions.

Even if the predictions were to work, he argued, he doubted that they would be of great use to presidents, 'at least in spheres where Presidents have greatest need.'

And fifth, Neustadt inferred from the weakness of institutional memory in the White House that 'the origins and possibilities and pitfalls of the institutional arrangements he inherits, to say nothing of the changes he may put in place in ignorance of what was tried before. Or rather, all too many are at hand, with partial knowledge and imperfect recollection' (2000b, p. 463).

Towards the end of his life, Neustadt reflected that his advice to colleagues in the academy had not been heeded — primarily because it had not been understood. His work was everywhere celebrated, but not everywhere carefully considered. As for practical politicians, presidents had more commonly read *Presidential Power* than appeared to have appreciated the fact and implications of its author's warnings about the presidency's weakness in authority. As John Maynard Keynes thought was often true of 'practical philosophers', so it may be said that Neustadt has influenced politicians and academics alike (1936, pp. 382–4). It is, however, overdue that the audiences of today should pay closer attention to Neustadt's works. We need — we still need — to take more seriously precisely what Neustadt had to say, how he set what he said in context, and thereby to recognise the richness of his writing for presidential analysis and for presidential craft in a separated system. At the time of its publication, one reviewer found *Presidential Power* 'not completely systematic, and not very scientific' (Price 1960, p. 736). Whether it was or remains good social science is arguably unimportant, however. What is of central significance is that Neustadt's work encapsulates priceless wisdom about the practical imperatives of sharing in the governing of a Madisonian system.

References

I. Berlin (1957) *Historical Inevitability* (Oxford: Oxford University Press).

G.C. Edwards III (2000) 'Neustadt's power approach to the presidency', in (eds.) R.Y. Shapiro, M.J. Kumar and L.R. Jacobs, *Presidential Power: Forging the Presidency for the Twenty-First Century* (New York: Columbia University Press).

E.O. Goldman and L. Berman (2000) 'Engaging the world', in (eds.) C. Campbell and B A. Rockman, *The Clinton Legacy* (New Jersey, NJ: Chatham House).

P. Cooper (2002) *By Order of the President: The Use and Abuse of Executive Direct Action* (Kansas, KS: University Press of Kansas).

F. Greenstein (1982) *The Hidden-Hand Presidency: Eisenhower as Leader* (New York: Basic Books).

W. Howell (2003) *Power without Persuasion: The Politics of Direct Presidential Action* (Princeton, NJ: Princeton University Press).

C.O. Jones (1995) 'A way of life and law', *American Political Science Review*, 89, 1, pp. 1–9.

— (2001) 'Professional reputation and the Neustadt formulation', *Political Studies Quarterly* 31 (June), pp. 281–95.

— (2002) 'Knowing what we want to know about the presidency', *Presidential Studies Quarterly* 32 (Dec.), pp. 710–19.

— (2003) 'Richard E. Neustadt: public servant as scholar', *Annual Review of Political Science* 6, pp. 1–22.

J.M. Keynes (1936) *The General Theory of Employment, Interest, and Money* (New York: Harcourt, Brace).

K.R. Mayer (2001) *With the Stroke of a Pen: Executive Orders and Presidential Power* (Princeton: Princeton University Press).

R.E. Neustadt (1956) 'The presidency at mid-century', *Law and Contemporary Problems*, 21, 4, pp. 609–45.

— (1960) *Presidential Power* (New York: John Wiley).

— (1990) *Presidential Power and Modern Presidents* (New York: Basic Books).

— (2000a) 'The weakening White House', *British Journal of Political Science* 31 (1), pp. 1–11.

— (2000b) 'A preachment from retirement', in R.Y. Shapiro, M.J. Kumar and L.R. Jacobs (eds.), *Presidential Power: Forging the Presidency for the Twenty-First Century* (New York: Columbia University Press).

R.E. Neustadt and E.R. May (1988) *Thinking in Time* (New York: Free Press).

D.K. Price (1960) 'Review of *Presidential Power*', *American Political Science Review* 54 (3), p. 736.

J. Raz (ed.) (1990) *Authority* (Oxford: Blackwell).

G. Robinson (2001) *By Order of the President: FDR and the Internment of Japanese Americans* (Cambridge, MA: Harvard University Press).

A. Rudalevige (2005) *The New Imperial Presidency: The Resurgence of Presidential Power after Watergate* (Ann Arbor, MI: University of Michigan Press).

S. Skowronek (2005) 'Leadership by definition: first term reflections on George W. Bush's political stance', *Perspectives on Politics*, 3, pp. 817–31, Dec.

4
Tenure reform and presidential power: the single six-year term proposal

Niall A. Palmer

Introduction

During the 20th century, a series of rapid changes transformed the presidency, affecting not only its raw power and influence upon other political institutions but also, crucially for an office defined as much by image as by constitutional authority, its status in the eyes of the American public and news media. From the turn-of-the-century administration of Theodore Roosevelt to the Lyndon Johnson presidency in the 1960s, George Reedy notes, 'commitment to the presidential concept' by politicians, voters and the news media became so pronounced that Americans were 'virtually incapable of thinking of the United States in other terms' (1976, p. 229). Progressives frequently encouraged the trend towards greater presidential influence as a useful means of bypassing entrenched conservatism in national and state legislatures but many on the political right were disturbed by the expansion of executive power, viewing it as both cause and consequence of liberal interventionism and as a threat to the equilibrium of constitutional government.

The experiences of Vietnam and Watergate created a broad, albeit temporary, consensus across the ideological spectrum that presidential power should be restrained. Achieving this goal, however, proved problematic. In the unstable political and economic environment of the late 1970s, the damaged institution inherited by Gerald Ford and Jimmy Carter struggled to function effectively. Weak party organisations, decentralisation of power in Congress, a newly aggressive and cynical media, disengaged voters, and interest group hyper-pluralism combined to generate widespread perceptions that the political system was failing to deal with the nation's problems. Calls for a renewed sense of national purpose, starting with more inspirational and effective leadership from the White House, showed that the 'president-centric' approach to national politics was alive and well in the late 1970s, but no identifiable consensus existed as to the nature or extent of the changes required to improve the quality of executive leadership. Whatever their impact, intended or otherwise, upon executive authority, legislated reforms in the last quarter of the century, such as the Budget and Impoundment Control Act of 1974 or the Line-Item Veto Act of 1996 (later ruled unconstitutional by the Supreme Court in *Clinton v. City of New York*, 1998) were invariably limited in their impact by the narrowness of their scope or judicial review. Reformers on both sides of the ideological divide consequently came to believe that more fundamental change was needed to enhance the authority of the presidency and restore its capacity to provide clear and creative leadership.

A long-standing idea for executive branch reform envisages a constitutional amendment replacing the current arrangement of two elected four-year terms for the president with a single, non-renewable, six-year term. To its supporters, this offers the opportunity to recalibrate some of the dynamics of executive power, bringing the office closer in concept to the original designs of the nation's founders while repairing the damage done to public esteem for the office by some of its recent occupants. Additionally, ending the president's preoccupation with re-election and diluting the impact of partisanship on decision-making would, it is claimed, remove two of the major systemic obstructions to bold and imaginative leadership. To critics of the reform, such notions are not only unworkable but blatantly anti-democratic. A single, non-renewable term, they argue, would isolate the presidency by de-coupling it from the traditional sources of political legitimacy upon which it relies for its authority. It would reduce the president's ability to engage on equal terms with other political institutions and actors and destabilise the traditional checks and balances of the constitutional system by removing the presidential re-election cycle while leaving the congressional cycle intact. Finally, critics contend, the reform idea is underpinned by a focus on presidential authority and independent initiative which moves the nation further away from, not closer to, the ideals of the founders.

Background

The single-term proposal, described by political scientist Theodore Lowi as 'the panacea that will not die', has been debated for over two centuries (1985, p. 195). Delegates to the Philadelphia convention indicated their early approval for the principle of tenure limitation by voting in favour of a single, seven-year term for the new national executive in May 1787. Subsequently, however, they endorsed the proposal for perpetually renewable four-year terms which emerged from the Committee on Unfinished Business later in the convention. In 1826, Representative Joseph Hemphill of Pennsylvania became the first of many members of Congress to reinstate the idea via a constitutional amendment (Congressional Research Service 2004, p. 2). The constitution of the Confederate states adopted the formula for its presidency in 1861. Moreover a number of US presidents endorsed the idea of removing the presidential re-election prerogative. They included Andrew Jackson, James Polk, Grover Cleveland and Benjamin Harrison in the 19th century, and William Taft, Lyndon Johnson and Jimmy Carter in the 20th century.[1] After the principle of constitutionally limited tenure was adopted in 1951 through the Twenty-second Amendment, which restricted the president to two elected terms in office, the frequency with which single, six-year term proposals appeared in Congress declined. During the 1980s, the Committee For Single Six-Year Presidential Term — whose founding members included former Attorneys General Herbert Brownell and Griffin Bell (members of the Eisenhower and Carter administrations respectively), former Nixon Treasury Secretary William Simon and former Carter Secretary of State Cyrus Vance — continued to press for reform.[2] Although the committee made little headway in persuading Congress to take up a constitutional amendment, the term-limitation concept continued to provoke discussion among politicians, historians, political scientists and reporters, fuelled, in part, by the Republicans' 1994 midterm election pledge to introduce term limits for Congress members.

The appeal of the six-year term rests partly on its simplicity — the deployment of one structural reform to counter a range of perceived faults in the contemporary political system — and partly on its advocates' capacity to adapt their arguments to differing political environments. Tenure reform is recommended as a remedy against presidents who push resentfully at the boundaries of their constitutional authority in order to expand presidential power, as exemplified by Lyndon Johnson, Richard Nixon and George W. Bush. Yet, it is also prescribed for 'weaker' presidencies beset by external pressures or internal contradictions, as exemplified by Jimmy Carter, George H.W. Bush and — arguably — Barack Obama. The latter condition is, in fact, the main concern of reformers. In this, their campaign differs, both in nature and design, from the effort which produced the Twenty-second Amendment in 1951. Where the *prima facie* purpose of that constitutional change was to check presidential expansion and demagoguery, six-year term advocates primarily highlight the dangers of a politically and institutionally *weakened* presidency. Their arguments therefore tend to focus mainly upon the perceived

---

[1] Reformers sometimes add Warren Harding and Dwight Eisenhower (and Richard Nixon frequently) to this list. However, both Harding and Nixon later changed their minds (Nixon issued a public retraction) while Eisenhower expressed sufficient reservations over the motives and wisdom underlying the Twenty-second Amendment to raise questions over the depth of his commitment to a single, six-year term.

[2] Also active on the committee's behalf were actor Charlton Heston and senior executives from AT&T, Ford, PepsiCo and the New York Stock Exchange.

discrepancies between the *ideal* and the *actual* — between uplifting visions of the executive's potential and its too-often disappointing realities.

The narrative underpinning the reform case depicts a gradual erosion of executive power during the second half of the 20th century that restricted the president's capacity to shape the nation's political agenda. According to reform supporters, this development resulted from the combination of changes in the wider political environment and certain systemic reforms. Its consequence was to generate deadlock and instability in the American political process and weaken the presidency as a source of national political leadership and moral inspiration.

Franklin D. Roosevelt's 12-year administration signalled a historic shift in the power balance between the presidency and Congress. The crises of the Great Depression and World War II called for rapid, centralised and coordinated decision-making that Congress was ill-equipped to provide. Increasingly, Americans looked to the presidency as the 'legitimating center of the national political order, the primary repository of national hopes and ambitions' (Heclo and Salomon 1981, p. 287). Under FDR, the 'stewardship' model of presidential leadership (the prototype for which had been trailed by the active-interventionists Theodore Roosevelt and Woodrow Wilson) permanently displaced the older 'Whig' concept of presidential power (Korzi 2003) to become the standard by which all future presidents would operate. As political scientist Stephen Skowronek observed, however, 'expectations had been heightened, but since the basic constitutional structure had not changed, modern American government appeared to have placed incumbents in difficult straits' (2008, pp. 7–8). Despite the office's theoretical dominance during its post-1933 'imperial' phase, successive presidents struggled to manage their expanded domestic and international responsibilities and the needs of the federal government's greatly enlarged client base. Other systemic factors further complicated the president's task of summoning order from chaos in the 1970s and beyond. These included the volatile legislative environment resulting from the decline of the seniority system in Congress, the dramatic rise in the size and influence of lobbying operations on Capitol Hill, the decline in party-line voting and rising bureaucratic resistance to executive-led reform. Presidents and other executive-branch actors were increasingly forced to engage in micro-bartering for their victories, altering legislative proposals in response to interest group demands and constructing makeshift coalitions in Congress on an issue-by-issue basis. Consequently, legislation was often flawed or unworkable.

The growth of television and the tendency of the news media to accentuate the public focus upon the presidency as the dynamic centre of national political power aggravated these problems — enhancing expectations of presidential performance and deepening disappointment at its failure. The presidents of the late-20th-century governed, as William Leuchtenburg notes, 'in the shadow of FDR' but were hard-pressed to match either the dynamism of his first 100 days or the long-term impact of his policies (2001). By the 1970s, reformers contend, the ability of the president to define and pursue broad visions for the nation had been so obstructed that the fashionable liberal concept of 'presidential government' was, to all intents and purposes, illusory. 'Far from being in charge', Hugh Heclo observed at the end of the decade, 'the president must struggle even to comprehend what is going on' (Heclo and Salomon 1981, p. 284).

Vietnam and Watergate generated an anti-executive backlash in the media and on Capitol Hill. New restrictions, some more effective than others, were placed upon presidential autonomy in foreign and domestic policy while confrontational media coverage eroded much of the deference previously shown to the office of the presidency. This latter development, reformers suggest, impeded attempts by Ford and Carter to utilise the unique capacity of the presidency for defining broad national goals and articulating policy choices. By the end of the Carter administration, a consensus appeared to be growing that fundamental reform would be necessary to salvage presidential authority. Shortly before Ronald Reagan's first inauguration, *Newsweek* published a lengthy article assessing the crisis facing the modern executive. The office, it noted, had 'in some measure defeated the last five men who have held it' and was now 'becoming a game nobody can win' (1981, p. 25).

Neither Reagan's capacity to redefine the national agenda nor the ability of Bill Clinton and George W. Bush to win re-election muted the reform critique. Rather, its advocates claim, each of these presidents highlighted, in different ways, the weaknesses of the modern institution — from Clinton's reliance on focus groups and sacrifice of ideological principles for electoral ends to the questionable legality of Bush's heightened national security powers and the use of divisive 'wedge tactics' to secure re-election. Before Reagan, no president since Eisenhower had completed eight years in office. By 2009, three presidents had served two full terms in office but the presidency, in the view of reformers, remained a 'broken' institution.

The case for reform

The single six-year term proposal combines *two* changes to presidential tenure in one measure. The first — ending the president's right to seek re-election — is intended to enhance both his measurable impact upon the policy process and the less tangible, but equally important, 'moral authority' to which all presidents aspire but which relatively few have achieved in recent years. Reformers believe that cynicism arising from suspicions that the president's actions and speeches are motivated by electoral self-interest would be reduced, thus strengthening the executive's hand in negotiations with Congress and improving its image in the media. Public faith in the institution of the presidency would rise as presidents were more associated with altruistic, principled leadership based upon the broader national interest.

The second element of the reform — the lengthening of the president's term from four to six years — seeks to foster stability and coherence in the political process by permitting the executive more time to introduce, oversee and adjust key policy initiatives while also reducing the scope for bureaucratic resistance to reforms.

A closer examination of these goals allows us to understand the ways in which reformers seek to address current systemic problems through the reshaping of political perception and behaviour. It also highlights the contentious interpretation of presidential power which lies at the heart of the reform case.

The electoral cycle

The removal of incumbent presidents from the electoral cycle appears, at first glance, to be simply an extension of the constitutional status quo existing since the passage of the Twenty-second Amendment. The two reforms differ fundamentally, however, in their primary aim. The amendment was passed by the Republican-controlled 80th Congress in 1947, after the death of FDR. Although Dwight Eisenhower considered it 'in large degree an act of retroactive vindictiveness against … Roosevelt rather than the result of judicious thinking about the institutions of the Republic', the amendment's sponsors maintained that the option of perpetual re-election encouraged the cultivation of personality cults (Murphy 1972, p. 254). Further, the accumulated bureaucratic and judicial appointments of multi-term presidents threatened to extend their partisan influence for years beyond the lives of their own administrations, restricting their successors' ability to chart their own course. A heavy dose of 'institutional opportunism' certainly motivated the amendment. The Eightieth Congress, the first GOP-led Congress since 1931, was hostile to New Deal-initiated liberalism, under whose banner FDR and Truman had made the presidency into a powerful force for economic activism and social reform. Also at work was a more deeply rooted mistrust of executive power which had influenced American political development since the late 18th century (Gregg 2000, p. 92). Bowing to arguments that the right of voters to reward or reject presidents at the ballot box remained sacrosanct, reformers stopped short of eliminating re-election altogether. Heavy stress was laid, however, on the importance of respecting the precedent set by George Washington of retirement after two terms and Thomas Jefferson's expressed hope that 'should a president consent to be a candidate for a third election, I trust he would be rejected on this demonstration of ambitious views.'[3]

The single-term proposal differs from the Twenty-second Amendment in its intention to liberate and augment, rather than restrict, presidential power. By closing off the re-election option, reformers hope to 'take the politics out of the presidency ... to elevate the presidency above selfish or factional ambitions' in order to facilitate firm, disinterested, and visionary leadership (Cronin 1980, p. 354). Time and again, it is claimed, important domestic and diplomatic initiatives are 'warped' by the re-election imperative, with necessary sacrifices and bold vision subordinated to voter preferences. William Quandt, though unconvinced by many of the reformers' arguments, concedes that one consequence of the two-term system has been 'a foreign policy excessively geared to short-term calculations, in which narrow domestic political considerations often outweigh sound strategic thinking' (1986, p. 826).

Illustrating this point, Jimmy Carter, who supported tenure reform during and after his occupancy of the White House, maintained that his efforts to secure the release of American hostages from Tehran in 1979–81 were hampered by the necessity to fight off Senator Edward Kennedy's challenge to his re-nomination in spring 1980 and by the general election campaign against Ronald Reagan. Resentment of the 'intrusion' of electoral calculations in foreign policy seems to have been widespread in the top echelons of Carter's administration. Former National Security Adviser Zbigniew Brzezinski and Secretary of State Cyrus Vance concurred that, in Vance's words, 'bad decisions are made under the pressures of months of primary elections ... at home and overseas, we are frequently seen as inconsistent and unstable' (Quandt 1986, pp. 829–30).

The full impact of the distorting influence of re-election campaigns was detectable, reformers contend, in American policy towards Vietnam in the last weeks of the Kennedy administration. According to former JFK-staffer Kenneth O'Donnell and Democratic Senate Majority Leader Mike Mansfield, the president had resolved by the fall of 1963, to withdraw US military personnel from South Vietnam but could not contemplate an announcement to that effect before the 1964 elections for fear of inviting accusations of weakness from Republican opponents (Buchanan 1988, p. 131). Presidential *activity*, rather than inactivity, has also been criticised for its electoral implications. Attacked in some quarters as 'gratuitous military action for political reasons', the air-strikes ordered by President Bill Clinton on Iraq in September 1996

---

3 Quoted by Senator Hiram Johnson of California, a Republican Progressive, in a CBS radio broadcast, 'The third term issue: the soul of America', New York, 18 Oct. 1940. Located at www.ibiblio.org/pha/policy/1940/1940-10-18a.html.

reaffirmed reformers' belief that crucial strategic decisions in foreign policy are too often shaped by presidential concern with re-election.[4]

Identical problems, it is argued, obstruct policy formulation at home. Necessary decisions are often deferred by administrations because of their electoral implications. Treasury Secretary William Simon recalled a preparatory session for the 1976 State of the Union address at which bold tax and welfare proposals were considered. President Ford initially approved the proposals: 'Boy, I agree with this one hundred percent. We're going to do it.' Immediately, Simon noted, 'the political advisors' heads snapped around, and he added, "Next year." Of course, "next year" never came for us' (O'Connor and Henze 1984, p. 12). Equally significant was Ford's announcement of his intention to pardon Richard Nixon, within weeks of succeeding the disgraced former president in August 1974, and his early announcement that he would run for re-election in order not to appear a 'lame duck' president. The Nixon pardon, in this context, appeared to some as a deliberate effort to clear the way for Ford's re-election bid by preventing the former president's trial from dominating newspaper headlines in 1975–6 (Werth 2006).

The manipulation of legislative agendas to suit re-election timetables is also held to obstruct innovative policymaking by encouraging a rushed, ad hoc approach to governance. Under a single six-year term, claim supporters of this constitutional reform, the Task Force established by Bill and Hillary Clinton in 1993 to examine options for a radical overhaul of the health care system would have had more time to explore viable legislative strategies, consult cabinet officials and cultivate public opinion. Instead, to save time and debate, it deliberated *in camera,* cut corners by failing to coordinate cost estimates with Treasury forecasts and spent relatively little time canvassing grassroots public opinion. Officials later attributed this strategy to the need to push a cohesive package through Congress as fast as possible before the midterm elections. For the sake of speed, the chance for major reform of health care provision during a period of single-party control of government was lost.

Reform supporters present Clinton's capitulation to congressional Republicans on both welfare reform and the Defense of Marriage Act (DOMA) in 1996 as further evidence of the negative consequences of re-election pressures. In both cases, they were less disturbed by his abandonment of core liberal principles, since their primary notion is that presidents should be able to 'do what is right even if this meant that their party would lose votes … or their own political future would be damaged' (Cronin and Genovese 2004, p. 329). Rather, the issue was Clinton's *motivation* for the abandonment and the subsequent cost to public trust in the presidency. Two of the president's

---

4   French President Jacques Chirac claimed the air-strikes were designed to help Clinton 'look tough before the presidential election.' See T. Branch, *Clinton Tapes*, p. 394.

senior liberal advisers resigned in protest at White House backing for the welfare bill while Clinton's approval of DOMA undermined years of work by Democrats cultivating the trust of gay voters. In both cases, reformers claim, public faith in principled presidential leadership suffered as a consequence of Clinton's electoral calculation.

Re-election pressures have accumulated over time and now threaten to divert the attention not only of presidents but also of other political actors and the news media from important policy issues. Nomination rules reforms in the 1970s, for example, increased the number of presidential primary contests held by Republicans and Democrats, forcing candidates to start exploratory committees and fundraising initiatives years, rather than months, in advance of the convention. This backward momentum often distracts the media from its responsibility to inform the electorate of key political developments and debates. As political scientist Burke notes, 'The situation is increasingly debilitating for a sitting president as attention now focuses on the upcoming presidency earlier and earlier each election cycle' (2009, p. 4). As a consequence, reformers contend, innovative leadership from the White House and the implementation of key policy goals must be squeezed into an 18-month window of opportunity at the outset of a president's tenure or risk being lost altogether.

Term extension and 'moral authority'

In calling for a presidency 'more scrupulous and less prone to self-interested political motives', Jimmy Carter emphasises the potential of tenure reform as a solution to the dilemmas confronting Clinton and other presidents seeking re-election (Schack 1996, p. 757). Increased public respect for the office, he contends, would confer on the president 'greater moral authority and credibility, and perhaps greater influence on ... policy formulation' (Congressional Research Service 2009, p. 22). Presidents would, by implication, feel more confident in promoting their core beliefs and defending administration priorities against pressures from Congress or special interests. Reformers stress Franklin Roosevelt's maxim that the presidency is 'pre-eminently a place of moral leadership' (quoted in Cronin 1980, p. 1) and it is this belief, not simply the aim to save the president time and angst in policymaking, which constitutes the radical core of the case for a single, six-year term. Reformers do not seek merely to tinker at the margins of executive influence but to effect a fundamental change in presidential behaviour and in responses to, and perceptions of, executive power by other political actors.

It is, perhaps, unsurprising that Carter's arguments dwell particularly on notions of credibility and moral authority. His 1976 election campaign, conducted in the aftermath of Watergate, criticised the corruption and patronage endemic in Washington and attacked the 'old politics' of power-bargaining with party bosses and special interests. In office, he rejected the combative partisanship and extensive use of patronage characteristic of his two Democratic predecessors, Harry Truman and Lyndon Johnson. Instead, Carter sought to emphasise the national and moral, rather than sectional or partisan, aspects of executive leadership. As Representative Barber Conable (R-New York) put it, less than sympathetically, the president often 'just decided what was right and announced it' (*Newsweek* 1981, p. 29). Some senior Carter administration officials, including Griffin Bell, later attributed much of the blame for the ultimate failure of this approach to the reluctance of Congress and the media to separate Carter's actions as president from his electoral interests as titular head of the Democratic party. Carter himself complained that journalists and Congress members were too inclined to 'dispute or contradict the president on the issues for strictly political reasons' (Davis 1987, p. 435).

Ineligibility for re-election, from this perspective, improves the president's ability to frame policy debates in broader national and moral terms, making more egregious acts of political self-interest, such as Clinton's approval of DOMA, unnecessary. 'Trust' and 'moral authority' are regarded by reformers as equal in importance to the popular vote as a power resource for the presidency. As Lawrence Schack notes, 'A President who is not trusted cannot be effective. If re-election pressures subvert credibility and foster skepticism, the presidency is continually undermined, thereby precluding effective government' (1996, p. 758).

A second important benefit claimed by supporters of tenure reform is the extension of the minimum term for presidents from four to six years. As Godfrey Hodgson observes, 'It is always election year in Washington' (1980, p. 210). Under current arrangements, the constraints of presidential and congressional election cycles cut deep into the time available to pass legislation. By the spring of an administration's second year, House members and a third of senators are increasingly distracted by primary challenges in their home district. They are less receptive to presidential initiatives unless these carry some tangible electoral benefit and may be overtly hostile to them if they carry significant risk. Even if the campaign does not produce an opposition-controlled Congress (an outcome which had serious implications for Clinton after 1994 and Bush after 2006), the president's own political capital is still likely to have fallen sufficiently by the third year of the administration to embolden his opponents in Congress to delay or defeat administration bills in order to diminish his re-election prospects.

As Lyndon Johnson told a staffer in 1965, 'You've got to give it all you can, that first year ... You've got just one year when they treat you right and before they start worrying about themselves' (Edwards 2009, p. 121). Yet, the first year of a new presidency is often fraught with problems and most administrations require a settling-in period to learn the ropes, notably with regard to locating the levers of power, testing media management strategies, developing congressional liaison operations and staffing their departments. During this phase, mistakes are often made, from which, under a four-year term, there is little time to recover. The early months of both the Carter and Clinton administrations were marred by the early bungling of congressional relations and tactical errors in dealing with legislative priorities such as energy and health care.

Compounding these problems is the inevitable bureaucratic 'drag' on the president's policy agenda — a resistance to change which hardens as a four-year term progresses. Since federal government agencies are generally more 'loose confederations of semi-autonomous bureaux', than monolithic, centrally coordinated structures, it is difficult for the president, within a four-year time span, to control their activities (Marchand 1984, p. 201). By the middle of the third year, the rate of policy implementation tends to slow, pending the outcome of the next election. During this time, presidents focus on achievable short-term gains, rather than radical reforms, regardless of their importance to the nation.

In summary, the six-year term is presented by its advocates as an empowering and facilitating device, not a restricting one, with the potential to raise the president above partisanship, providing him with both the time and the tools to govern in the national interest. In their assessment, this re-empowerment of the presidency, resulting from its enhanced 'moral authority', would make a substantial difference to the dynamics of national politics and the quality and dignity of executive leadership.

The case against reform

The proposal for a single, six-year term traditionally draws strong opposition from a majority of politicians as well as political scientists, historians and journalists, who contend that institutional or behavioural dysfunction cannot be corrected by a single, structural adjustment. The radicalism of the reform, moreover, is criticised as excessive — 'tantamount to an argument', Buchanan suggests, 'that the only solution to a broken arm is amputation' — and more likely to *diminish*, not increase, the stature of the presidency (1988, p. 134). To its detractors, the idea fails to account for the complexity of political and institutional relationships, misconstrues the role of the presidency in those relationships and is, at base, a fundamentally anti-democratic measure.

The electoral cycle

Critics of reform broadly accept that re-election pressures can negatively impact upon presidential foreign and domestic policy-making. However, they contend that the prospect of a second encounter with the electorate — and the reward or punishment for successes or failures — also exerts a positive influence over presidential behaviour. Presidents are compelled to re-examine their priorities, recalibrate policies in response to shifting trends in public opinion and regain the trust of alienated voter groups. Examples of positive recalibration, it is claimed, are as numerous as the negative examples identified by reformers. Political scientist Beth Fischer suggests, for example, that the 1984 re-election campaign induced an unexpectedly conciliatory tone in the president's foreign policy statements during the Reagan administration, beginning with Ronald Reagan's radio broadcast of 16 January calling for 'greater cooperation and understanding' between the US and the Soviet Union. In her assessment, this departure from the aggressive Cold War rhetoric of the first three years of the Reagan presidency was partly influenced by the need to 'appeal to moderate voters who had been disturbed by the president's hardline rhetoric' (1997, p. 496). The motivation behind other positive foreign policy actions, such as Nixon's visit to China or the Clinton peace mission in Northern Ireland, could also be attributed to the desire of both presidents to bolster their foreign policy records for electoral gain. More importantly, critics note, definitions of 'positive' or 'negative' outcomes are a matter of partisan or ideological perspective. The early withdrawal of troops from Vietnam by President Kennedy, for example, would have represented a 'negative' rather than 'positive' outcome to Republican conservatives and to supporters of traditional containment theory across both major parties. Similarly, Reagan's softened rhetoric, which paved the way for arms reduction treaties with the Soviet Union in the later 1980s, attracted praise from moderates and liberals but was deplored by neoconservatives, such as Irving Kristol, as a misguided strategy that threw away valuable military and strategic advantages over the communist bloc. On a related point, some of the most controversial executive decisions on foreign policy, including the 1961 Bay of Pigs invasion, the 'secret bombing' of Cambodia in 1969, and the 1989 invasion of Panama, occurred during the first year of the presidential terms of Presidents Kennedy, Nixon and Bush Snr. (Karol 2009, p. 53). None of these actions could realistically be ascribed to re-election pressures and none would have been prevented under a single, six-year term.

While opponents of reform do not necessarily disagree with Quandt's contention that 'foreign policy issues are likely to be assessed at the White House in terms of whether or not they can help advance the incumbent's re-election bid' (1986, p. 832), they regard the problem as exaggerated. Re-election inevitably affects strategic planning to an extent, but is not necessarily the decisive factor in every case. Instead, as Buchanan argues, the influence of the re-election campaign is 'sometimes bad, sometimes good and sometimes irrelevant' (1987, p. 135).

Another flaw in the reform case is its tendency to overlook the potential impact of re-election, which projects not only backward into the first term but also *forward* into the second. Clinton's re-election in November 1996, for example, was instrumental in providing the president with fresh leverage against members of Congress who opposed compromise with the White House on the issue of deficit reduction. House Republicans had attempted to wrest the initiative on fiscal policy from the president after the GOP victory in the 1994 midterms, resulting in a stalemate and partial government 'shutdown' in 1995. With Clinton's re-election and opinion polls indicating that a majority blamed Republicans for the impasse, senior Republicans were persuaded to accept a negotiated compromise which produced the first budget surplus for nearly three decades in 1999. Re-election therefore has the capacity to re-energise administrations, providing fresh political capital and impetus for their legislative agenda and sometimes stimulating a realism in Congress that enhances political stability.

Reformers are inclined to dispute this point, arguing that the record of presidential failure or corruption during second terms (from the weakened political clout of Dwight D. Eisenhower and George W. Bush to the Watergate, Iran-Contra and Monica Lewinsky scandals) undermines the case for re-election. Critics point out, however, that the seeds of all three second-term scandals were planted during the *first* years of the Nixon, Reagan and Clinton administrations, a problem unlikely to be avoided by introducing a single, six-year term. Further, opponents of reform lay most of the blame for the lame-duck status of second-term presidents squarely upon the negative impact of the Twenty-second Amendment and suggest repeal of the amendment would go some way to removing the need for passage of a second, more draconian, term limitation measure.

President and party

A non-renewable term, critics argue, would also be likely to increase the political isolation of the president as a consequence of the de facto electoral divorce of the executive branch from the party organisation. The prospect of re-election serves as a constant reminder to presidents of the realities of institutional and political interdependence. Notably, two prominent supporters of the single six-year term — Richard Nixon and Jimmy Carter — were among those presidents least inclined to welcome such reminders. Both frequently resisted pressures to engage in party-building activities and mediate intra-party disputes. Re-election staff at the Committee to Re-elect the President (CREEP) maintained a contemptuous distance from the Republican National Committee and congressional campaign committees throughout 1972, in accordance with Nixon White House directives, CREEP 'grabbed all the political contributions … leaving little or nothing for congressional or state candidates' (Ambrose 1989, p. 498). Similarly, Carter 'did not encourage new Democratic talent or ideas' and 'neglected both the mechanism and the vision of the party.' The apathy generated among Democratic activists by White House disinterest in party priorities was a key factor driving Edward Kennedy's challenge to the president's re-nomination in 1980. This also ensured that after his election defeat, Carter would 'disappear like dew on a hot day' insofar as his own party was concerned' (*Time* 1980, p. 28).

Despite the impact of reforms to candidate selection rules, growth of interest groups, and the executive's use of modern media tools to connect directly with voters, party organisations remain powerful bulwarks, helping presidents to weather voter hostility, media antagonism and congressional investigations. Partisan loyalty was essential in shoring up Democratic congressional support for Bill Clinton during the 1998–9 impeachment hearings and helped protect Ronald Reagan's support base at his administration's low point during the 1986–7 Iran-Contra scandal. This was partly due to the efforts made by both presidents to maintain the semblance of a working relationship between the White House and the national party. Although their strategic synchronisation was often erratic, the two remained committed to traditional partisanship as the lynchpin of democratic politics. Perhaps coincidentally, both served two full terms and both publicly opposed adoption of the single, six-year term.[5]

Carter, conversely, treated the national Democratic party as something of an albatross around his neck. For its critics, tenure reform threatens multiple repetitions of the Carter experience. National and state party organisations would feel less obliged to remain loyal to presidents who declared their 'independence' from party interests after their election to a single term. This reconfiguration of the party-executive relationship would also embolden party leaders in Congress to take greater control of policy-making and deprive the White House of its traditional influence over the party's machinery, patronage and nominating conventions (Willis and Willis 1952, p. 480). The significance of this weakened influence was not lost on Richard Nixon, who switched sides in the single, six-year term debate some years after leaving office. Justifying his reversal, Nixon argued that a single term would only accelerate the weakening of respect for the president's authority since other political actors 'will know that the day will soon come when he can no longer do something to them or for them' (1990, p. 209).

The president-party relationship would, therefore, be radically weakened by tenure reform, compelling presidents to rely more heavily on plebiscitary leadership via the mobilisation of public and media support. This argument, of course, runs directly counter to reformers' claims that ending presidential re-elections would *decrease* the destabilising influence of constantly changing trends in popular and partisan opinion. According to critics, tenure reform

---

5   Reagan publicly opposed *any* form of term limitation and, after leaving office in January 1989, became titular head of a campaign to repeal the Twenty-second Amendment.

would have the effect of 'freeing the president from party but not from popularity', a development that would not guarantee enhanced public respect or political effectiveness for the presidency (Lowi 1985, p. 196). As political scientist George Edwards points out, Bill Clinton discovered, to his cost, the limits of the president's ability to 'use public support as leverage to overcome known political obstacles' during the 1993–4 health care reform debates (2009, p. 196).

Abolishing presidential re-election, of course, would not remove the influence of partisan campaigning on Washington politics. Despite the security of tenure enjoyed by a six-year president, the congressional re-election cycle would continue unaltered, with all House members and one-third of the Senate facing re-election every two years. This new disjunction could only increase the political and psychological distance between Congress and the White House. Senators and Representatives would continue to renew or lose their mandates at regular intervals, permitting Congress to claim closer adherence to changing trends in public opinion. The president's mandate, however, would age irreversibly from the moment of his inauguration — a process that could only work to his disadvantage as his term progressed. Midterm elections are generally seen as referenda on incumbent administrations but also have an energising impact upon Congress. Where some midterms (1998, 2002) may inflict minimal damage on the president's party, and may even strengthen it, others (1994, 2006, and 2010) can substantially undermine presidential support in one or both chambers, encouraging opportunistic resistance to administration policies in the new Congress. Under the system of renewable four-year terms, the possibility of the president's re-election will afford at least a modicum of protection against the problem of the 'ageing mandate'. Without the ability to match the legislature's mandate-renewal cycle, however, the president would quickly appear out of touch with public opinion, lose essential bargaining power and seem less relevant in policy debates than the parties and interest groups who had consulted repeatedly with the electorate. Accordingly, the lame-duck status already afflicting post-1951 second-term presidents could begin even earlier in a six-year, non-renewable term.

Reformers' faith in structural manipulation seems badly misplaced therefore. Congress, still working to its own electoral calendar, would be less inclined to comply with White House requests or directives which conflicted with its own, more partisan, goals and could hardly resist asserting the superiority of its 'updated' mandate. Enhanced 'moral authority' would not compensate the White House for this new disadvantage. As political scientists Erwin Hargrove and Michael Nelson note, 'New rules will not cause legislators to follow presidents' (1984, p. 270). Instead, the unreformed congressional election cycle would present presidents with an uncomfortable dilemma — either to remain above the fray during midterm campaigns or to campaign for their allies in Congress. The first option would simply reinforce a general perception of the presidency's isolation from current political debate. The second would require it to engage in precisely the kind of partisan activity which, reformers argue, eroded executive credibility in the first place.

In summary, to opponents of reform, the single, six-year term is a bad fit for America's political system as currently constituted. Without further substantial constitutional changes to address the string of unintended consequences which, critics believe, would follow tenure reform, the office of the presidency would lose much of its political clout, becoming still more dependent for its continued influence on focus groups and media support.

Politics and the presidency

Underlying the debate over the impact of re-election campaigns on policy and institutional relationships, critics identify a more fundamental difference of opinion over the nature of politics itself — labelled by Bruce Buchanan the 'politics is good' versus 'politics is bad' argument (1987, p. 135). Reform advocates aim to increase the president's 'moral authority' through careful cultivation of a dignified, non-partisan image which elicits respect and trust from the public. They exhibit distaste for the obligations of routine partisan politics, at least to the extent that these involve the executive. During the Carter administration, Press Secretary Jody Powell admitted the president 'enjoys building a consensus with the public more than with the legislature' (McCleskey and McCleskey 1984, p. 133). White House relations with Congress in the Carter years were notable for the 'inadequate use of the carrot-stick trade-off', the combination of arm-twisting and inducement which the president considered demeaning to executive dignity (Ayres 1984, p. 135). Carter's 'Rose Garden' re-election strategy was instead designed, probably unwisely, to transmit the message that the president was too busy governing the nation to indulge in the distraction of appealing to the electorate. This negative view of the participation of sitting presidents in election campaigns reaches back to the early days of campaigns for the single, six-year term. At the height of the Progressive era, California Senator John D. Works, an early reform supporter, denounced the spectacle of a president running for re-election as 'degrading to the President himself ... [it] brings his great office into disrespect.'[6]

For opponents of reform, in contrast, Schack suggests that politics is 'good' (1996, p. 767). The fundamental premise underpinning modern liberal democracies is assumed to be the duty of elected officials, from the president downwards, to maintain close contact with the electorate, from whom power and legitimacy are drawn. To ensure executive leadership remains responsive,

6 Senator John D. Works, speech on 'Presidential term', *Congressional Record* 49, 10 Dec., 1912 (Washington DC: Government Printing Office), p. 404.

presidents must continually interact with public opinion on many levels — through elections, focus groups, websites, press conferences and opinion polls as well as through other institutions and agencies such as Congress, political parties and interest groups. As the chronicler of the imperial presidency, Schlesinger Jr., declared regarding the importance of re-election, 'Few things have a more salubrious effect on a president's … sensitivity to public concerns than the desire for re-election.' The efforts presidents must make to engage with the modern electorate are arduous and time-consuming but escape from this interaction is deemed neither practical nor desirable. They must persist or forfeit altogether their claim to represent the active electorate or the broadly defined national interest. Placing the presidency above politics, Schlesinger concludes, is 'plainly hostile to the genius of democracy' (2004, p. 388).

Opponents of reform often base this part of their case upon Alexander Hamilton's claim, in *Federalist #72*, that 'desire of reward is one of the strongest incentives of human conduct'.[7] For Hamilton, the very concept of term limitation is potentially harmful to the practice of democracy. The obligation to submit to regular interim judgement by the electorate encourages presidents to conduct themselves in ways which attract sufficiently broad public approval to secure re-election. Buchanan concurs that this 'power of anticipated approval' should never be regarded as a distraction, still less a burdensome by-product of modern mass politics, but as a crucial means by which 'democratic control is most tangibly, consistently and meaningfully exercised' (1987, p. 138).

The prospect of re-election acts as an efficient method for constraining leaders who may be tempted to behave irresponsibly or corruptly in their conduct of the nation's affairs. Here, Hamilton notes, the founders' agreement upon a constitutional arrangement of *renewable* four-year terms for presidents was necessary in order 'to make their interests coincide with their duty'. If presidents no longer feared repudiation at the polls, those 'inducements to good behavior' which, he freely admits, spring from the selfish hope of political reward, would be eliminated. Once released from such worries, presidents 'might not scruple to have recourse to the most corrupt expedients to make the harvest as abundant as it was transitory.'[8]

Contemporary writers reiterate Hamilton's fears of the corruptive potential of term limitation but go further, expressing concern at the possible consequences of increased isolation of the Oval Office from the stimuli of interaction with the electorate. Negative psychological traits, such as petulance, paranoia, arrogance and stubbornness, would be magnified by further distancing the president from the electorate. Term limitation has already clearly demonstrated

---

7   A. Hamilton, '72: the same view continued in regard to the re-eligibility of the president', in Hamilton, *Federalist 72*, p. 414.
8   Ibid.

its inability to mitigate this problem. As Schlesinger points out, Congress, in passing the Twenty-second Amendment, ignored Hamilton's warnings by institutionalising the 'lame duck' second term. The amendment did nothing, however, to prevent the three major late-century political scandals which followed.

Equally disturbing to critics is the implication that American government requires the services of a 'philosopher-king' in the Oval Office. Conflicting perceptions over the ideal *character* of the presidency, like those concerning the nature of democratic politics outlined above, lie at the heart of the debate over reform. Reformers and their opponents adhere to starkly differing interpretations of the ideal role for the chief executive within the American political system, a difference hinted at in Weeks' 1913 attack on presidential electioneering and more fully expounded by Jimmy Carter. Underpinning the entire reform critique is an urge to return the presidency to a more 'dignified' phase of its history, before the rise of competitive party systems compelled presidents to rely upon partisanship, patronage and political bargaining to achieve their objectives. Under early presidents, particularly Madison and Monroe, aloofness from political street-fighting was considered an essential virtue — enabling presidents to retain public confidence by avoiding the appearance of partisan bias or preference in sectional rivalries. The 'popular presidency', as defined by Ralph Ketcham and exemplified in more recent years by Dwight Eisenhower, cultivates and stores public approval by avoiding divisive issues, facilitating compromise between rival groups and rhetorically downplaying the importance of narrow ideological perspectives or party agendas in favour of appeals to altruism and national unity. Rather than behaving as the victor in a contest between bitter rivals, the 'popular' president 'gains office … by seeming not to have a partisan program at all' (Ketcham 1987, p. 226).

Diametrically opposed to this model is the 'partisan presidency', exemplified by Andrew Jackson and later presidents such as Woodrow Wilson, FDR, Ronald Reagan, and George W. Bush. Presidents of this ilk embrace and pursue party interests, often treating partisan goals and the national interest as synonymous. The strength of this approach, and its success in eclipsing the 'popular' model, derives from its willingness to *spend*, rather than simply accumulate, the authority and credibility gained through popular support. As the American political environment changed rapidly through the 19th and 20th centuries and absorbed far higher levels of mass participation, most modern occupants of the presidency felt it necessary to accept *competitive* coexistence with other political actors and institutions. As suggested earlier, the expansion of federal authority elevated the status of the national government's chief executive until he appeared to frame and direct much of the nation's political dialogue.

Nevertheless, reform critics point out, the political system is not, and was never intended to be, president-centred. To reorder institutional relationships for the convenience of the president's 'moral authority' not only overestimates the power of a single structural change but places undue emphasis on presidential performance as a measure of the health and fitness of the system as a whole. Without a wholesale redesign of the constitutional balance of powers, scaling back, in particular, the role of parties and interest groups, there can be no return to the days of Monroe. 'If we have learned anything in recent years', Cronin and Genovese note, 'it is that the doctrine of presidential infallibility has been rejected' (2007, p. 469).

The complex challenges facing all presidents must be confronted and overcome through the exercise of superior political skills. Some presidents have aspired to rise above the partisan fray but, historian James MacGregor Burns reminds us, 'They have failed because the office is political in every sense of the word' (1965, p. 270). By a combination of luck and judicious husbanding and deployment of political resources, some presidents will succeed in pushing legislation through Congress and maintaining healthy opinion poll ratings. Others will fail. It is difficult to conceive that a single, six-year term would have tempered the vicious mindset of the Nixon White House, changed Jimmy Carter's attitudes towards patronage and bartering, or offset George H.W. Bush's flawed communication skills. The moral authority prized by Carter, critics contend, must be earned, spent and, if possible, renewed. It cannot be conferred by a constitutional amendment which, in the view of many political scientists such as Thomas Cronin, remains nothing more than 'an illusory quick fix' for a complex, deeply rooted set of institutional and political problems (quoted in Petracca 1992, p. 660).

Conclusion

There is something strangely un-American about the proposal for a single, six-year presidential term. Indeed, the deployment of term limits at any level of the American political system often seems incongruous in a political culture which thrives on *mano a mano* combat and celebrates the power of the ballot in rewarding or punishing elected officials. The nature of the single, six-year term proposal itself reflects this contradiction. Term-limitation reflects a thread of suspicion towards executive authority which runs through the American political psyche, yet reformers' seek to *enhance,* not to restrict, that authority. Support for this reform, unlike support for the Twenty-second Amendment, derives from frustration that presidents appear more powerless than dictatorial. According to its advocates, the only practical solution to this problem is to re-invent the presidency as an essentially non-partisan force dedicated to conciliation and visionary leadership and less susceptible to the destabilising influences that complicate modern mass politics.

As such, the reform is far more radical than it appears at first sight. As a solution to the problems afflicting contemporary American politics, however, it is badly flawed. Its interpretation of the nature and purpose of presidential leadership is idealistic but entirely out of step with modern public and media expectations of the office. The experiences of Jimmy Carter and, more recently, Barack Obama suggest that a sober, above-the-fray stance has limited utility as a power resource. Public support, unfiltered and unorganised by political parties or special interests, remains an unstable commodity and a poor substitute for an ideologically committed base. Moreover, severing the electoral connection between presidents and voters would inevitably increase the sense of psychological isolation which has plagued holders of the office since George Washington. In some respects, reformers' preoccupation with 'detachment', 'respect', and 'moral authority' as the ideal foundations of executive influence reflect an urge to return the presidency to its paternalistic, early-19th-century roots, but the nature of modern mass democracy makes such a project not only impossible but also ill-advised.

'Stripped of its romance', *Newsweek* observed in January 1981, 'the history of the American Presidency is a record of long passages of muddling through and intermittent episodes of greatness' (p. 26). Advocates of tenure reform overlook this fact in their persistently negative view of conventional political activity and their in habitual tendency to identify 'good' government with the president's ability to get his own way. As William Quandt notes, '[F]requent elections and the concept of popular sovereignty were all meant to limit abuses of power, not to make it easy for a president to govern' (1986, pp 835–6).

Opponents of reform, including the present author, acknowledge that much is wrong with the modern American political system and with the theory and practice of executive power. For them, a single, six-year presidential term — embodying antiquated concepts of leadership and bringing with it a string of unintended consequences — would do little to solve these problems and could only be a backward step for American democracy.

References

M.G. Abernathy, D.M. Hill and P. Williams (eds.) (1984) *The Carter Years: The President and Policy-Making* (London: Frances Pinter).

S. Ambrose (1989) *Nixon: The Triumph of A Politician 1962–1972* (New York: Simon and Schuster).

Q.W. Ayres (1984) 'The Carter White House staff', in Abernathy, Hill and Williams (eds.), *The Carter Years*, pp. 144–64.

T. Branch (ed.) (2009) *The Clinton Tapes: A President's Secret Diary* (London: Simon and Schuster).

B. Buchanan (1988) 'The six-year one term presidency: a new look at an old proposal', *Presidential Studies Quarterly* 18 (1), pp. 129–42.

J. P. Burke (2009) 'The evolution of the George W. Bush presidency', in M.J. Rozell and W. Gleaves (eds.), *Testing the Limits: George W. Bush and the Imperial Presidency* (Lanham, MD: Rowman and Littlefield), pp. 3–22.

J.M. Burns (1965) *Presidential Government: The Crucible of Leadership* (Boston: Houghton Mifflin).

Congressional Research Service (2004) *CRS Report for Congress: Presidential and Vice Presidential Terms and Tenure*, Thomas H. Neale (Washington DC: CRS).

— (2009) *CRS Report for Congress: Presidential Terms and Tenure: Perspectives and Proposals for Change*, Thomas H Neale (Washington DC: CRS).

T. Cronin (1980) *The State of the Presidency* (Boston: Little, Brown).

T. Cronin and M.E. Genovese (2004) *The Paradoxes of the American Presidency*, 2nd edn. (New York: Oxford University Press).

— (2007) '"If men were angels ...": presidential leadership and accountability', in (eds.) J. Pfiffner and R.H. Davidson, *Understanding the Presidency* (New York: Pearson Longman).

J.W. Davis (1987) *The American Presidency: A New Perspective* (New York: Harper & Row).

G.C. Edwards (2009) *The Strategic President: Persuasion and Opportunity in Presidential Leadership* (Princeton, NJ: Princeton University Press).

B.A. Fischer (1997) 'Toeing the hardline? The Reagan Administration and the ending of the Cold War', *Political Science Quarterly* 112 (3), pp. 477–96.

G.L. Gregg II (2000) 'Whiggism and presidentialism', in P.G. Henderson (ed.), *The Presidency Then And Now* (Lanham, MD: Rowman and Littlefield).

A. Hamilton, J. Madison, J. Jay (1987 reprint) *The Federalist Papers* (London: Penguin).

E.C. Hargrove and M. Nelson (1984) *Presidents, Politics and Policy* (Baltimore, MD: Johns Hopkins University Press).

H. Heclo and L.M. Salomon (eds.) (1981) *The Illusion of Presidential Government* (Boulder, CO: Westview Press).

G. Hodgson (1980) *All Things to All Men: The False Promise of the Modern American Presidency* (London: Weidenfeld & Nicolson).

D. Karol (2009) 'Resolved, the 22nd Amendment should be repealed', in (eds.) R.J. Ellis and M. Nelson, *Debating the Presidency: Conflicting Perspectives on the American Executive* (Washington, DC: CQ Press).

R. Ketcham (1987) *Presidents Above Party: The First American Presidency, 1789–1829* (Chapel Hill, NC: University of North Carolina Press).

M.J. Korzi (2003) 'Our chief magistrate and his powers: a reconsideration of William Howard Taft's "Whig" theory of presidential leadership', *Presidential Studies Quarterly* 33 (2), pp. 305–24.

W. Leuchtenburg (2001) *In the Shadow of FDR: From Harry Truman to George W. Bush* (New York: Cornell University Press).

T.J. Lowi (1985) 'Presidential power: restoring the balance', *Political Science Quarterly* 100 (2), pp. 185–213.

D. Marchand (1984) 'Carter and the presidency', in Abernathy, Hill and Williams (eds.), *The Carter Years*, pp. 192–207.

McCleskey and McCleskey (1984) 'Carter and the Democrats', in Abernathy, Hill and Williams (eds.), *The Carter Years*, pp. 125–43.

P.L. Murphy (1972) *The Constitution in Crisis Times, 1918–1969* (New York: Harper & Row).

Newsweek (1981) 'The presidency: can anyone do the job?', 26 Jan., pp. 25–9.

R. Nixon (1990) *In the Arena: A Memoir of Victory, Defeat and Renewal* (New York: Simon & Schuster).

A. O'Connor and M.L. Henze (1984) *So Great A Power to Any Single Person: The Presidential Term and Executive Power* (Washington, DC: Jefferson Foundation).

M.P. Petracca (1992) 'Predisposed to oppose: political scientists and term limitations', *Polity* 24 (4), pp. 657–72.

W.B. Quandt (1986) 'The electoral cycle and the conduct of foreign policy', *Political Science Quarterly* 101 (5), pp. 825–37.

G. Reedy (1976) 'The presidency in 1976: focal point of political unity?', *Journal of Politics* 38 (3), pp. 228–38.

L. Schack (1996) 'Note: a reconsideration of the single, six-year presidential term in light of contemporary electoral trends', *Journal of Law and Politics* 12 (4), pp. 749–73.

A.M. Schlesinger (2004) *The Imperial Presidency* (New York: Houghton, Mifflin, Harcourt).

Time (1980) 'Is there life after disaster?', 17 Nov., pp. 28–9.

B. Werth (2006) *31 Days: Gerald Ford, the Nixon Pardon and A Government in Crisis* (New York: Anchor Books).

P.G. Willis and G.L. Willis (1952) 'The politics of the Twenty-second Amendment', *Western Political Quarterly* 5 (3), pp. 469–82.

5
The politics of the US Budget: a metaphor for broken government?

Iwan Morgan

Money is, with propriety, considered as the vital principle of the body politic; as that which sustains its life and motion and enables it to perform its most basic functions.
Alexander Hamilton, *Federalist* #30 (1788)

If politics is regarded in part as conflict over whose preferences shall prevail in the determination of national policy, then the budget records the outcome of that struggle.
Aaron Wildavsky (1964)

As Alexander Hamilton had foreseen during the campaign to ratify the new Constitution and political scientist Aaron Wildavsky confirmed some 180 years later, the federal budget is the foremost index of political reality in the United States. Its allocation of funds to public programmes is the principal determinant of the size and scope of national government. Through the instrument of taxation, it determines how much money will be transferred from the private sector to the public sector and how the costs of government shall be distributed within society. Finally, its operation of a deficit or surplus governs how much of the present expenses of government will be passed on to the future. These issues have been central to American politics since the inception of the republic because they are fundamental battlegrounds for competing political values, party identities and notions of the national interest. In essence, therefore, controversy rather than consensus has been the consistent characteristic of fiscal debate. However, this has reached a new level of intensity in the early 21st century to the extent that the budget has become a metaphor for the incapacity of American government to address issues of vital significance to the nation's future.

Put simply, the United States is staring into an abyss of unsustainable public debt unless its government can balance its outlays and receipts in the medium term. The crisis may not be imminent but there are already clear indications of its development. The Congressional Budget Office (CBO) has estimated that the public debt as a share of Gross Domestic Product (GDP) could well exceed its historic peak (reached at the end of World War II) of 109 per cent in 2023 and approach 190 per cent by 2035. In the assessment of this non-partisan agency, which has a reputation for realism rather than hyperbole, 'The explosive path of federal debt ... underscores the need for large and rapid policy changes to put the nation on a sustainable fiscal course' (2011, p. x).

While there has been widespread agreement during Barack Obama's term as president that something has to be done to avert fiscal crisis, there is in equal measure disagreement over what course of action is necessary to this end. The partisan and ideological divisions that underlie this dissensus have prevented the executive and legislative branches of American government from working together to address a fundamental threat to the continuation of the nation's prosperity and power as the 21st century unfolds. This chapter places this imbroglio in historical and political context to explain why the budget has become such a divisive problem and to assess the prospects for its resolution.

The old politics of budget accommodation

Scholars should desist from offering a 'good old days' scenario but it is difficult to understand America's current fiscal impasse without some reference to the past. In essence modern American budgeting was born with the passage of the Budget and Accounting Act of 1921. Prior to this, the fiscal process was haphazard, unsystematic and largely dominated by Congress — but it worked because government costs were relatively small and import tariffs provided a dependable source of revenue. As a result, other than in exceptional circumstances of war and recession, the United States habitually operated a balanced budget for the first 140 years since the Constitution endowed the federal government, specifically the Congress, with the 'power of the purse.' This engendered a dichotomous American credo that balanced budgets represented republican virtue and small government, while deficits threatened to corrupt founding values (Kimmel 1958; Savage 1988).

The introduction of a new system of budgeting reflected a change in fiscal circumstances. Federal costs, particularly for defence, grew significantly in the early 20th century. The declining volume of tariff revenues as America became an industrial power in its own right necessitated development of a new source of government funds in the form of direct taxation of personal and corporate income in 1913. Finally, the massive expansion of public debt resulting from America's participation in World War I required more rigorous management of interest repayment than the old procedures allowed (Ippolito 2003).

Though confirming Congress's power of the purse, the 1921 reform endowed the president with responsibility for creating a budget plan to inform the legislature's deliberations on taxation and spending and created the Bureau of the Budget (BoB) to help in this task. This measure did much to establish the modern presidency's status as programmatic and political leader. Holding strategic responsibility for setting the fiscal agenda under its aegis, the president henceforth was required to estimate the aggregate costs of government programmes that the nation needed and the means to pay for these. Democratic presidents from Franklin D. Roosevelt through to Lyndon Johnson capitalised on this to build up expensive domestic and national security programmes. Although political conflict over the budget increased in the new system, this was never on a scale that made it unworkable. The capacity of conservatives in both congressional parties to constrain presidential domestic ambition through their influence within the committee system was a powerful incentive for political compromise. Moreover, a broad consensus emerged as America rose to global superpower status on the need for strong defence, which consumed the lion's share of spending from the 1940s through the 1960s. National security imperatives also drove the transformation of the hitherto elite personal income tax into a mass tax in World War II, which provided bountiful revenues for post-war programme development (Ippolito 1990; Morgan 1995; Brownlee 1996).

Also important in promoting budget accommodation in the mid 20th century was the recognition that deficits were useful tools of economic management in line with new Keynesian doctrines. While unbalanced budgets had provoked significant controversy in the Great Depression, their contribution to economic growth in World War II generated post-war consensus about their value in countering recession, a function that gained *de facto* legitimacy from the Employment Act of 1946. Further assisting their acceptance, deficits were neither large nor chronic in the post-war quarter century. Balanced and unbalanced budgets were virtually equal in number from 1947 to 1961 and deficits were small, if regular, in the 1960s. It was significant that the two largest post-war deficits — in recession-affected Fiscal Year (FY) 1959 and Vietnam-affected FY 1968 — were both followed by balanced budgets (Stein 1996; Morgan 2009).

The new politics of budgetary intransigence

The transition to intensified budget conflict occurred in the 1970s. The initial roots of dissensus were planted by stagflation, the simultaneous incidence of stagnation and inflation that made this decade the most miserable for the economy since the 1930s. With Keynesian formulae seemingly incapable of solving this new problem, deficits lost their legitimacy as instruments of economic purpose. Indeed, conservative activists who became increasingly active in Republican ranks, conservative economists and business interests charged that they aggravated inflation in the cause of funding big government. To make matters worse, the fiscal gap grew significantly wider in this period, in part because erratic economic growth (there were recessions in 1970, 1974–5, 1980 and — most severely — in 1981–2) did not generate sufficient revenue to keep pace with rising government costs (Roberts 1984; Collins 2000).

Related to this problem was the changing composition of federal spending. Driven by Great Society programme development, domestic outlays overtook defence as a budget share in FY1971, a lead that widened in the next 40 years and more — regardless of the military expansions of Ronald Reagan and George W. Bush. Moreover, the expansion of existing entitlements like Social Security and the development of new ones like Medicare and Medicaid in the 1960s reduced the discretionary element of the budget that was subject to the control of the annual appropriations process. In FY1960, payments to individuals that were mandated by statute law made up 26.2 per cent of federal outlays; their share had risen to 47.1 per cent in FY 1980 and to 58.9 per cent in FY2000. Meanwhile, bigger deficits resulted in larger interest payments on the national debt, whose budget share rose from 7.5 per cent in FY1960 to a late-20th-century peak of 15.4 per cent in FY1996. In essence, therefore, more than 70 per cent of federal expenditure went on automatic rather than discretionary outlays by the end of the century compared to some 40 per cent in FY1970. This development undermined budget suppleness, making deficit control more difficult and constraining federal capacity to respond to new problems (Ippolito 2003; Schick 2007)

The combined effect of these developments was, in economist Herbert Stein's words, 'the disintegration of fiscal policy' (1995, pp. 155–63; 1996). Hitherto, US budgeting had been rule-driven in its focus on fiscal aggregates — whether in pursuit of balanced-budget imperatives from the 1790s through the 1920s or in calculation of the level of deficit (or surplus) best suited to economic needs in the Keynesian era from the 1930s through to the 1960s. The coincidental decline of Keynesianism and the change in budget make-up shifted fiscal attention from aggregates to composition. Without an agreed-upon new rule to guide them, budget policy-makers became increasingly concerned to protect their programme preferences in the shrinking portion of the budget that they still controlled. While Republicans prioritised big defence, Democrats supported social and infrastructure programme expansion. Taxation also grew increasingly contentious as rising domestic costs undermined its national security rationale: Republicans demanded tax cuts to boost economic growth and constrain big government, while Democrats wanted to preserve tax levels in order to fund their domestic priorities.

Institutional development facilitated intensification of budget conflict from the 1970s onward. Increased incidence of divided party control of government was critical in this regard. One or other party had simultaneously held the presidency and both houses of Congress for all but ten years from 1921 to 1968, but in only six years from 1969 to 2000. This diffusion of partisan power encouraged intransigence rather than compromise in pursuit of partisan fiscal aims.

Budget reforms in the 1970s unintentionally had the same effect. The Nixon administration in 1970 refashioned the BoB, originally a mainly technocratic agency, into the more politicised Office of Management and Budget to promote presidential fiscal aims. Hitherto reliant on individual standing committees to develop the budget piecemeal, the legislature responded by seeking to increase its strategic power over budget policy-making and oversight. The Congressional Budget and Impoundment Act of 1974 established budget committees in both chambers, required approval of a congressional budget resolution and created the CBO to assess presidential fiscal recommendations. The new system proved unwieldy, susceptible to partisan dispute and rarely capable of producing an agreed budget by the start of the fiscal year (1 October). Its shortcomings necessitated reliance on Continuing Resolutions to provide government with operating funds until a formal budget was delivered (Ippolito 1990, 2003).

The most disturbing policy development associated with the new budget politics was the explosion of the federal deficit in the 1980s and early 1990s. Claiming a conservative mandate from his 1980 landslide election, Ronald Reagan promoted the largest tax reduction in American history (the Economic Recovery and Tax Act of 1981) and the largest defence expansion since the Korean War. However, he was unable to persuade the Democrat-controlled House of Representatives to enact domestic economies required to pay for this. This engendered a cycle of large deficits that annually averaged 4.3 per cent Gross Domestic Product (GDP) in FY1982–FY1993, a higher level than pertained in the depressed 1930s and greatly exceeding the 1.1 per cent annual average of the 1960s.

Nevertheless, government was not yet broken insofar as the budget was concerned because the scale of fiscal problems was not so vast as to preclude deficit-reduction initiatives that broadly protected the political priorities of the main institutional and partisan actors. While steadfastly refusing to surrender his personal tax cuts, the core of his political philosophy, Ronald Reagan agreed business tax increases and tax loophole closures in 1982 and 1984 as part of deficit-control compromises with the House Democrats and Senate Republicans. On the recommendation of a blue-ribbon commission, he also accepted higher social security taxes in 1983 to protect the solvency of the pensions programme. He then signed a bipartisan congressional measure, the Balanced Budget and Emergency Deficit Control Act of 1985, which projected deficit elimination in annual instalments without touching personal taxes and entitlements. Though routinely circumvented by the White House and Congress, this legislation kept the pressure on them to address the fiscal gap by providing an index of progress to which financial markets paid close heed. With the Federal Reserve pushing up interest rates as a safeguard against the inflationary consequences of deficits, George H.W. Bush and the congressional Democratic leadership agreed a new budget deal in 1990 whereby the president accepted income tax increases for high earners in return for domestic spending restraint. However, conservative Republicans, an increasingly significant force in the congressional GOP, regarded this compromise as a betrayal of the Reagan legacy. The result was a new cycle of budgetary confrontation that foreshadowed developments in the Obama presidency (Schier 1992; Hager and Pianin 1996; Morgan 2009).

Worried that inflationary concerns about the deficit continued to affect long-term interest rates charged by the bond market, the principal source of the loan investment that was vital for economic growth, Bill Clinton prioritised its reduction in his first year as president. In contrast to the recent trend towards bipartisanship, however, his 1993 five-year $433 billion omnibus package of spending cuts and tax increases was entirely reliant on congressional Democratic support for its narrow enactment. Blaming Bush's acceptance of higher taxes for the GOP's loss of the presidency, congressional Republicans rejected further compromise on the deficit if this entailed tax hikes.

In the 1994 midterms the Republicans took control of both houses of Congress for the first time since 1954 with a campaign focused against the Clinton tax increases as the epitome of tax-and-spend liberalism and a drag on economic growth. House Republican candidates also signed up to the Contract with America manifesto that promised huge spending retrenchment to pay for not only a balanced budget but also massive tax cuts. The large cohort of freshmen elected on this pledge offered a foretaste in the 104th Congress (1995–6) of the militancy of the Tea Party Republicans elected in 2010. Led by Speaker Newt Gingrich (Georgia), the GOP-controlled House dragged the Republican Senate along in its wake into budget confrontation with Clinton, who was determined to protect social programmes from evisceration. The refusal of both sides to compromise their core positions resulted in failure to agree a budget or a continuing resolution to fund services temporarily. This resulted in two partial shutdowns of government in late 1995 and early 1996. In the battle for public opinion, however, Clinton succeeded in portraying his opponents as ideological extremists who were intent on destroying popular social programmes to pay for tax cuts for the rich. Beating a retreat, Republican congressional leaders eventually agreed a budget that conformed to presidential preference (Hager and Pianin 1996; Strahan and Palazzolo 2004; Rae 1998).

In his second term, however, Clinton himself took the lead in seeking a bipartisan budget fix that would give him a legacy of preparing America to meet the fiscal challenges of the 21st century. The Balanced Budget Act and the Tax Reduction Act of 1997 seemingly indicated a political rapprochement to eliminate the deficit, economise on spending and offer middle-income tax cuts. Whereas these measures projected a balanced budget within five years, a stockmarket-driven economic boom that resulted from the Federal Reserve's reduction of short-term interest rates produced it within one year. Bountiful tax receipts generated a four-year cycle of surplus budgets in FY1998–2001, the longest sequence since the 1920s, raising expectations that continued surpluses would entirely eliminate the public debt early in the new century. However, this rosy scenario produced a new budget stalemate over whether to invest the projected surplus in shoring up the Social Security trust fund, as Clinton wanted, or new tax cuts, as the congressional Republicans demanded (Palazzolo 1999; Gillon 2008).

The expectation of vast surpluses stretching ahead into the new century was short-lived. The budget swung sharply from a surplus of 2.4 per cent GDP in FY2000 to a deficit of 3.6 per cent GDP in FY2004, a fiscal deterioration of 6 per cent GDP unmatched in peacetime since the Great Depression cycle of FY930–FY1934. The first blow to fiscal optimism was the so-called dot-com recession of 2001, a result of the stockmarket collapse of overvalued 'e-company' shares, which blew away the revenue harvest on which surplus projections had depended. In addition to this cyclical development, structural policy decisions promoted by President George W. Bush further entrenched the renewal of deficits. The massive 2001 and 2003 tax cuts, the increase in military outlays resulting from the war on terror and the Iraq conflict, and huge increases in spending on domestic programmes that conformed to Bush's big-government conservatism contrasted markedly with the relative fiscal restraint of the 1990s.

Politics reinforced this return to the red but in this instance the driving force was single, rather divided, party control of government. The Republican-controlled Congresses of 2001–06 (only the Senate was not under GOP control for an 18-month period in 2001–02) largely supported the agenda of a Republican White House, even agreeing to outlay increases in health care, infrastructure and other domestic programmes that were deemed advantageous to party fortunes. George W. Bush's only major fiscal defeat occurred in 2005 over his plans to partially privatise Social Security in an attempt to contain the long-term effects of an ageing population on the public purse. The unpopularity of this proposal, combined with doubts about its fiscal efficacy, led to its abandonment by the GOP-led Congress. However, the outcome left unresolved the vexing issue of how to cope with rising entitlement costs when the abnormally large generation of baby-boomers born in the aftermath of World War II (1945–65) increasingly reached retirement age as the 21st century progressed (Morgan 2010; Owens 2010; Waddan 2010).

The debt-ridden future

As his presidency neared its end, George W. Bush loudly proclaimed that the deficit was once more under control and the budget was on track to being balanced by FY2012. Having promised to halve the gap between outlays and receipts over the course of his second term, he appeared to have delivered on his pledge one year early when it shrank to 1.2 per cent GDP in FY 2007. However, this proved another illusion about the fiscal future. Even without the economic crisis that blighted Bush's final year in office, America's finances were in reality heading towards future unsustainability. According to the projections of numerous government agencies, the public debt was set to mushroom to dangerous levels in the second quarter of the 21st century without a correction of fiscal course (Government Accountability Office, 2007). Seeking to popularise this message, the Peter G. Peterson Foundation, a balanced-budget advocacy group, promoted a documentary movie, *I.O.U.S.A.* (2008), that warned of the debt threat to the nation's future.

The roots of the fiscal problem were twofold — the inexorable growth of entitlement spending, and the increasing inadequacy of revenues to cover rising costs. According to the Government Accountability Office, GDP was set to increase by 71 per cent in real terms from 2007 to 2032, but Social Security, Medicaid and Medicare costs would grow respectively over the same period by 137 per cent, 224 per cent and 235 per cent (2007). Conservative economist Bruce Bartlett estimated that tax revenues would need to deliver *immediately and forever* an additional 8.1 per cent GDP above their 30-year average of 18.4 per cent GDP to cover the entitlement-driven fiscal gap. This would be equivalent to a tax increase of 81 per cent a year for all taxpayers, something that was both economically undesirable and politically impossible (2009).

With pension outlays driven upwards by the progressive ageing of the population and health care costs per beneficiary rising along historic trends, aggregate spending on Social Security, Medicaid and Medicare was projected to rise even under moderate assumptions from 9 per cent GDP in FY2008 to 19 per cent GDP in FY2050. Without correction of fiscal course, these three programmes and defence are likely to consume all federal revenues by 2031, leaving all other programmes (including interest repayments on the public debt) to be funded from the deficit. The fiscal future could be even bleaker if Medicare and Medicaid outlays grow on a faster track to account for 22 per cent GDP by 2050, a scenario that is by no means unrealistic (Concord Coalition 2009; Kogan et al. 2008). It is these two entitlement programmes that are most difficult to control because they are sensitive both to health care cost inflation (the result of improving but increasingly expensive medical technology, drugs, and personnel quality) and population ageing. A top CBO official warned in congressional testimony in 2009, 'The rate of growth of spending on health care is the single greatest threat to budgetary balance over the long run and such spending will have to be controlled in order for the fiscal situation to be sustainable in future decades' (Sunshine 2009).

As the Bush presidency drew to a close, a host of budget watchdog organisations lined up to warn of impending financial crisis if nothing was done to correct course. One of these, the Center on Budget Policy and Priorities (CBPP), typically estimated that the annual deficit would rise from 4.6 per cent GDP in FY2020 to 9.4 per cent GDP in FY2030, to 14.7 per cent in FY2040, and to 21.1 per cent GDP in FY2050. The corollary growth of interest payments would be 3.2 per cent GDP, 5.4 per cent GDP, 8.7 per cent GDP, and 13.7 per cent GDP. The effect would be to drive up the public debt-GDP ratio in each of these four years to: 67 per cent, 108 per cent, 179 per cent, and 279 per cent. Even these scary figures came to be regarded as underestimates as the effect of the economic crisis of 2007–09 on government finances became clearer (Kogan et al. 2008).

Owing to the difficulty of coordinating its separate institutions, the American political system has rarely shown the capacity for long-term planning without the impulse provided by an imminent threat. It is unclear whether the doom-laden fiscal projections being produced by governmental and non-governmental agencies would have resulted in public policy change to address a problem whose actual effects would not be felt for some years to come. However, the Great Recession of 2007–09, sparked by the financial crisis that resulted from the implosion of the sub-prime mortgage market, had a profound effect on the fiscal agenda. In FY2009, anti-recession spending drove federal outlays up to 25 per cent GDP, the highest level since World War II, and the decline in economic activity flattened revenues to 14.9 per cent GDP, the lowest level since FY1950. The record peacetime deficit of 10 per cent GDP (the previous peak was 6 per cent GDP in FY1983) represented a fiscal deterioration of 8.8 per cent GDP in two years. Over the same period, the public-held debt rose from 36.2 per cent GDP to 53.5 per cent GDP, the highest level since 1952, when the US was still paying for its massive World War II borrowing (Office of Management and Budget 2011). It was widely recognised that fiscal recovery would be a long and difficult process. 'The next president will inherit a fiscal and economic mess of historic proportions. It will take years to dig our way out', warned Senate Budget Committee chair Kent Conrad (D-North Dakota) in late 2008 (Uchitelle and Pear 2008). The foretaste of the indebted future also focused attention on the need to pre-empt the long-term deterioration of the nation's finances.

Fiscal impasse

In the transition period between his election and inauguration as America's 44th president, Barack Obama outlined what would be his administration's twin-track fiscal policy approach of operating large deficits to boost economic recovery in the short-term and constraining debt expansion in the long-term. On 7 December 2008, he avowed, '[W]e can't worry short-term about the deficit. We've got to make sure the stimulus is large enough to get the economy moving.' A few days earlier, however, he had announced that 'as soon as the recovery is well underway, then we've got to set up a long-term plan to reduce the structural deficit and make sure we're not leaving a mountain of debt for the next generation' (Obama 2008; Bixby 2008). However, the new administration's capacity to deliver this strategy fell foul of political conflict over the deficit.

At first sight, the Obama administration seemingly held the advantage in the battle to shape the budgetary agenda. Combined with his party winning increased majorities in both houses of Congress in 2008, Obama's victory with the largest popular-vote margin for a Democrat since 1964 seemingly provided him with a strong mandate to deal with the nation's inter-related economic and fiscal problems. Also encouraging was the legacy of bipartisan action to deal with the economic crisis during the final year of the Bush presidency. A Republican White House and Democratic Congress had cooperated in promoting a number of initiatives, most notably the Troubled Assets Relief Program (TARP) that committed the Treasury to take up to $700 billion of mortgage assets onto its books to help banks hit by toxic sub-prime loans.

The new administration hit the ground running by securing enactment within a month of taking office of the American Recovery and Reinvestment Act (ARRA) of 2009, the largest stimulus measure in US history with three-year costs of $787 billion. However this represented the high-water mark of the Obama White House's fiscal success because it revealed the limitations of the bipartisanship that was essential for further progress. In reality, the renewal of political conflict had been entirely predictable. In 2008 the Bush White House and the congressional Republicans had refused to countenance a spending stimulus to boost the economy. Viewing this as a smokescreen to renew big government, they insisted that tax cuts were the only viable means to promote recovery. The nearly two-to-one ratio of spending increases to tax cuts in ARRA's provisions consequently aroused strong GOP opposition. Not a single Republican voted for the measure in the House and only three did so in the Senate. The ARRA also provoked the ire of the wider conservative movement as a new expression of wasteful big-government liberalism at best and socialist intent at worst. Slamming the earmarks that some Democrats had written into the bill to benefit their home states, right-wing talk radio show presenters like

Rush Limbaugh decried it as a 'porculus' bill (Hall and Jackson 2009; Brannon 2009; *Economist* 2009).

The revisions that the Obama administration made to the FY2010 budget plan inherited from the Bush administration further deepened the partisan divide. The White House estimated that its proposals would bring the deficit down to 3 per cent GDP in FY2013, effectively achieving primary balance (equilibrium between outlays and receipts not counting interest payment on the public debt). To this end, its plan featured reduction of military costs for operations in Afghanistan and Iraq and revenue enhancement from the scheduled expiry of the Bush tax cuts for high earners and corporations (while maintaining those for other income groups at a 10-year cost of $1.1 trillion). Administration projections were immediately challenged by the independent CBO on grounds that they overestimated economic growth and did not include costs for Obama's proposed health care insurance programme. In its estimate the presidential plan would keep the deficit in excess of 5 per cent GDP for a decade, resulting in the debt-GDP ratio growing to 82.4 per cent GDP by FY2019 (Office of Management and Budget 2009; Congressional Budget Office 2009).

With the administration on the defensive over its deficit calculations, Republicans focused attention on the domestic spending initiatives in the plan that estimated $500 billion in new expenditure over ten years for energy, education and other public investment programmes. House Minority Leader John Boehner (R-Ohio) charged that the Obama budget was 'a move to a big socialist government' that piles 'debt on the backs of our kids and grandkids.' The GOP and its supporters also warned that the Obama plan would ultimately necessitate higher taxes for all Americans. On 15 April 2009, Freedomworks, a conservative group led by onetime Republican congressional leader Dick Armey, organised thousands of anti-tax 'tea parties' across the nation. 'There's no way that he can do the spending he does and cut taxes', Armey declared, 'People know that spending inevitably means more taxes' (Montgomery 2009a, 2009b).

The early skirmishing on the budget hardened into entrenched stalemate over how to deal with the larger debt problems facing the nation. Without doubt, Obama overestimated the prospects for bipartisanship and remained too long above the fray in the hope of its emergence. His failure to develop a plan outlining the Democratic agenda for long-term debt reduction added grist to charges from the GOP and conservative media outlets like Fox News that the administration was using the recession as a smokescreen for enlarging government. The president's pursuit of a wide-ranging domestic agenda, including a new health care insurance entitlement that seemed the antithesis of fiscal restraint, also prevented clear-cut focus on budgetary issues. As a consequence of all this, it was the Republicans who gained the upper hand in the battle for public opinion. According to Ipsos-McClatchy opinion surveys, the Democrats had a 30-point lead as the party more trusted to deal with the deficit at the start of 2008, but the Republicans had a seven-point lead by the end of Obama's first year in office (Fox News 2009; *Economist* 2010a).

Effectively recognising that the conventional political process could not deliver progress on long-term debt, Obama established the National Commission on Fiscal Responsibility and Reform (NCFRR) by executive order in February 2010 to produce solutions. A number of blue-ribbon bodies had been instituted to address entitlement problems over the course of the previous 30 years. Only the Social Security Commission of 1982 had truly been a success in terms of its recommendations being enacted into law because the Reagan White House and the House Democrats had a mutual interest in ensuring pension programme solvency. Other bodies either did not produce findings with bipartisan credibility or their recommendations fell foul of partisan conflict. The NCFRR started life facing the same bullet because of the manner of its establishment. As initially proposed by its bipartisan co-sponsors, Senator Kent Conrad and Senator Judd Gregg (R-New Hampshire), its findings would have had the full force of a legislative proposal that would be subject to an up-or-down congressional vote without possibility of amendment. The refusal of House Speaker Nancy Pelosi (D-California) to surrender congressional authority over Social Security reform prevented establishment of the commission on such terms in 2009. Obama's commitment to its creation in 2010 coincided with the Democrats' loss of their supermajority in the upper house when the GOP won the special Massachusetts Senate election necessitated by the death of liberal champion, Edward Kennedy. Now unable to win Senate support for this body, the president instituted it through executive order, which did not guarantee the legislature's consideration of its proposals (Broder 2009; Henry 2010).

Co-chaired by former Clinton chief of staff Erskine Bowles and former Republican senator Alan Simpson, the NCFRR had a membership of 18 that consisted of nine Democrats, eight Republicans and one Independent. Its recommendations had to be agreed by 14 of these to be eligible for consideration by Congress, a supermajority requirement that would prove impossible to achieve. The final report, produced in December 2010, called for $3.9 trillion of cuts over ten years to reduce the deficit to 1.2 per cent GDP in FY2020 and their continuation to eliminate it entirely by FY2035. The savings were to come from spending cuts, revenue enhancement and diminished interest payment on a declining public debt in a ratio of 2:1:1. The bulk of expenditure economies, totalling some $1.7 trillion, were to come equally from defence and domestic programmes. Social Security reductions would flow from progressively increasing the retirement age to 70 and payroll tax increases for higher earners, while health care economies affected both providers and beneficiaries. Comprehensive tax reform to close tax loopholes would also allow for some lowering of rates (National Commission 2010). The NCFRR report only received support from 11 members because partisanship disrupted its operation. Significantly, five of those members backing it no longer held elective office and two others were retiring from Congress at the end of the current session. In contrast, members who were continuing as officeholders voted six to four against, among them Senator Max Baucus (D-Montana) and Representative Dave Camp (R-Michigan), the chairs of the tax-writing committees in the incoming Congress (*Economist* 2010b).

By the time the report was unveiled, the political landscape had changed dramatically as a result of the stunning Republican success in the midterm elections of 2010. The GOP took control of the House with a 242-193 majority, in the process picking up 63 seats that represented the largest midterm gain by any party since 1938, and slashed the Democrat lead in the Senate to 53-47. A goodly number of the Republican victors, particularly in the House, associated directly or indirectly with the Tea Party grassroots movement that had helped to shape the election outcome. This new populist force had emerged in opposition to ARRA, the Obama health care plan and other new spending initiatives promoted by the administration and the congressional Democrats. Its supporters wanted a restoration of founding values that they equated with small government, low taxes, balanced budgets and limited public debt (*The Hill* 2010; Rasmussen and Schoen 2010; McGregor 2011).

The Tea Party's supporters and other freshmen elected with its strong backing, who enjoyed influence far beyond their numbers in the 112th Congress, promised to be uncompromising in pursuit of these aims. In addition to making up one-third of the House GOP caucus, they could count on support from not only established GOP conservatives but also senior party figures wary of being seen as unsympathetic. In the Senate, for example, there were only four avowed Tea Party Republicans but the movement's success in ousting three-term senator Bob Bennett in the Utah primaries of 2010 was a powerful incentive against risking its wrath (Drew 2011a). As a consequence, the already-strong partisan divisions over fiscal issues grew even more intense.

The dysfunctionality of American politics and government on the budget reached a new low with the debt-limit controversy in the summer of 2011. As the dollar size of the public debt grows, Congress is required to raise the permissible debt ceiling, a vote that is usually a matter of routine in order to prevent government default. While some European countries, notably Greece, were locked into or tottering on the verge of a 'can't-pay' sovereign-debt crisis, the United States government came close to a 'won't-pay' version. Playing what was in effect a game of debt blackmail, the House Republicans made the raising of the debt limit over the current level of $14.2 trillion conditional on acceptance of their fiscal aims. Commenting on their strategy, political analyst Norman Ornstein remarked: 'If you hold one-half of one-third of the reins of power in Washington and are willing to maintain ... [party] discipline even if you bring down the entire temple around your own head, there is a pretty good chance that you are going to get your way' (Steinhauer 2011).

The Democrats were the ones to blink first. A deal was finally hammered out between the White House and Speaker John Boehner just in time for the president to sign the bill on 2 August 2011, the day the Treasury had warned that it would run out of cash to meet its obligations. This mandated a two-stage increase of the debt limit by $900 billion in August/September and by $2.4 trillion in total. It also required an immediate cap on discretionary spending to save $2.1 trillion, including spending cuts of $917 billion, over the next decade. In addition a 12-member congressional committee — equally composed of Republicans and Democrats — would be convened to find $1.5 trillion in further deficit reductions over ten years by 23 November 2011, which Congress then had to approve within one month. If it failed to reach agreement or its proposals were rejected by Congress, this would automatically trigger spending retrenchment of $1.2 trillion, drawn equally from defence and domestic programmes, to commence in 2013 and grow in volume over a ten-year period (Sahadi 2011).

At one level, the outcome showed that old-fashioned bargaining could still work. The Republicans put the onus for deficit reduction entirely on discretionary spending, the Democrats protected social programmes and entitlements, and Obama gained a reprieve from debt-ceiling blackmail until the 2012 presidential election (and perhaps his presidency) is over. Overall, however, the negative consequences far outweighed the benefits. As ever, deal-making entailed both parties safeguarding rather than slaughtering their sacred cows, whose sacrifice is necessary for long-term fiscal salvation. Predicting this outcome, one critical commentator remarked, 'The answer will have to be a fudge ... [that] would do nothing to address the long-term problem, but it would avoid an immediate debt-ceiling collision. One would call that success. This is what Washington has come to' (Crook 2011).

The short-term spending cuts targeted in the debt-limitation deal, coming mainly from defence, law enforcement, and other discretionary areas, will not significantly halt debt growth to dangerous levels. The outcome also makes it likely that this tactic will be a 'new template' — the words of Senate Minority Leader Mitch McConnell (R-Kentucky) for budget coercion. 'In the future', he declared, 'any president, this one or another one, when they request us to raise the debt ceiling, it will not be clean any more ... we will go through the process again and see what we can continue to achieve.' Such words indicated no recognition that the shoe might be on the other foot if a Republican president faced a Democratic Congress. Nor did they acknowledge that the debt-limit imbroglio had caused jitters on the world's money markets and created economic uncertainty at home and abroad at a time when recovery from the global recession was patently fragile. In a sad commentary on American political folly, Standard & Poor downgraded the US government's credit rating from AAA to AA+ because the recent brinkmanship showed American governance had become 'less stable, less effective and less predictable.' No one expected that this would affect America's capacity to borrow, but it still signified the global financial community's growing concern that excessive partisanship could make the US an unreliable borrower in the future (*Economist* 2011a, 2011b; Drew 2011b).

Is a new budget politics possible?

Anticipation of a new budget politics that places constructive engagement with the nation's deep-seated fiscal problems ahead of partisanship is based more on hope than expectation. Bipartisan deficit-reduction initiatives in the past were only possible when the two parties could reach agreement without compromising their core concerns on avoiding personal tax increases in the case of the Republicans and protecting social programmes, including entitlements, in the case of the Democrats. The sole agreement that contravened this political reality — George H.W. Bush's tax-increasing concession in the 1990 budget deal — only served to reinforce adherence to the established orthodoxy.

The most significant bipartisan budget initiative of the Obama era also conformed to this pattern. In December 2010 the president agreed a deal with GOP congressional leaders to preserve the George W. Bush tax breaks for all income groups for two years, thereby compromising on his stated goal of letting them expire for the wealthiest two per cent of households. In return, he obtained the extension of emergency unemployment benefits and a two per cent reduction of payroll taxes for every worker, both for the full year (2011), to boost economic recovery. Instead of being covered by pay-go obligations, the combined two-year cost of $900 billion of this package would be financed through borrowing that would expand the public debt (Montgomery and Murray 2011).

At the time of writing the United States lacks a fiscal policy that is helpful to either economic recovery or debt reduction. The former is a short-term problem, the latter is a medium-/long-term one, and each should be treated as such. As the 2010 budget deal seemingly recognised, but the 2011 debt-limitation deal did not, deficit reduction is self-defeating if it runs counter to economic recovery. Political posturing about the size of the current fiscal gap is harmful to economic growth, without which tax revenues will remain anaemic, thereby resulting in increased public indebtedness. In the light of this, it is worth noting that the short-term spending cuts mandated by the debt-limit deal is likely to knock 0.3 per cent from growth in 2012 and failure to renew the payroll tax cut and unemployment benefit extension could cost a further 1.4 points. This contraction would coincide with the loss of ARRA stimulus through its scheduled expiry in late 2011 (*Economist* 2011a).

In the medium-/long-term, effective debt reduction will require not only entitlement reform to control outlays but also revenue enhancement. If the Democrats have to swallow the former, the GOP cannot close its eyes to the necessity of the latter. This is the 'grand bargain' that needs to be struck, but whether the Republicans have the political capacity to compromise and the Democrats have the political savvy and clout to make them do so is open to question. Moreover, if President Obama has shown the vision to differentiate between short-term and long-term fiscal requirements, he has not displayed the skill needed to shape the debt-reduction agenda in line with his preferences. However, his lack of consistent engagement with the battles over budget issues means that he has not made a firm stand to fight for his convictions. Obama's failure to develop a long-term budget plan of his own has also conceded the political advantage to his opponents.

It has to be acknowledged, however, that the 44th president 'inherited the in-box from hell ... [and] faces the opposition from hell' (*Economist* 2011c). Whether any other occupant of the Oval Office could have done better in these circumstances is a matter of conjecture. The utter lack of bipartisanship in Congress was further underscored by the inability of the 'bipartisan' supercommittee established after resolution of the debt-limitation imbroglio to propose an agreed route to fiscal sustainability. The rock on which this body foundered was increased taxation. The Democrats insisted on tax hikes for the better-off in return for entitlement retrenchment. All six GOP members of the supercommittee, in common with virtually every other Republican congressman and senator, were signatories of a pledge demanded by Grover Norquist, president of Americans for Tax Reform, not to support a single tax rise, however small. Anyone breaking ranks on this had received clear warning of facing a tough primary challenge against a handpicked Norquist candidate backed with his organisation's ample funds. It was small wonder, therefore, that Senator John Kerry (D-Massachusetts), the 2004 presidential candidate, dubbed this tax lobbyist the 13th member of the supercommittee (Calmes and Steinhauer 2011; Rushe 2011; MacAskill 2011).

In these circumstances some analysts advocated procedural reform to facilitate the task of debt reduction. One idea gaining increased credence was biennial budgeting to reduce the time spent on developing a budget and conversely allow greater time for oversight. Under this schema, the first session of a Congress would be devoted to setting priorities and establishing programme funding levels and the second would focus on oversight and long-term planning, which would allow for evaluation and possible elimination of unnecessary programmes to the consequent benefit of deficit control. To its supporters, who include Senators Kent Conrad and John Thune (R-South Dakota) biennial budgeting would also allow for more accurate assessment of long-term funding needs, in contrast to the current practice of producing unrealistic assumptions that are routinely ignored in future years. Conversely critics charge that this reform would open the way to undisciplined supplementary spending in the second year to meet supposedly emergency needs (Isenberg 2011).

Another proposal that has received congressional investigation is to insert the president into the Congress's budget process by making its budget resolution a law that he could sign or veto. Supporters consider this a means of enhancing institutional budget co-ordination and facilitating compromises to resolve areas of disagreement earlier in the budget process. As critics like former CBO director Rudy Penner observed, however, this ignores the reality that the president and Congress would be unlikely to reach early agreement over the budget, so the current lengthy process of budgeting would be replicated. Others note that if such an agreement were possible, there would be no need for procedural reform in the first place (Kogan 2011).

Still others like Francis Fukuyama (2011) despair of politicians being able to reach agreement over the party-defining issues at stake in debt reduction. Accordingly they advocate taking the supercommittee process one stage further by populating it with technocrats capable of making politically neutral decisions in the nation's best interests. According to Fukuyama, such a body could make 'painful trade-offs' that would be submitted to Congress for a binding up-down vote on the entire package. Attractive though this idea appears, it ignores the problems of divided government and the difficulties of selling elite-defined sacrifice to the mass of ordinary Americans who will bear the brunt of austerity. In essence debt-reducing solutions that seek to de-politicise the budget ignore the reality that it is a highly political entity.

If the budget is a political document, the route to fiscal sustainability has to lie in political compromise and bipartisanship. Unfortunately, it is difficult to envisage the United States making substantial political progress on budget problems anytime soon, even if the economy continues on track to recovery (something by no means certain at the time of writing). The current White House incumbent is likely to desist from asking the nation to face up to painful choices until the 2012 presidential election is done and dusted. If Obama is re-elected, history indicates that second-term presidents have less political capital to pursue their goals than first-term ones. Intimating this in graphic terms after the failure of the supercommittee, Grover Norquist predicted that he would be a dead duck rather than just a lame one because a politically astute Republican party would not be 'cutting [him] any slack' (MacAskill 2011). Even a new president is likely to face a polarised Congress in which party margins are very tight. Moreover, there is no reservoir of public support for fiscal sacrifice on which political leaders can draw to legitimise compromise in pursuit of a debt-reduction agenda. Polls consistently reveal a dichotomy between overwhelming popular support for a balanced budget and overwhelming popular opposition to entitlement reduction and higher taxes. The partisan division in Washington on this score largely reflects that in the country. An *Economist*/YouGov poll, conducted amid the debt-ceiling crisis, found that 55 per cent of respondents favoured having a congressman who 'compromises to get things done' as against 45 per cent who did not. However, the margin for Democratic identifiers was 68-32 percent, while Republican identifiers by the very same margin wanted a congressman who 'sticks to his principles, no matter what' (*Economist* 2011d).

Winston Churchill, one of 20th-century America's greatest admirers, famously quipped, 'You can always rely on America to do the right thing once it has exhausted all the alternatives.' The US stance on debt reduction is testing the validity of this observation. Perhaps it requires a sovereign debt crisis whereby it cannot support borrowing without paying huge interest rates to nervous creditors to make it do the right thing. The only trouble with this scenario is that the scale of fiscal correction needed by the time such a crisis ensues will be vastly greater even than what is presently required. In essence, therefore, the budget has become the litmus test of American government's capacity to deal with future problems, one that it is presently failing. The politics of the debt issue raises fundamental questions about whether the United States can be governed in a rational way to safeguard its future prosperity and power.

References

B. Bartlett (2009) 'The 81% tax increase', *Forbes*, 15 May 2009, www.forbes.com/2009/5/14/taxes-social-security-opinions-columnists-medicare.html.

R. Bixby (2008) 'Congress in a glass house', *Washington Post*, 4 Dec., A21.

I. Brannon (2009) 'The troubling return of Keynesianism', *Cato Institute Tax and Budget Bulletin* 52 (Jan.).

D. Broder (2009) 'Hiding a mountain of debt', *Washington Post*, 29 March, A15.

E. Brownlee (1996) *Federal Taxation in America: A Short History* (New York: Cambridge University Press).

J. Calmes and J. Steinhauer (2011) 'As sides dig in, panel on deficit has an uphill fight', *The New York Times*, 25 Sept.

R. Collins (2000) *More: The Politics of Economic Growth in Postwar America* (New York: Oxford University Press).

Concord Coalition (2009) *Designing a Framework for Economic Recovery and Fiscal Sustainability* (Washington, DC: Concord Coalition).

Congressional Budget Office (2009) *A Preliminary Analysis of the President's Budget and an Update of CBO's Budget and Economic Outlook* (Washington, DC: CBO).

— (2011) *CBO's 2011 Long-Term Budgetary Outlook*, www.cbo.gov/publication/41486/.

C. Crook (2011) 'America's deepening default chasm', *Financial Times*, 22 May, p. 9, www.ft.com/comment/columnists/clivecrook/.

E. Drew (2011a) 'Obama and the House radicals', *New York Review of Books*, 15 April, www.nybooks.com/blogs/nyrblog/.

— (2011b) 'What were they thinking?', *New York Review of Books*, 18 Aug.

Economist, The (2009) 'The end of innocence', 21 Feb., p. 50.

— (2010a) 'Barack Obama's first year: reality bites', 16 Jan., pp. 24–6.

— (2010b) 'The president's deficit commission: no cigar', 11 Dec., p. 56.

— (2011a) 'The debt-ceiling deal: no thanks to anyone', 6 Aug., pp. 33–5.

— (2011b) 'America's downgrade: looking for someone to blame', 13 Aug., pp. 31–2.

— (2011c) 'Lexington: an underperforming president', 6 Aug., p. 37.

— (2011d) 'The debt ceiling (continued): glum and glummer', 30 July, pp. 33–4.

Fox News (2009) 'Obama shatters spending record for first year presidents', 24 Nov., www.foxnews.com/politics/2009/11/24/obama-shatters-spending-record-year-presidents/.

F. Fukuyama (2011), 'America's political dysfunction,' *The American Interest*, Nov./Dec., pp. 125–7.

S. Gillon (2008) *The Pact: Bill Clinton, Newt Gingrich, and the Rivalry That Defined a Generation* (New York: Oxford University Press).

Government Accountability Office (2008) *U.S. Financial Future and Fiscal Briefing*, www.gao.gov/cghome/d08446cg.pdf.

— (2007) *The Federal Government's Financial Health: A Citizen's Guide to the 2007 Financial Report of the U.S. Government*, www.gao.gov/financial/fy2007financialreport.html.

G. Hager and E. Pianin (1996) *Mirage: Why Neither the Democrats Nor the Republicans Can Balance the Budget, End the Deficit, and Satisfy the Public* (New York: Times Books).

M. Hall and D. Jackson (2009) 'Stimulus slammed as Dems' agenda', *USA Today*, 17 Feb.

E. Henry (2010) 'Obama to create debt commission Thursday', CNNMoney, 17 Feb., http://money.cnn.com.

Hill, The (2010) 'Gallup: Tea Party's top concerns are debt, size of government', 5 July.

I.O.U.S.A (2008), www.iousathemovie.com.

D. Ippolito (1990) *Uncertain Legacies: Budget Policy from Roosevelt through Reagan* (Charlottesville, VA: University of Virginia Press).

— (2003) *Why Budgets Matter: Budget Policy and American Politics* (University Park, PA: Pennsylvania State University Press).

C. Isenberg (2011) 'Congress should seriously consider biennial budgeting', *The Hill's Congress Blog*, 15 Oct., http://thehill.com/blogs/congress-blog/economy-a-budget/.

L. Kimmel (1958) *Federal Budget and Fiscal Policy, 1789–1958* (Washington, DC: Brookings Institution).

R. Kogan (2011) 'A "joint" budget resolution? More harm than good', Off the Charts blog, Center on Budget Policy and Priorities, 14 Oct., www.offthechartsblog.org/author/richard-kogan/.

R. Kogan, K. Cox and J. Horney (2008) *The Long-Term Fiscal Outlook is Bleak: Restoring Fiscal Sustainability Will Require Major Changes to Programs, Revenues, and the Nation's Health Care System* (Washington, DC: Center on Budget Policy and Priorities).

E. MacAskill (2011) 'Republican lobbyist hails victory after spending deal fails', *The Guardian*, 23 Nov., p. 16.

R. McGregor (2011) 'Elephantine problem', *Financial Times*, 12 May, p. 11.

L. Montgomery (2009a) 'Battle lines quickly set over planned policy shifts', *Washington Post*, 1 March, A1.

— (2009b) 'America's tax burden near historic low; Despite Obama's pledge, some fear future hikes as debt grows', *Washington Post*, 16 April, A4.

L. Montgomery and S. Murray (2011) 'Obama, GOP reach deal to extend tax breaks', *Washington Post*, 7 Dec., A1.

I. Morgan (1995) *Deficit Government: Taxation and Spending in Modern America* (Chicago, IL: Ivan Dee).

— (2009) *The Age of Deficits: Presidents and Unbalanced Budgets* (Lawrence, KS: University Press of Kansas).

— (2010) 'Bush's political economy: deficits, debt and depression', in I. Morgan and P.J. Davies (eds.), *Assessing George W. Bush's Legacy: The Right Man?* (New York: Palgrave).

B. Obama (2008) 'Interview with Tom Brokaw on NBC's "Meet the Press"', *American Presidency Project*, 7 Dec., www.americanpresidency.org.

Office of Management and Budget (2009) *A New Era of Responsibility: Renewing America's Promise* (Washington, DC: OMB).

— (2011) *Budget of the United States Government: Historical Tables Fiscal Year 2012* (Washington DC: Executive Office of the President).

National Commission on Fiscal Responsibility and Reform (2010) *The Moment of Truth: The Report of the National Commission on Fiscal Responsibility and Reform* (Washington, DC: White House).

J. Owens (2010) 'Bush's Congressional legacy and Congress's Bush legacy', in I. Morgan and P.J. Davies (eds.), *Assessing George W. Bush's Legacy: The Right Man?* (New York: Palgrave).

D. Palazzolo (1999) *Done Deal: The Politics of the 1997 Budget Agreement* (Chappaqua, NY: Chatham House).

N. Rae (1998) *Conservative Reformers: The Republican Freshmen and the Lessons of the 104th Congress* (Monckton, NY: M.E. Sharpe).

S. Rasmussen and D. Schoen (2010) *Mad as Hell: How the Tea Party Movement is Fundamentally Remaking our Two-Party System* (New York: HarperCollins).

P.C. Roberts (1984) *The Supply-Side Revolution: An Insider's Account of Policymaking in Washington* (Cambridge, MA: Harvard University Press).

D. Rushe (2011) 'Defence and welfare cuts loom as budget committee deadlocked over $15tn deficit', *The Guardian*, 21 Nov., p. 23.

J. Sahadi (2011) 'Debt ceiling: what the deal will do', CNN Money, 1 Aug., http://money.cnn.com/2011/08/01/news/economy/debt_ceiling_breakdown_of_deal/.

J. Savage (1988) *Balanced Budgets and American Politics* (Ithaca, NY: Cornell University Press).

A. Schick (2007) *The Federal Budget: Politics, Policy, Process*, 3d edn. (Washington, DC: Brookings Institution).

S. Schier (1992) *A Decade of Deficits: Congressional Thought and Fiscal Action* (Albany, NY: State University of New York Press).

H. Stein (1995) *On the Other Hand ... Essays on Economics, Economists and Politics* (Washington, DC: AEI Press).

—— (1996) *The Fiscal Revolution in America: Policy in Pursuit of Reality*, 2nd rev. edn. (Washington, DC: AEI Press).

J. Steinhauer (2011), 'Debt bill is signed, ending a fractious battle', *The New York Times*, 2 Aug., A1.

R. Strahan and D. Palazollo (2004) 'The Gingrich effect', *Political Science Quarterly* 119, pp. 89–115.

R. Sunshine (2009) 'Statement on the Congressional Budget Office', *The Budget and Economic Outlook: Fiscal Years 2009 to 2019*, before the Committee on the Budget, U.S. Senate, January 8' (Washington, DC: Congressional Budget Office).

Time (2010) 'Judging Obama's first year issue by issue', 20 Jan., www.time.com/time/specials/.

L. Uchitelle and R. Pear (2008) 'Deficit rises, and consensus is to let it grow', *The New York Times*, 20 Oct., A1.

A. Waddan (2010) 'Bush and big government conservatism', in I. Morgan and P.J. Davies, *Assessing George W. Bush's Legacy: The Right Man?* (New York: Palgrave).

A. Wildavsky (1964) *The Politics of the Budgetary Process* (Boston, MA: Little, Brown).

6

Losing voice, losing trust: the partisan dynamics of public evaluations of government in an era of polarisation[1]

Brian F. Schaffner and John A. Clark

For much of the second half of the 20th century, conventional wisdom held that trust and confidence in the US federal government was in decline. The attention garnered by the Tea Party movement following Barack Obama's election as president in 2008 renewed concern about declining trust and rising anger with the political system. Yet, historical perspective reveals a different story: confidence in the American government has *not* been in *steady* decline; rather, it fluctuates greatly over time. In the aftermath of the terrorist attacks on 11 September 2001, for example, the percentage of citizens indicating that they 'trust the government in Washington to do what is right' at least most of the time rose to 64 per cent, nearly double the level before the attacks.

More importantly, simply looking at aggregated measures of confidence and trust in government masks important context regarding which citizens are distrustful or angry with the government. This question strikes at the very heart of what meaning should be taken from the relatively large proportion of Americans who express their distrust or anger in government. On the one hand, if there is a consistent block of Americans who are distrustful and angry with the federal government, then it might suggest a significant problem with the political system itself. On the other hand, if the composition of angry and distrustful citizens changes over time, then it suggests that these citizens have less of a problem with the system itself than with those who are currently in power.

This chapter provides important context to our understanding of the meaning of the public's distrust and anger with government. It shows that much of this anger and distrust can be explained by partisan dynamics; that is, Democrats tend to trust government less and be more angry about government

---

[1] Research assistance was provided by Arus Harutyunyan, Mihaiela Ristei Gugiu and Heather Forrest.

when Republicans are in control, while the opposite is true when Democrats control government. This pattern is driven not by reactions to policies enacted by the party controlling government, but by the loss of a voice in government. Furthermore, this tendency appears to have become even more pronounced with the rise in polarisation during the past decade. Thus, the anger towards government that found a voice with the Tea Party movement might be best characterised as frustrations felt by conservatives shut out of government following Democratic victories in 2008. Accordingly, anger and mistrust of government dropped, particularly among Republicans, following the GOP takeover of the House of Representatives in 2010.

Why do(n't) people trust the government?

The oft-cited decline in trust among American citizens has been a source of much research and debate among political scientists. Political scientists have generally measured trust with a survey question that asks respondents, 'How much of the time do you think you can trust the government in Washington to do what is right?' Respondents choosing either 'just about always' or 'most of the time' are typically referred to as those who trust the government, while those responding 'only some of the time' or 'never' are categorised as untrusting. This question has been asked by the American National Election Study (ANES) every two years since 1964. Figure 1 plots responses from this 50-year time series of responses. The figure shows that there was a sharp decline in the percentage of Americans saying they trusted the government 'just about always' or 'most of the time' from the late 1960s through to the early 1980s. However, this decline has not persisted; rather, levels of trust rebounded at the end of the 1980s and again a decade or so later.

Scholars have often equated responses to this traditional trust in government measure with general support for the political system. Thus, research has found that lower levels of trust are associated with support for minor party candidates in presidential elections (Koch 2003; Hetherington 1999); support for term limits in state legislatures (Karp 1995); and even an increased likelihood of owning firearms (Jiobu and Curry 2001). Higher levels of trust are associated with compliance with tax laws (Scholz and Lubell 1998); support for government spending; and a willingness to give elected officials the leeway to pass legislation (Hetherington 1998).

A variety of factors tend to be associated with whether American citizens trust the government. For example, the public tends to be more trusting when the economy is booming and less trusting when the nation is facing an economic downturn (Lawrence 1997). Levels of trust in government also tend to be affected by the crime rate (Chanley et al. 2000) or the percentage of the public that sees crime as an important problem facing the country (Chanley 2002).

Significant events also appear to influence trust. For example, the Watergate scandal is frequently cited as responsible for the drop in trust in the mid-1970s (see Figure 1). Political scandals do not always serve to erode trust, however. For example, Miller and Borrelli (1991) found little evidence that the Iran-Contra scandal in 1986 accounted for the drop in trust during the mid-to-late 1980s. Of course, events may have short-lived effects on the degree to which citizens trust government. In addition, citizens of different political outlooks may also differ in the way they react to these events.

Other events thought to affect levels of trust include threats from other countries in the international arena. Unlike scandals, these 'external threats' are expected to drive up levels of trust in government as citizens 'rally around the flag' in support of their country (Alford 2001, pp. 45–6). Perhaps the best example of this rally effect is the terrorist attacks on the World Trade Center and the Pentagon on 11 September 2001 (Chanley 2002; Hetherington and Nelson 2003). Indeed, the effect of 9/11 can be seen to some extent in Figure 1. When the ANES conducted its interviews in 2002, about a year after the attacks, 56 per cent of Americans reported that they trusted the government 'most of the time' or 'just about always'. These were the highest levels of trust that the ANES had recorded since 1968. However, the spike in trust in the

Figure 1: Trust in the federal government, 1968–2008
Source: American National Election Studies.

wake of 9/11 was relatively short-lived; by 2004, trust in government was back to where it had been in 2000.

In addition to these factors, scholars have demonstrated that when citizens tell survey researchers how often they trust the government in Washington to do what is right, their point of reference tends to be focused on who is presently controlling the government rather than the system of government itself. Miller (1974) argued that those most alienated by centrist policies — extremists on the left and right — were less trusting of government to do the right thing. Citrin (1974) countered that trust centred on individual political leaders more than the policies they enact. Indeed, as this chapter will show, Democrats and Republicans tend to be more likely to trust government when their own party holds the presidency (Citrin 1974; Anderson and LoTempio 2002).

Thus, the existing research examining trust in government suggests that partisanship plays an important role in determining who distrusts government. Yet, many of these conclusions were reached at a time when political parties had lost much of their relevance among the American public (Wattenberg 1981). By the first decade of the 21st century, there was a clear renewal of partisanship among the American public (Bartels 2000; Hetherington 2001). The public is not only more divided among party lines than it was in the past, but people also see the parties as being more divided as well. For example, according to the ANES, in 2004 and 2008, three-quarters of Americans said they saw important differences between the two major parties — the highest level since at least 1960. And because citizens are now more likely to see important differences between the parties, they are also more likely to care which side wins. Indeed, the percentage of Americans reporting that they 'care a good deal' who wins the presidential election was higher in the past two presidential elections than at any other point since at least 1952.

Since Americans now care a great deal more about which party is in control of the federal government, these feelings are likely to influence how they evaluate the government itself. If a member of one party is asked to evaluate a federal government controlled by the opposing party, it would not be surprising to find that he or she is less trusting of that government. Furthermore, in an era of intense partisanship, we might also expect some partisans to express even stronger negative sentiments about the federal government when their party is out of power. This chapter examines both of these dynamics by showing how fluctuations in trust in government have recently become even more subject to partisan dynamics, and then extending the analysis to show how partisanship has evoked even stronger and more emotional evaluations of government during this period of polarisation.

The partisan dynamics of trust in government

To gain a better understanding of the extent to which evaluations of government are influenced by partisanship, this analysis begins by examining three time series of trust in government separately for Democrats and Republicans. In each of these series, trust is measured using the question described above. Like most previous researchers, we combined those saying that they trusted the government in Washington 'to do what is right' either 'always' or 'most of the time' into an aggregate measure of trust.

To start with we used the ANES biennial data presented in Figure 1. As noted above, the ANES data provide 22 biennial time points from 1964–2008.[2] This time series gives a long-range view of trust over more than four decades. Figure 2 disaggregates the responses shown in Figure 1 into trust among Democrats and Republicans. Note that many of the long-term trends in trust appear to be relatively consistent across partisan groups. Trust in government declined throughout the 1960s and 1970s, recovered somewhat during the 1980s, then declined and recovered again in the late 1990s and early 2000s. By 2008, trust among both Democrats and Republicans was relatively low,

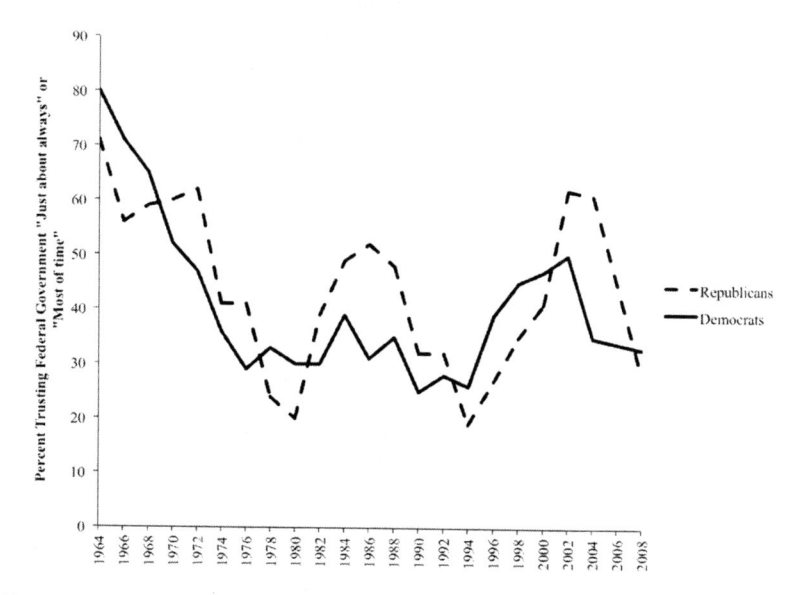

Figure 2: Biennial trust in government: 1964–2008
Source: American National Election Study.

---

2 Since ANES did not conduct interviews in 2006, that time point is missing from the analysis.

perhaps driven by declining economic conditions and fatigue with extended military conflicts in Afghanistan and Iraq.

Yet, within these long-term trends are some important partisan differences. Most significantly, the lines for Democrats and Republicans always cross when there is a change in the party controlling the presidency. Democrats are more trusting of the federal government during Democratic presidencies, as are Republicans during Republican administrations. This finding is consistent with previous research indicating that party control of the presidency was an important factor in determining levels of trust among partisans (Citrin 1974; Alford 2001).

Partisan groups also seem to react differently to events that may affect trust. With the biennial times series, it is difficult to see clearly how a single event creates movement in trust. The exception is the Watergate scandal that became daily news between 1972 and 1974. If ever an event took place that might erode citizens' trust in the federal government, Watergate was it. However, it is interesting to note the different reactions to this scandal among Republicans and Democrats: trust among the former fell drastically between 1972 and 1974, but among the latter it seemed unaffected by Watergate. While Democrats' trust in government did decline during this time period, the rate of decline did not depart from the trend during the previous five time periods. Democrats, who were far more likely to oppose the Vietnam War than Republicans, may already have felt estranged by US involvement in that conflict and the Nixon presidency in general. To them, Watergate may have been just one more reason to continue their deepening cynicism towards the federal government.

Similarly, the early 2000s witnessed significant polarisation in trust towards the federal government. The 2002 ANES registered high levels of trust among both Republicans and Democrats, largely due to the spike in trust that occurred in the wake of 9/11. However, by 2004, levels of trust had diverged along partisan lines. In that year, 61 per cent of Republicans reported that they trusted the federal government 'most of the time' or 'almost always', nearly unchanged from 2002. In the meantime, trust among Democrats had dropped 15 percentage points to just 35 per cent. Thus, 2004 witnessed the largest partisan gap in trust during the entire series.

What accounts for the large gap in trust between Republicans and Democrats in 2004? To be sure, partisan polarisation is an important part of the story. As Jacobson (2007) showed, the George W. Bush presidency was a particularly polarising one, and even by 2004 Democrats had grown frustrated with policies pursued by Bush and his fellow Republicans in Congress. Thus, it is possible that Democrats were losing trust in government as a result of the policies that had been produced by that government during the past several years. But it is also possible that it was not the policies at all. Rather, Democrats may have distrusted government as soon as they lost control of the Senate in 2002. With unified Republican control of government, Democrats may have felt shut out from policymaking at the federal level, a fact that would naturally leave them lacking trust.

Unfortunately, the biennial nature of the ANES data did not allow our research team to adjudicate between these two possibilities and forced the use of even more disaggregated time series data. With the second data source, movement in trust between 1991 and 2011 was examined using all available surveys from this period (nearly 90 in all). These data allowed movement in trust over shorter time intervals to be examined. The time series data was collected from the Roper Center's public opinion archives,[3] which importantly allowed the team to examine responses across different subsets easily, including different partisan groupings.

The examination of quarterly data on trust in Figure 3 presents a picture that reveals more variance in trust over shorter time intervals. For example, while Figure 1 indicates that trust rose steadily among all groups between 1994 and 2002, Figure 3 demonstrates that this increase in trust was actually subject to

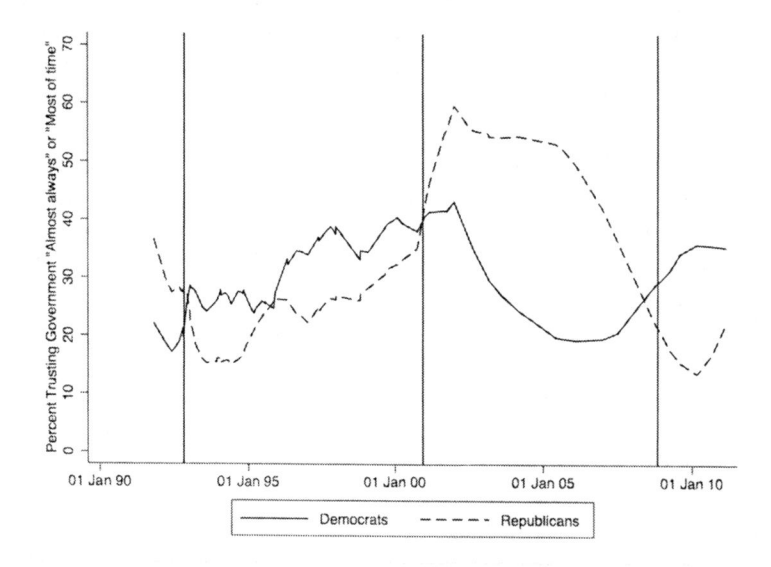

Figure 3: Partisanship and trust: 1991–2011
Data compiled by the authors from surveys available through the Roper Center and Lexis-Nexis. Lines plotted using Lowess smoothing. Vertical lines indicate dates of presidential elections that resulted in a change of the party of the president.

---

3   For surveys conducted prior to 2002, the Roper Center data was accessed via Lexis-Nexis. For more recent surveys, this data was accessed directly from the Roper Center website (www.ropercenter,uconn.edu/).

periodic ebbs and flows. Note that, as with the long view, Democrats became more trusting of the federal government during the Clinton presidency while Republicans were the more trusting group during both Bush presidencies. However, there are interesting variations within this pattern. Specifically, trust among Republicans increased steadily during the first year following the Republican takeover of Congress in 1994 (while trust among Democrats was steady during this period). Ultimately, this culminated in a moment where levels of trust between Democrats and Republicans was indistinguishable at the end of 1995. This rare convergence of partisan groups may have resulted from the government shutdown that occurred during that period. The strong stance taken by Republicans in Congress seemed to bolster trust among Republican citizens; however, trust in government among Democrats rebounded quickly during the subsequent months based on the popular view that Clinton and congressional Democrats had 'won' the budget showdown (Maraniss and Weisskopf 1996). Trust among Republicans declined in the months following this showdown.

As with the government shutdown, many of the significant movements in trust among the groups can be tied to particular events that are likely to have caused them. For instance, there was an increase in trust among both groups towards the end of 1997 coinciding with the signing of the balanced budget deal during that summer. The announcement of that legislation was met with favourable media coverage trumpeting the spirit of bipartisanship that had led to the accomplishment. Interestingly, the increase in trust among independents (not shown in the figure) was more pronounced than it was among either Democrats or Republicans. Independents may have felt particularly good about the bill because of its bipartisan nature since they tend to prefer it when both parties come together and compromise (Hibbing and Theiss-Morse 2001). The effect on trust among Democrats and Republicans may have been more muted since compromise meant sacrificing principles their side holds dear.

There was also a noticeable decline in trust among Democrats during the Monica Lewinsky scandal in 1998, while Republican trust remained steady during the same period. However, once the public's attention to the scandal waned and as the economy continued to strengthen, trust among both parties continued to rise until the 2000 presidential election, an event discussed in further detail below.

In addition to political events such as Watergate and budget showdowns, trust in government may also be affected by foreign threats to US security (Alford 2001; Chanley 2002). In fact, one of the largest movements in trust during the period covered in Figure 2 was the result of terrorist attacks on the World Trade Center and the Pentagon on 9/11. In the wake of these acts of terrorism, citizens were quick to support the government and its efforts to deal with the foreign threat. However, what is remarkable about the increase in trust after the attacks is how quickly it eroded in the months following the tragedy, particularly among Democrats. By the beginning of 2002, trust among Democrats was at about the same levels as it had been before the 2000 presidential election. In fact, with the biennial time series of trust in Figure 2, the effect of the 9/11 terrorist strikes are scarcely detectable among Democrats between 2000 and 2002.

While Democratic trust quickly eroded following the 9/11 bump, the same was not true for Republicans. In fact, trust among Republicans remained above 50 per cent until the beginning of 2006. Because of the persistent levels of trust among Republicans and the sharp decline among Democrats, trust following 9/11 quickly became as polarised as it had ever been. From 2002 through 2006, trust in government was about 20 to 30 percentage points higher among Republicans than it was for Democrats. Indeed, one of the most striking patterns from Figure 3 is how much larger the partisan gap in trust has become since 2000. From 1992 through 2000, the average difference in trust between Republicans and Democrats was just nine percentage points; since 2000, the average gap was more than 20 percentage points. This pattern is similar if the comparison is limited to trust during the two years of unified Democratic control of government in the 1990s (1993–4) to the years when one party or the other had unified control of the government in the 2000s (2003–06 and 2009–10). It suggests that trust-in-government fluctuations have become markedly more partisan in recent years.

Of course, the question still remains of why trust moves in a partisan way. That is, does trust in government decline among members of the out-party as a result of the policies enacted by the party in control of government, or do out-party members just react to losing a voice in government? If members of the out-party begin trusting the government less because of the types of policies enacted by the party that controls government, then we would not expect feelings of trust to change immediately after an election. Rather, under such a scenario, members of the out-party might become increasingly distrusting over time, as the majority party enacts more policies they find objectionable.

The patterns in Figure 3 suggest that the partisan dynamics of trust in government arise as a result of the out-party losing voice rather than as a response to policies enacted by the majority party. The three vertical lines in the figure indicate the date of a presidential election when party control of the presidency shifted. It is also worth noting that in each of these three cases (1992, 2000 and 2008), the outcome of the election gave a single party unified control of the federal government.[4] Note that in each of the three cases, levels of trust in government among partisans flips almost immediately upon the election result. In fact, in each case supporters of the party that won control of the government in the election became more trusting than those of the party that lost control before the actual handover in power even took place. Thus, Figure 3 provides fairly strong evidence for the notion that partisans lose trust in government as soon as they lose a voice in government, not as a response to the policies actually enacted by the new majority party.

An even more convincing demonstration of this dynamic is the 2000 National Annenberg Election Survey (Romer et al. 2004). For this survey over 38,000 interviews were conducted daily between 14 December 1999 and 20 January 2001. The intention was to study the dynamics of public opinion during the full course (and immediate aftermath) of a presidential campaign. Accordingly, the largest number of interviews were conducted during the several months preceding the November election. Respondents were asked the question about trust in government between 4 April 2000 and 20 January 2001. In all, nearly 25,000 Americans were questioned on how much they trusted the government during this time period.

The daily series from this dataset is particulary useful for examining how quickly trust changes among partisans once it has become clear which party has won or lost an election. Figure 4 presents this series. Consistent with the patterns shown up to this point, Democrats were about ten percentage points more trusting of the federal government than Republicans through most of the year. However, attitudes began to shift shortly after election day, even with the election unresolved. The two vertical lines mark the beginning and end of the recount by showing the date of the election and the date of the Supreme Court's decision in *Bush v. Gore*. Surprisingly, partisans did not become less trusting in government during the recount; rather, Democratic trust in government remained fairly constant while trust among Republicans actually began to increase. Within a week of the Supreme Court announcing its decision and Al Gore's concession, Republicans had become more trusting of government than Democrats. By inauguration day, trust was already about ten points higher among Republicans than it was for Democrats.

While not plotted in Figure 4, it is worth noting that independents seemed almost entirely unaffected by the recount controversy and the subsequent Supreme Court decision. Trust among them increased slightly throughout the process and did not dip following the Supreme Court decision. Thus, overall, independents did not seem to become more or less trusting of

---

4 Following the 2000 election, the Senate was split evenly, with Republicans owning the tie-breaking vote of Vice President Dick Cheney. Several months into this term, however, Senator James Jeffords broke with the Republican Party and became an independent, handing (tenuous) control of the Senate back to the Democrats until the 2002 elections.

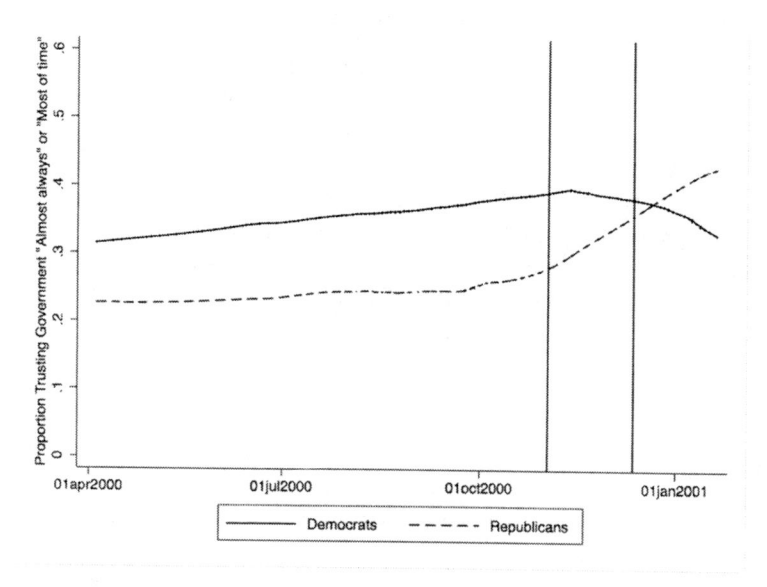

Figure 4: Daily trust: 14 December 1999–20 January 2001
Daily data compiled from the 2000 National Annenberg Election Survey. Lines plotted using Lowess smoothing. The first vertical line marks the date of the general election and the second line indicates the date that the Bush v. Gore *decision was handed down by the Supreme Court.*

government during the disputation. This lack of movement may indicate that independents paid little attention to the controversy and cared less about its outcome. Independents do tend to pay less attention to politics and they also tend to care less about which party controls the government (see, for example, Flanigan and Zingale 2002, pp. 83–8). Thus, it is not surprising to find that the recount wrangle did little to change the degree to which they trusted the federal government.

Overall, Figure 4 underscores two important points about attitudes towards the federal government. First, despite the chaos surrounding the Florida recount and concerns that it might erode the public's faith in the political system, trust in government actually ticked upwards during this episode. At a minimum, this suggests that the public's trust in the political system is not easily shaken, even by a contested result. Second, it does not take very long at all for trust among partisans to respond to a change in party control. Indeed, Democrats did not wait to see what kinds of policies Republicans would enact after gaining unified control of the federal government. Their trust in government dropped as soon as they knew that unified Republican control was imminent.

Partisanship and anger with government

To this point in the chapter, investigation has focused on how partisanship strongly conditions trust in the federal government. While the concept of trust in government has been extensively studied by political scientists, less attention has been paid to other evaluations of the political system. Yet, with the increasing polarisation in American politics, a non-trivial portion of the American public appears increasingly willing to express quite extreme views towards the federal government. In 1997, the Pew Center for the People and the Press began asking Americans the following question:

> Some people say they are basically content with the federal government, others say they are frustrated, and others say they are angry. Which of these best describes how you feel?

In 1997, 29 per cent of Americans said that they were 'basically content' with the government, 56 per cent reported that they were 'frustrated', and 12 per cent responded that they were 'angry'. By September 2010, nearly one in four Americans said that they felt 'angry' with the federal government.

To be sure, expressing anger at the federal government seems to be quite a bit more of an indictment than merely stating that one only trusts the government 'some of the time'. News organisations rightly took these strong sentiments seriously and focused on this anger as evidence of a more fundamental problem with the political system. However, as with measures of trust in government, it is important to understand whether anger at government is truly indicative of increasing dissatisfaction with the political system, or if it is merely an expression of frustration from those who affiliate with a party that is shut out of the government.

To gain more leverage on this particular question, this chapter turns to three snapshots of public opinion captured from 2006 to 2011. This timeframe is useful for the purposes of this analysis because it provides three different conditions: in 2006, Republicans held unified control of Congress and the presidency; in 2009, the Democrat party had control of both branches; and in 2011, Republicans regained control of the House of Representatives, creating divided government. In evaluating how concerned we should be with this anger at the federal government, it is important to know whether the same people were angry in each of these years, or if the composition of angry citizens fluctuated with changes in partisan control of the government.

Figure 5 shows the results from three different surveys conducted by the Pew Organization in October 2006, September 2010 and March 2011. The overall level of the bars indicate the percentage of respondents who said they were angry with the federal government and the shaded areas within the bars indicate what proportion of these citizens were Democrats, Republicans, or independents.[5]

Notably, overall levels of anger were relatively similar in 2006 and 2010; in both cases, about one in five respondents said that they were angry with the federal government. What changed in this short time period was *who* was angry. In 2006, Democrats made up about three-quarters of those who reported that they were angry with the federal government, while very few Republicans expressed similar views. Four years later, with Democrats in control of the federal government, the situation was reversed. At this point, there were very few Democrats who expressed anger, but many more Republicans who did so. Finally, the onset of divided government in 2011 reduced the proportion of those who were angry with the federal government by one-third. For the most part, this drop in anger resulted from Republicans being much less likely to express this opinion in 2011 than they had been the previous year.

In sum, the patterns in Figure 5 are fairly similar to those presented in the analysis of trust in government. There is not a large group of Americans who are consistently angry with the federal government; rather, the composition of

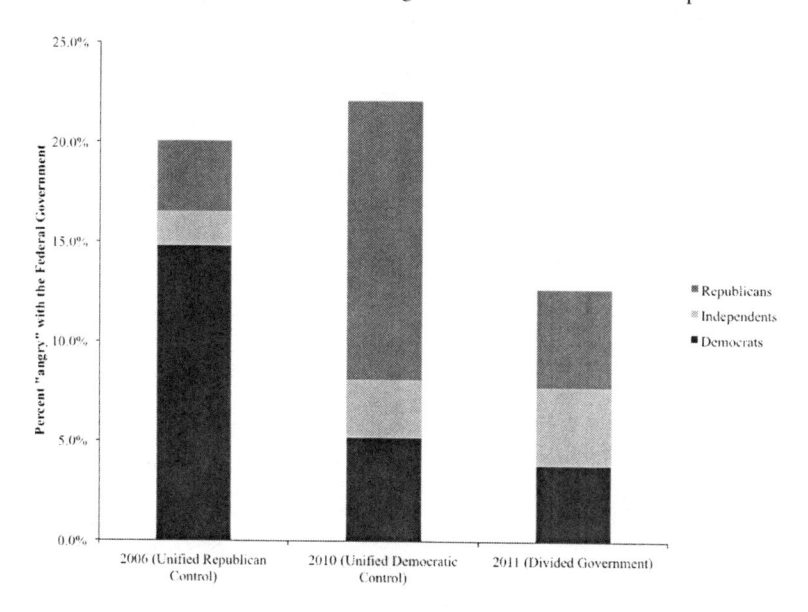

Figure 5: The partisan composition of citizens who are angry with government, 2006–11
Source: Surveys conducted by the Pew Center for the People and the Press.
Note: Independents stating that they 'lean' towards a particular party are included as partisans in these calculations.

5   Respondents who initially said that they were independents but then said that they leaned towards one party are treated as partisans.

angry Americans fluctuates quite significantly with changes in partisan control of government. Democrats were angry in 2006 when Republicans had unified control of government and Republicans were angry in 2010 when the opposite was true. Divided government in 2011 gave both parties a voice in the federal government, thereby reducing the number of angry partisans.

To further buttress these findings, a multivariate model was used to examine which factors are the strongest predictors of whether an individual is angry with the federal government. Specifically, the relative importance was examined of five statements that respondents were asked to evaluate as being either a major problem or a minor problem with elected officials in government. Those statements were:

1. They care only about their careers
2. They are influenced by special interest money
3. They are not willing to work together and compromise
4. They are not careful with the government's money
5. They are out of touch with regular Americans

Controlling for partisanship, ideology and other demographic variables, the research team found that the most important factor influencing whether an individual was angry with government was agreement that the 'out of touch' statement was a major problem. Those giving this response were three times

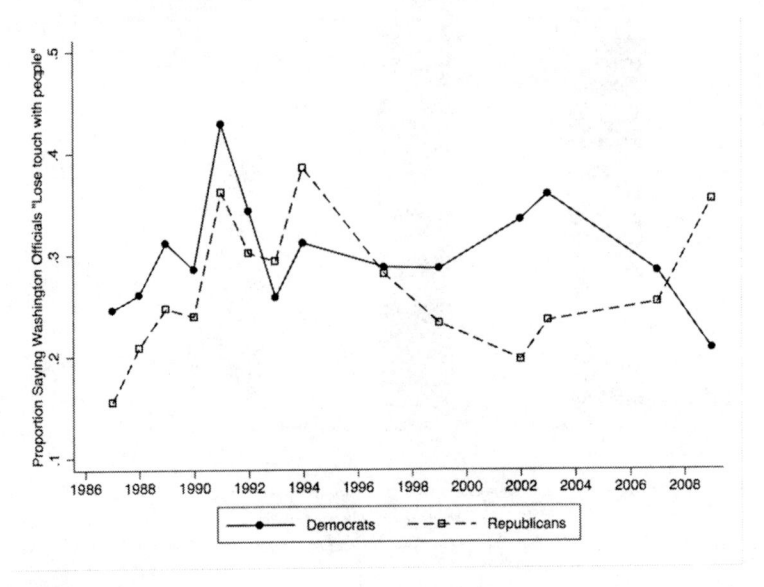

Figure 6: Percentage of Democrats and Republicans who 'completely agree' with the statement that elected officials in Washington 'lose touch with the people pretty quickly'. Source: 14 Pew surveys conducted over a 22-year period.

more likely to be angry with government than those seeing it as a minor problem. This is consistent with the notion that the majority of these negative sentiments are fuelled by partisans who feel shut out of a government controlled by the other party. These partisans view themselves as 'regular Americans' and they see a government populated with elected officials who do not represent their interests.

Indeed, viewing the government as 'out of touch' also appears to be influenced by partisanship over time. Figure 6 shows the percentage of Democrats and Republicans who 'completely agreed' with the statement that 'generally speaking, elected officials in Washington lose touch with the people pretty quickly' in 14 different surveys conducted by Pew over a period of 22 years. Notably, feelings that elected officials are out of touch appear to move in much the same way as trust and anger in government. Members of the party not in control of the presidency are more likely to think that public officials are out of touch, but the differences have become more pronounced in the past decade and the gap is largest when one party has unified control of government. Thus, partisans are more likely to feel that elected officials are out of touch when their preferred elected officials are out of power, and, especially in an era of heightened polarisation, this leads them to express more anger with the government.

Conclusion

Are low levels of trust and high levels of anger indicators that something is fundamentally awry with the American political system? Our view is that they are not. While indicators such as these should be carefully followed by individuals tasked with assessing the health of American democracy, it is at least as important to fully understand what it really means when an American tells a pollster they they trust the federal government 'only some of the time' or that they feel 'angry' with that government. We have shown that there is not a single large group of Americans that is consistently distrustful or angry with the government; rather, this group fluctuates significantly from year-to-year depending on which party is currently in control of that government. Furthermore, these partisan dynamics have become even more pronounced since the turn of the century with the rise of polarisation in the electorate.

Even though our analysis has suggested that these views are not an indictment of government itself, they do serve as yet another reminder of both the positive and negative consequences of polarisation in the US. On the positive side, polarisation has increased passions among the electorate, leading citizens to become more interested in politics and to participate more as a result. As just one example, individuals who said that they were angry with the federal government in 2010 were also significantly more likely to vote. These were hardly individuals who are disaffected from politics; rather, they were engaged partisans who were intent on regaining a voice in government.

On the negative side, polarisation has seemingly increased animosity, particularly among partisans. It also appears to have reduced the number of partisans who are even willing to give the other side a chance at governing. As this chapter has shown, partisans do not wait to see what kinds of policies the other party produces once they take control of the government; rather, they immediately become less trusting and more angry with the government. This fact likely makes it more difficult for politicians to build broad coalitions by engaging members of the other party. President Barack Obama, who ran in 2008 on a promise to restore bipartisanship in Washington, discovered just how difficult polarisation has made such a task. His efforts to reach out to the opposition party on issues like financial regulation and health care reform were frequently rebuffed by Republicans and criticised by liberals in his own party. Ultimately, much of Obama's agenda passed without any GOP support during the first two years of his presidency. Only after the return to divided government following Republican victories in 2010 have both sides been forced to take bipartisanship seriously. What remains to be seen is whether such compromise is even possible in contemporary American politics.

References

J.R. Alford (2001) 'We're all in this together: the decline of trust in government, 1958–1996, in (eds.) J.R. Hibbing and E. Theiss-Morse, *What Is It About Government that Americans Dislike?* (New York: Cambridge University Press).

C.J. Anderson and A.J. LoTempio (2002) 'Winning, losing, and political trust in government', *British Journal of Political Science* 32, pp. 335–51.

L.M. Bartels (2000) 'Partisanship and voting behavior, 1952–1996', *American Journal of Political Science* 44, pp. 35–50.

V.A. Chanley (2002) 'Trust in government in the aftermath of 9/11: determinants and consequences', *Political Psychology* 23, pp. 469–83.

V.A. Chanley, T.J. Rudolph and W.M. Rahn (2000) 'The origins and consequences of trust in government: a time series analysis', *Public Opinion Quarterly* 64, pp. 239–56.

J. Citrin (1974) 'Comment: the political relevance of trust in government', *American Political Science Review* 68, pp. 973–88.

W.H. Flanigan and N.H. Zingale (2002) *Political Behavior of the American Electorate*, 10th edn. (Washington, DC: CQ Press).

M.J. Hetherington (1998) 'The political relevance of political trust', *American Political Science Review* 92, pp. 791–808.

— (1999) 'The effect of political trust on the presidential vote, 1968–96', *American Political Science Review* 93, pp. 311–26.

— (2001) 'Resurgent mass partisanship: the role of elite polarization', *American Political Science Review* 95, pp. 619–31.

M.J. Hetherington and M. Nelson (2003) 'Anatomy of a rally effect: George W. Bush and the war on terrorism', *PS: Political Science and Politics* 36, pp. 37–42.

J.R. Hibbing and E. Theiss-Morse (2001) 'Process preferences and American politics: what the people want government to be', *American Political Science Review* 95, pp. 145–53.

G.C. Jacobson (2007) *A Divider, Not a Uniter: George W. Bush and the American People* (New York: Pearson Longman).

R.M. Jiobu and T.J. Curry (2001) 'Lack of confidence in the federal government and the ownership of firearms', *Social Science Quarterly* 82, pp. 77–88.

J.A. Karp (1995) 'Explaining public support for legislative terms', *Public Opinion Quarterly* 59, pp. 373–91.

J.W. Koch (2003) 'Political cynicism and third party support in American presidential elections', *American Politics Research* 31, pp. 48–65.

R.Z. Lawrence (1997) 'Is it really the economy, stupid?', in (eds.) J.S. Nye Jr., P.D. Zelikow and D.C. King, *Why People Don't Trust Government* (Cambridge, MA: Harvard University Press).

D. Maraniss and M. Weisskopf (1996) *'Tell Newt to Shut Up!'* (New York: Touchstone).

A.H. Miller (1974) 'Political issues and trust in government: 1964–1970', *American Political Science Review* 68, pp. 951–72.

A.H. Miller and S.A. Borrelli (1991) 'Confidence in government during the 1980s', *American Politics Quarterly* 19, pp. 147–73.

D. Romer, K. Kenski, P. Waldman, C. Adasiewicz and K. Hall Jamieson (2004) *Capturing Campaign Dynamics: The National Annenberg Election Survey* (New York: Oxford University Press).

J.T. Scholz and M. Lubell (1998) 'Trust and taxpaying: testing the heuristic approach to collective action', *American Journal of Political Science* 42, pp. 398–417.

M.P. Wattenberg (1981) 'The decline of political partisanship in the United States: negativity or neutrality?' *American Political Science Review* 75, pp. 941–50.

7

Two years of achievement and strife: the Democrats and the Obama presidency, 2009–10

Alex Waddan

In the aftermath of the midterm elections of November 2010 Republicans were triumphant and Democrats downcast. The outcome certainly constituted a so-called 'wave' election with the results apparently more meaningful than those represented by the more regular ebb and flow of midterm campaigns. There is nothing very surprising about the president's party losing seats in a midterm election, but the scale of the setback suffered by the Democrats was shocking. The loss of 63 seats in the House of Representatives was the heaviest in that chamber for either party since 1938, while six Senate seats were also lost (in addition to Edward Kennedy's former seat in the Massachusetts special election earlier in the year). From January 2011, therefore, control of the governing institutions in Washington DC was divided between the two parties, with the Tea Party-fuelled Republican majority in the House avowedly committed to frustrating what it deemed Obama's socialistic impulses and ensuring that he was a one-term president. The Senate remained in Democrat hands, but with a much reduced, and politically cowed, majority. The prospects for purposive collaborative action were very slim indeed.

Yet, two years earlier, a period of effective governance had looked possible, if in traumatic economic circumstances. Amidst much anticipation Senator Barack Obama was waiting, as President-elect, to enter the White House and his fellow Democrats had reinforced the congressional majorities initially attained in the 2006 midterm elections. The electorate had apparently repudiated the Republicans and given the incoming president the authority to correct the nation's troubled course and deal decisively with George W. Bush's troubled legacy. As the 2010 midterm elections signified, this scenario did not come to pass. Instead, the majority of those casting their ballots expressed disapproval with the course of public policy charted by Obama and the Democratic majority in Congress.

In examining the first two years of Barack Obama's tenure of the White House, this chapter starts by reviewing initial expectations that his could be a transformative presidency that would not only change public policy but also long-term political trends in the mould of Franklin Roosevelt and Ronald Reagan. It then considers the Obama administration's policy record by focusing on two legislative successes that generated a fierce political backlash — the American Recovery and Reinvestment Act (ARRA), also known as the stimulus bill, and the Affordable Care Act (ACA), better known as health care reform (or, as derided by conservative opponents, Obamacare).

By any standard these were substantive policy initiatives and legislative accomplishments. A response to economic crisis, ARRA was a three-year package of stimulus initiatives carrying an unprecedented price tag of $787 billion to boost recovery from the worst recession since the 1930s. Health care reform, on the other hand, fulfilled a long-time Democratic goal. The ACA aimed to reduce significantly the numbers of Americans without health insurance as well as imposing new rules preventing insurance companies from rejecting coverage of people with existing health problems. In addition, it sought to curb health care inflation, thereby alleviating the cost burden placed on American business and government alike. Finally, the chapter considers why Democratic success in enacting these ground-breaking measures exposed them to the political backlash that found cogent expression in the outcome of the 2010 midterm elections.

An emerging Democratic majority?

When Barack Obama was elected president few commentators predicted a GOP comeback two years hence. Indeed there was considerable debate as to whether the Democrats' success in recapturing the White House, and consolidating the large midterm congressional gains, marked 2008 as a realigning election that signified the beginning of a new political era in which they would hold majority party status. This was in line with the predictions of political commentators John Judis and Ruy Teixeira (2004; 2005). In their assessment the temporary national security advantage that the 9/11 terrorist attacks had given the Republicans would eventually give way to economic security anxiety that would benefit the Democrats. According to them, the higher job churn, the decline of well-paying blue-collar employment, and worries about employment-related fringe benefits such as health care insurance, would push voters towards the Democrats. This was because it was the party likely to mitigate the excesses and inequalities of the market through government intervention designed to protect not just the poor but also an increasingly uneasy middle class. By the same token, they anticipated that the GOP's cultural conservatism, which was widely interpreted as having helped

George W. Bush's re-election (Nather 2004; Dionne 2006) would further limit its appeal to voters increasingly focused on jobs rather than socio-moral issues.

By 2008 the Judis and Teixeira thesis no longer appeared to be the somewhat one-eyed statement of liberal optimism of its original iteration. The two analysts had forecast that the new Democratic majority would consist of a diverse collection of voter groups: so-called 'post-industrial professionals' — namely, those involved in professions such as teaching, nursing and computing; women; large proportions among minorities — with a particular emphasis on the growing number of Latino voters; and an equal share of the white working class. Some critics had charged that it would be difficult to hold such a heterogeneous coalition together because of the diverse interests of its component parts (Miller and Schofield 2008). It was also evident that not every group was moving towards the Democrats as predicted. In 2008 Obama still trailed McCain by 18 points among working class white voters, and in the 2010 congressional midterms the GOP advantage among that demographic widened significantly to 30 points (Teixeira 2011).

For the most part, however, the post-2008 election analysis concentrated on the people who had voted for the Democrats, and in particular for Obama, rather than those who had not. Obama won 53 per cent of the overall vote — hardly a landslide but the biggest margin of victory for a Democrat since 1964. This was also the first time since then that a Democratic candidate had won over half the votes cast, other than for Jimmy Carter's 50.1 per cent share in the Watergate-affected 1976 race. In this context, therefore, Obama's popular-vote victory was as convincing as Democrats could expect and was reinforced by his healthy lead (365 to173) in the Electoral College.

The voter coalition that elected Obama had various components. He enjoyed the overwhelming support of younger voters, including two-thirds of voters aged under 29 and 69 per cent of first-time voters. He also won women voters by a 56 to 43 per cent margin and, unusually for a Democrat, even gained a majority of male voters, albeit very narrowly (*The New York Times* 2008). A majority of college-educated voters supported him, including two-thirds of those with postgraduate qualifications. As political scientist John White noted, 'The collapse of support for the Republicans among the most highly educated has made the backing Democrats receive from today's new "creative class" a dominant feature of the electoral landscape' (White 2009, p. 232). In addition, African-American support for the Democratic candidate rose from its normally very high level of around 90 per cent to an extraordinarily high 95 per cent. Moreover, two-thirds of Latino voters went for Obama, marking a sharp swing back to the Democrats after George W. Bush had taken 40 per cent of their ballots in 2004. In contrast, Obama's share of the white vote was an unimpressive 43 per cent, just two per cent better than in 2004 (*The New

York Times 2008). Nevertheless, his lead among other groups enabled him to carry states considered to be reliable Republican turf, notably North Carolina, Virginia and Indiana. Having gone to George W. Bush by 20 points in 2004, the latter now entered the Democratic column for the first time since 1964 (Sabato 2009).

Overall, therefore, albeit with some caveats about the continuing problems in attracting white male voters (Kuhn 2007), there seemed grounds to believe that a new Democratic majority was taking shape. According to Judis:

> The three main groups in the new Democratic majority are professionals (college-educated workers who produce ideas and services), minorities (including African-Americans, Latinos, and Asian-Americans), and women (particularly working, single, and college-educated women). These groups, which overlap in membership, are also the key components of the new post-industrial economy (2009a).

In this context giddy Democratic partisans were not alone in their belief that 2008 was a potentially decisive election. Devotees of electoral realignment theory also felt a rush of blood because it evidenced a shift in voting behaviour at a time of national trauma (Key 1955; Burnham 1970; Sundquist 1983). There seemed to be new life in a concept that had seemingly lost currency because it was difficult to identify a specific realigning election after 1932 despite the nation's political course undergoing significant change since then (Mayhew 2002).

The 2008 exit polls suggested that the most common concern uniting Obama voters was a desire for change. Plenty of other data supported the belief that a new political era had dawned with his victory. A Pew Research Center pre-election poll in 2008 put Democratic Party identification at 38 per cent compared to the Republican Party's 28 per cent. Furthermore, a Rasmussen poll around the same time showed that Democrats were more trusted than Republicans on a range of issues. They had leads over the GOP of 13 per cent on the economy, 19 per cent on education, 20 per cent on health care and 12 per cent on social security. They even led on the normally solid Republican issues of taxation by five points and national security by three points.

Such high poll ratings were always likely to be unsustainable, but more substantively the incoming Obama presidency seemed to have the opportunity to overcome political gridlock. The problems of governance in the contemporary United States have been well documented (Steinmo and Watts 1995; Nivola and Brady 2006), especially given the heightened partisanship in Congress since the early 1990s (Aldrich and Rohde 2001; Sinclair 2006). In addition, the extended use of the filibuster has increasingly come to mean that a supermajority of 60 is the necessary marker of capacity to enact bills in the Senate, excepting when legislation can be bundled into a reconciliation bill that bypasses that obstructive manoeuvre (Wawro and Schickler 2006). What turned out to be solid Republican opposition to Obama in Congress was also predictable in view of the GOP's shift to the right and the decline of its moderate wing (Hacker and Pierson 2005). Certainly the 44th president could not have expected the kind of legislative support from a group of congressional Republicans that Ronald Reagan had received from so-called Boll Weevil Southern Democrats during the early months of his first term.

On the other hand, the Democrats had a comfortable majority (257 against 178) in the House of Representatives. They could also rely on the support of the party-switching Arlen Specter of Pennsylvania (who joined their ranks in April) and independents Jo Lieberman of Connecticut and Bernie Sanders of Vermont in the upper chamber. When Al Franken was finally declared the victor over Republican incumbent Norm Coleman in Minnesota in July (after some eight months of legal wrangles over the count that gave him a 312-vote majority), the Democrats could muster a potentially crucial 60 votes in the Senate.

If Obama's party was still short of parliamentary-style discipline, political analyst Rhodes Cook insisted that this was 'Not your father's Democratic Congress'. This was not just a reference to the post-war divisions between Southern segregationists and Northern liberals over civil rights. There had been a significant change in the make-up of the congressional Democratic Party since the more recent time of Bill Clinton's presidency that improved the chances of it behaving like a unified majority. According to Cook:

> In January 1993, Southern Democrats comprised nearly one-third of the party's number in the House and more than one-quarter in the Senate. Nowadays, the Southern component of the Democratic majority is less than one quarter in the House and barely 10 per cent in the Senate. The Democrats have made up for their Southern losses by gaining congressional seats in the party's liberal beachheads on the two coasts (2009).

In addition to apparent popular approval, including an expressed desire for change from the status quo, and the greater degree of coherence within the party's congressional ranks, the administration was presented with a set of circumstances that seemingly demanded a decisive political and policy response. This is not to suggest that politicians wish to inherit an economic crisis of the magnitude of the one facing the United States at the start of 2009, but in the now infamous words of President-elect Obama's White House Chief of staff Rahm Emmanuel: 'You never want a serious crisis to go to waste ... What I mean by that is that it's an opportunity to do things you could not do before' (Leonhardt 2010).

In its final months the Bush administration had pursued a variety of different strategies in response to the danger of financial-sector meltdown after the collapse of investment bank Lehman Brothers. Insurance giant AIG was given almost unlimited funds in order to stay afloat. Hastily put together by Treasury Secretary Henry Paulson to bail out the financial sector, the Troubled Assets Relief Program was enacted after its initial defeat in the House of Representatives had been instrumental in causing the Dow Jones industrial average to drop over 770 points (Kuttner 2010). In the circumstances more dramatic, concerted and coherent government intervention seemed to be the order of the day. Moreover there was major concern that the downturn was not just a cyclical recession. Historical examples suggested that economic crises brought on by a collapse of the financial sector would be longer lasting and more severe (Reinhart and Rogoff 2009).

This was clearly, therefore, not a happy inheritance but, in this context as indicated by Emanuel's words, the economic crisis seemed to offer the opportunity for a political reordering in the wake of the 2006 and 2008 elections. The Democrats seemingly had good grounds for confidence that their moment, as predicted by Judis and Teixeira, was at hand. The Republicans, equally, had cause for concern that their long-held fears of Americans turning to government for protection against economic risk were about to be realised. Voicing such anxiety back in 1993, conservative strategist Bill Kristol had advised unyielding Republican opposition to Bill Clinton's health care reform:

> [It will] re-legitimize middle-class dependence for 'security' on government spending and regulation It will revive the reputation of the party that spends and regulates, the Democrats, as the generous protector of middle-class interests. And it will at the same time strike a punishing blow against Republican claims to defend the middle-class by restraining government (quoted in Johnson and Broder 1997, p. 234).

Obama: a president of reconstruction?

Given the circumstances as he entered office, it seemed reasonable to regard Obama as a potentially transformative president, or in Stephen Skowronek's terminology, a president of reconstruction (1993). These are presidents elected at times of high crisis when the pre-existing political order does not any longer seem to have adequate political or policy responses to the problems at hand. In turn, there is a public demand for a new set of solutions — and, if successfully applied, these become the new normal with corresponding political reward for the architects of that innovation. Skowronek highlights the concept of reconstruction by referring to the presidencies of Thomas Jefferson, Andrew Jackson, Abraham Lincoln and Franklin Roosevelt:

> A great opportunity for presidential action was harnessed at these moments to an expansive authority to repudiate the established governing formulas ... The order-creating capacities of the presidency were realized full vent in a wholesale reconstruction of the standards of legitimate national government (1993, p. 37).

Skowronek's typology of presidential leadership considers the possibilities open to presidents on the basis of the institutional and ideological characteristics of their political inheritance (Beland and Waddan 2006; Ashbee and Waddan 2009). In his assessment, the historical legacies passed on to each president do much to determine how much scope a particular president has to leave his or her own distinctive mark on the American polity. All presidents enter office determined to establish the significance of their own leadership, of course. According to Skowronek, however, each one's 'political authority turns on identity vis-à-vis the established regime' (1993, p. 34). If the existing regime is in good institutional and ideological health then presidents committed to that regime will have the opportunity to further that project. Matters are more complicated, however, should a new president be either in opposition to a healthy regime or affiliated with a declining regime. In the former case, a president has to play a skilful political game in order to survive and is unlikely to leave a substantive programmatic legacy. In the latter scenario, presidents are burdened by inherited policy commitments that lack legitimacy, as illustrated by Herbert Hoover and Jimmy Carter.

For Skowronek, the presidents with the greatest *potential* political authority, and those who are remembered as the most important, are the ones who can repudiate a failing political order. The prime example of a 20th-century 'reconstructive' president was Franklin Roosevelt. Ronald Reagan can also potentially be cast in this mould but his case is more problematic. According to Skowronek, Democratic control of the House throughout his tenure (and the Senate in 1987–9) inhibited his capacity for reconstruction (1993, p. 422). Nonetheless, the 40th president's Republican successors acted as affiliates of the 'Reagan revolution' in seeking to build on its foundations. George H.W. Bush and George W. Bush portrayed themselves as affiliates of the conservative political regime initiated by the 40th president. Meanwhile, Bill Clinton's 'third way' approach and 'New Democrat' identity were pre-emptive strategies for operating within a still-ascendant conservative political order. In 2008, however, amidst the prevailing economic chaos, that paradigm appeared to have exhausted itself and the election results of that year suggested a popular repudiation of the existing political discourse.

In this context, a critical question became whether President Obama and congressional Democrats could establish an alternative political narrative that robustly repudiated the Republican regime orthodoxy and laid the foundations of a new political order. In testing this scenario, it is important to think of the different ways in which a policy can be deemed transformative. Most clearly, a transformative policy would be an effective remedy for a particular problem, setting in place its own policy legacies and consequently delineating new boundaries for future policy options. A transformative policy would also be likely to be popular and have the capacity to shift public opinion in support of its commitments. The effect would be to institutionalise the new agenda as part of the long-term political architecture, thereby changing the range of ideas about how policy should be developed and the manner in which political actors and interest groups treat particular policy areas (Beland and Waddan 2006; Ashbee and Waddan 2009).

So what was the policy agenda and what were the legislative accomplishments of the White House and the Democratic Congress between January 2009 and January 2011? A number of measures that had seemingly transformative potential were enacted in this period. The most significant were the economic stimulus and the health care reform, so it is important to examine how they were conceived, passed into law and then received.

The stimulus bill

When it became law in February 2009, the American Recovery and Reinvestment Act (ARRA) projected $787 billion of outlays on economic recovery measures. The measure was rapidly enacted by the new administration working with congressional Democrats. Illustrating the lack of consensus regarding economic solutions, ARRA won barely any bi-partisan support, other than from three Republican senators (but this sliver of endorsement was sufficient to pre-empt a filibuster threat). However, the more general Republican opposition was reinforced by the manner in which ARRA appeared to constitute a major break in the prevailing orthodoxy about the primacy of market economics. In February 2008 the Bush administration had pushed its own stimulus package through Congress, valued at about $168 billion, but this had mostly taken the form of tax cuts and so had not antagonised the conservative faithful. On the other hand, ARRA involved significant spending projects and seemed to herald a revival of the politics and policies of New Deal liberalism (Ashbee and Waddan 2011). When signing it into law in February 2009 President Obama described it as 'the most sweeping economic recovery package in our history' (quoted in Crummy and Sherry 2009) and a *New York Times* report described it as a 'striking return of big government' (Herszenhorn 2009).

John Judis, later to lament the president's lack of bold initiatives (2011), saw the stimulus as a potential radical re-wiring of the role of the state in the economy. Even if it were not the presidential intention to bring about such a change, 'the sheer size' of the intervention meant that government's role in economic affairs would increase significantly:

> Obama's stimulus program and its budget are going to lift overall government spending from the 30s to well over 40 per cent of GDP. [The] 2009 budget, along with other public spending, could reach 45 per cent of GDP. That's in response to a crisis, but as has happened before, the extent of government intervention is likely to remain permanent.
>
> At the least, the Obama budgets will shift even more dramatically the balance of economic power away from the private and toward the public sector. The American relationship of state to economy will begin to look more like that of France and Sweden (Judis 2009b).

Two years later, however, this idea that ARRA had the capacity for transformational political impact seemed much less convincing. That was partially because the economy remained slow to recover. The White House unwisely offered projections of how the stimulus package would help keep unemployment in relative check at eight per cent (Romer and Bernstein 2009). Though more an economic forecast than a promise, this created a hostage to fortune that Republican leaders turned against the administration when the unemployment rate went above this figure. Republican House Whip Eric Cantor asserted in July 2009: 'Clearly, the stimulus or so-called stimulus plan that spent almost $800 billion has not worked. We were promised — the president said we would keep unemployment under 8.5 per cent. We're now over 9.5 per cent on our way to 10 per cent. We have had a massive hemorrhaging of jobs in this economy' (PBS Newshour 2009). Whether or not Cantor was fairly interpreting the administration's predictions, the unemployment data helped fuel the impression that the stimulus had done little or nothing to boost recovery.

In March 2009, a month after ARRA was enacted, unemployment had already reached 8.6 per cent. A year later the figure was 9.7 per cent, equating to 15 million people, though this in fact represented a slight decline from the high of 10.1 per cent in October 2009 (U.S. Department of Labor 2010a). Beyond these figures, and in addition to the official tally of the unemployed, there were significant numbers of underemployed and others who had stopped looking for work. In March 2010 an estimated 9.1 million workers who wanted to be in full-time employment had part-time jobs. A further 2.3 million were described by the Department of Labor as being 'marginally attached to the labor force', meaning that they wished to work but had not actively sought a job in the four weeks prior to the compilation of the unemployment data. Of those about one million were described as 'discouraged workers', meaning that they had effectively stopped looking for work because they believed that no jobs were available for them (U.S. Department of Labor 2010b, p. 2). Adding up all these numbers meant that in October 2009 17.4 per cent of American workers were either unemployed or under-employed (Peck 2010).

Despite these unpromising indicators, the White House insisted that the stimulus was a success:

> Following implementation of the ARRA, the trajectory of the economy changed dramatically. Real GDP began to grow steadily starting in the third quarter of 2009 and private payroll employment has increased by nearly 600,000 since its low point in December 2009 (Council of Economic Advisors 2010).

Whatever the merits of this argument, there was plenty of scope for the administration's conservative adversaries to attack ARRA's underlying rationale. As one of these charged:

> The centerpiece of Obama's short-term stimulus program is a massive $787 billion fiscal program he signed into law last spring. By all accounts, this legislation was poorly crafted. However, poorly crafted or not, as short-term economic stimulus it was doomed from the outset as it is based on the erroneous assumption that deficit spending can increase total demand in a slack economy (Foster 2009).

In this way Republicans used ARRA's alleged failure to pin 'ownership' of the stuttering economy on the administration. They also developed a more general narrative about its supposedly wasteful spending. Drawing up a list of one hundred spendthrift projects, Senator Tom Coburn (R-Oklahoma) complained that the money was being spent 'repairing bridges nobody uses, building tunnels for turtles, and renovating extravagant train stations in remote areas' (*Tulsa Beacon* 2009).

Simultaneously — interestingly — an alternative critique grew on the left. The sense that ARRA was a significant and game-changing intervention (Judis 2009b) was challenged by commentators who considered it an inadequate response to a severe recession that not only demanded but also created the opportunity for bold action by government (Kuttner 2010, p. 73). The left's frustration was reinforced by the lame-duck Congress's vote after the midterm election to extend George W. Bush's tax cuts which were due to expire at the end of 2010. The administration claimed that in return it had bargained for a mini-stimulus in the form of extending eligibility for unemployment benefit for the long-term unemployed, but the agreement was clearly more attractive to conservatives than liberals. Lamenting this turn of events, the liberal columnist and economist Paul Krugman asked how cutting taxes rather than increasing government spending had emerged as the antidote to the economic downturn:

> The answer from the right is that the economic failures of the Obama administration show that big-government policies don't work. But the response should be, what big-government policies?
>
> For the fact is that the Obama stimulus — which itself was almost 40 per cent tax cuts — was far too cautious to turn the economy around ... Put it this way: a policy under which government employment actually fell, under which government spending on goods and services grew more slowly than during the Bush years, hardly constitutes a test of Keynesian economics (2010).

In the wake of GOP midterm success, however, conservative voices drowned out this liberal critique.

Many economists agree that ARRA had a positive, if limited, impact on employment (Congressional Budget Office 2011), but it received little credit for this. Whatever the reality of what would have happened without the stimulus to unemployment and to programmes such as Medicaid that benefited from ARRA funds (Waddan 2010), the stimulus did not revitalise popular demand for Big Government intervention in economic policy. In a December 2010 poll, for example, only 35 per cent of respondents approved of the way that the president was handling the economy against 58 per cent disapproving (American Research Group 2011). In its own defence, the administration insisted that it had used the best policy tools available in what was a very tough economic environment. Even if true, this was a very hard political sell — elections are not won on the slogan of 'Things are bad, but could be worse'.

Health care reform

As Vice President Joe Biden put it, the ACA was indeed a 'big f---ing deal' (*Huffington Post* 2010). On the other hand, it is impossible to assess its real effects as yet because so much of its implementation is delayed until 2014, while some elements will take up to a further five years to come into force. Continued posturing about the legitimacy, both popular and constitutional, of the ACA — with many Republicans keen to maintain health care policy as a debating point throughout the 2012 elections — also shrouded understanding of its real impact. It is possible, however, to identify the aims of the legislation, to explain the difficulties of getting the bill passed and to assess why — at least in the short term — enacting comprehensive health care reform has had negative political consequences for the Democrats.

The ACA had two broad aims: first, to bring about near universal health insurance, and second to reduce the ever-escalating cost of health care provision in the United States. In 2008 nearly 15 per cent of America's population was uninsured and many millions more were underinsured, leaving them exposed to financial ruin or worse if illness required expensive treatment (Thorne and Warren 2008). Yet, health care spending in the US accounted for 16 per cent GDP, compared with 8.7 per cent GDP in the United Kingdom, 11.2 per cent GDP in France, and 10.5 per cent in Germany (OECD 2010). It is to be expected that America would spend more of its GDP on health care than other nations since there is a correlation between a country's wealth and its proportionate expenditure on health. The problem is the level of relative excess spending and the limited value added by it. A McKinsey Global Institute study found that in 2006 the United States spent $2.1 trillion on health care, which amounted to 'nearly $650 billion more ... than peer OECD countries, even after adjusting for wealth.' In return the US 'has some of the best hospitals in the world. Cutting edge drugs are available earlier, and waiting times to see a physician tend to be lower' (McKinsey Global Institute 2008, pp. 10–11). In terms of health outcomes measured by life expectancy and infant mortality, however, the United States was no better than peer OECD nations.

Moreover America's spending on health care showed every sign of getting higher and higher, producing a potentially unsustainable squeeze on both private companies providing insurance for their employees and federal and state governments paying for the different public programmes. In 1970, for example, Medicare consumed 3.5 per cent of the federal budget, but by 2000 its share was 12.1 per cent (Moon 2006, p. 38). Shortly before passage of ACA, the Congressional Budget Office warned: 'The biggest single threat to budgetary stability is the growth of federal spending on health care — pushed up both by increases in the number of beneficiaries of Medicare and Medicaid (because of the aging of the population) and by growth in spending per beneficiary that outstrips growth in per capita GDP' (2010, p. 21). State governments feel the strain of Medicare costs even more than the federal government (Goldstein and Balz 2011). In Fiscal Year 2010 their aggregate outlays on this programme constituted 21.8 per cent of their total expenditure (National Association of State Budget Officers 2011, p. 2). Health care costs also hurt American business as companies offering employee health care plans have to grapple with the ever-rising costs of this benefit. Exemplifying this burden, Starbucks spent more on insuring its workers than it did on coffee by 2005 (Morris 2006). Businesses looking to reduce their costs had the option of passing more of the expense for insurance on to employees or no longer offering insurance, but the effect would be to add to the ranks of the uninsured or force more people to join public health care programmes.

Reforming this system had been a core commitment for many Democrats dating back at least to President Truman's failed efforts (Blumenthal and Morone 2009). However, they have disagreed among themselves over whether the priority is to reduce the number of uninsured or to contain costs. For all the work done by health economists and health policy experts, finding a politically viable solution to these problems remained elusive. Liberal Democrats, for example, had long championed a single-payer plan but this was highly unlikely to find enough support in Congress to be a realistic policy option. In addition to the policy problems, previous efforts to deliver on the promise of reform had turned politically sour, most emphatically for Bill Clinton, whose proposed Health Security Act turned into a policy dead end and a political catastrophe (Hacker 1997; Skocpol 1997). Nevertheless, Obama arrived in the White House promising major reform. During the primary battle the campaign for comprehensive change had been led by Senator Hillary Clinton (New York) and former South Carolina senator John Edwards, but Obama made it his own priority when running against John McCain (Jacobs and Skocpol 2010, pp. 34–8).

Tracing ACA's progress through Congress provides a remarkable insight into the US legislative process. The passage of ARRA involved considerable negotiation and compromise, but the urgency of doing something to address the economic crisis prompted the main political actors to resolve their differences quickly and get the stimulus enacted and into effect (Ashbee and Waddan 2011). There was no such swift resolution when it came to health care reform. The ACA only emerged after a protracted and tortured passage that at various points looked as if it would stall.

The House eventually agreed a package by mid-November 2009, but Senate debate dragged on throughout the year as Majority Leader Harry Reid (Nevada) tried to hold together 60 votes. There were protracted negotiations during the summer as the Senate Finance Committee devised its version of reform. At this point the administration was still trying to get some Republican support, even as conservatives outside the Beltway launched ferocious attacks against 'Obamacare' (Urbina 2009). Efforts to get some bipartisan imprint on reform yielded hardly any return. Senator Olympia Snowe (Maine) was the lone Republican vote for the Senate Finance Committee bill, but she reasserted her partisanship by supporting GOP efforts to prevent its final enactment. Eventually on 24 December, the upper chamber approved a package but, with each individual Democratic senator virtually having a personal veto, this measure differed considerably from the House version.

Arguments consequently raged within the Democratic caucus over a diverse range of issues. In particular, the House bill included the so-called 'public option', a government scheme available through the state insurance exchanges to help low-income Americans access insurance, but there was no such commitment in the Senate bill. Jo Lieberman (I-Connecticut) and some conservative-leaning Democratic senators, whose support was crucial to achieving the necessary supermajority, made it clear that its inclusion would be a deal-breaker for them. Even in the House, Speaker Nancy Pelosi (California) struggled to hold her caucus together as pro-choice and pro-life Democrats argued over the potential for public funding for abortions (*Washington Post* 2010).

The difficult task of reconciling the two health care bills became even harder when the Democrats lost their Senate supermajority in early 2010. In the special Senate election in Massachusetts necessitated by the death of health care reform champion Edward Kennedy, Republican Scott Brown scored a stunning victory in winning a seat that his Democratic predecessor had held since 1962. This gave the GOP the magic number of 41 votes in the Senate that enabled them to maintain a filibuster. As Democrats pondered again being thwarted in their efforts at health reform, President Obama exercised decisive leadership in pressurising the House leadership to enact the Senate version of reform. Despite her reservations about the Senate bill, Pelosi eventually agreed that this was the most effective way forward and worked hard to get the votes necessary. After passing the Senate bill the House also voted through a series of 'fixes' to that legislation that were sent on to Senate to vote through as a 'reconciliation' measure that did not allow for a filibuster. President Obama celebrated the moment following final passage of the legislation: 'When faced with crisis, we did not shrink from our challenge — we overcame it. We did not avoid our responsibility — we embraced it. We did not fear our future — we shaped it' (*Washington Post* 2010, p. 62).

The ACA was certainly a momentous legislative achievement. Obama's sentiments, however, were not universally shared and, reflecting the increasingly deep partisan divisions, opponents of the measure refused to reconcile themselves to a post-reform world. Republican hostility remained unremitting and legal challenges were quickly launched questioning the ACA's constitutionality, particularly the so-called 'individual mandate' whereby people would be compelled to buy themselves insurance (Balkin 2010). With these critiques finding some popular resonance, opposition to ACA became a key theme for Republicans in the 2010 campaign. Reinforcing the logic of this line of attack, Obama's approval ratings appeared to move 'in sync with the relative prominence of the health care debate' (Saldin 2010, p. 8). Depressingly for the administration, the more that health care came to the fore, the further down the president's numbers went.

Unsurprisingly this engendered some second-guessing about whether Obama had made the correct judgement when prioritising health reform. This came not just from opponents of reform but also from supporters. Among the latter, Joe Klein reflected:

> In 2008, Barack Obama wins a smashing electoral victory, largely because the public believes he's a calm, cool adult who can lead the country out of

an economic crisis. But for some crazy reason, he decides to focus much of his attention on passing a universal health care plan that has been the long-term dream of his party. This, despite polls that indicate nearly 80% of the public are satisfied with the health care they already have. The plan passes, but it's so complicated, the public isn't sure what's in it (and is wondering why the President hasn't focused similar attention on the economy), and Obama's party is clobbered in the 2010 elections (2011).

Countering this, reform supporters maintain that they will be vindicated in the long-term as more aspects of ACA begin to be implemented, thereby enabling the public to see its virtues.

This contention begs the question of whether the ACA will be a transformative reform. Even assuming that the bill is substantially implemented, the extended time frame required for this will long delay assessment of whether it will take its place in the pantheon of social welfare reform alongside Social Security and Medicare and thereby realign middle-class support in favour of the Democrats. As it is, the ACA is relatively clear about how it will increase access to insurance through a major expansion of the Medicaid programme and the creation of so-called state health insurance exchanges where low-income households will be able to buy insurance packages with government subsidies. In terms of controlling costs, however, the methodology is less clear and less convincing (Beland and Waddan forthcoming).

Conclusion

Unsurprisingly, the long-term implications of the 2010 election results were interpreted in alternative ways depending on partisan perspective. Some conservative analysts looked at the data and surmised that these elections represented an important shift — an illustration of the American public moving to the political right. Polling analyst Jay Cost argued that the voters had reaffirmed the conservative drift in American politics witnessed through the early years of the George W. Bush presidency (Cost 2010). Liberal commentators, in contrast, saw the results as an exaggerated case of midterm blues, noting that the 1938 results marked only a temporary reversal in the march of the New Deal coalition that dominated the American political landscape for 30 years.

Which of these competing narratives is more accurate will only be realised over time, but some things were clearly discernible in November 2010. First, Democratic hopes that the 2008 elections had represented a decisive turning point in their favour were at best put on hold, if not dashed. On the other hand, a second feature of the political landscape was that the Republican gains came with serious qualifications. The exit polls suggest that the outcome represented a repudiation of the Democrats rather than a positive endorsement of the Republicans. A majority of voters still 'expressed unfavourable views of the GOP', even while voting for them (Brownstein 2010, p. 28). This certainly casts doubt on the notion that the Republicans had a mandate of their own. Finally, the 2010 vote was evidently the third 'wave' election in succession to those of 2006 and 2008 results, which pointed to a volatile and discontented electoral mood rather than a voter affirmation of either party.

This does not gainsay the reality that the Obama presidency achieved a significant record of legislative success in its first two years, highlighted most notably by ARRA and ACA. It is evident, however, that neither reform transformed the political landscape in favour of the Democrats in the short term. Both measures may constitute good public policy but, along with the failed effort at cap and trade legislation, they provided political ammunition for the White House's adversaries (Saldin 2010). With regard to the longer-term test of transformation — whether new policies themselves become part of the established institutional framework — it is too early to make any definitive judgement on ARRA or ACA. It may be that a future generation of historians will compare them with the major pieces of New Deal legislation, as parts of a bigger picture that changed patterns of governance in the United States, but that time seems some considerable distance away.

References

J.H. Aldrich and D.W. Rohde (2001) 'The logic of conditional party government: revisiting the electoral connection', in L.C. Dodd and B.L. Oppenheimer (eds.), *Congress Reconsidered*, 7th edn. (Washington, DC: CQ Press), pp. 269–92.

J. Allen and J. Gerstein (2010) 'Liberal Democrats to Obama: fight harder', *Politico*, 12 Dec., www.politico.com/news/stories/1210/46054.html.

American Research Group (2011) 'Obama's overall job approval drops', www.americanresearchgroup.com/economy/.

E. Ashbee and A. Waddan (2009) '"You never want a serious crisis to go to waste": the Obama presidency, institutional constraints and political opportunities', unpublished paper presented at Copenhagen Business School, Dec. 2009.

— (2011) 'The passage of ARRA and the character of the contemporary American state', unpublished paper presented at the Mid-West Political Science Association, Chicago.

J. Balkin (2010) 'The constitutionality of the individual mandate for health reform', *New England Journal of Medicine*, 11 Feb., pp. 482–3.

D. Beland and A. Waddan (2006) 'The social policies presidents make: pre-emptive leadership under Nixon and Clinton', *Political Studies* 54 (1), pp. 65–83.

— (forthcoming) 'The Obama presidency and health insurance reform: assessing continuity and change', *Social Policy and Society*.

D. Blumenthal and J. Morone (2009) *The Heart of Power: Health and Politics in the Oval Office* (Berkeley, CA: University of California Press).

R. Brownstein (2010) 'Past as prologue', *National Journal*, 6 Nov., pp. 28–32.

W.D. Burnham (1970) *Critical Elections and the Mainsprings of American Politics* (New York: Norton).

R. Cook (2009) 'Not your father's Democratic Congress', *Sabato's Crystal Ball*, 19 Feb., www.centerforpolitics.org/crystalball/articles/frc2009021901/.

Congressional Budget Office (2010) *The Budget and Economic Outlook: Fiscal Years 2010 to 2020* (Washington DC: Congress of the United States), www.cbo.gov/ftpdocs/108xx/doc10871/01-26-Outlook.pdf.

— (2011) *Estimated Impact of the American recovery and Reinvestment Act on Employment and Economic Output from January 2011 through March 2011* (Washington DC: Congressional Budget Office), www.cbo.gov/ftpdocs/121xx/doc12185/05-25-ARRA.pdf.

J. Cost (2010) 'Back to the Bush coalition: where have we seen this majority before?', *Weekly Standard*, 15 Nov., www.weeklystandard.com/articles/back-bush-coalition_515074.html?page=1/.

Council of Economic Advisors (2010) *The Economic Impact of the American Recovery and Reinvestment Act of 2009 Fourth Quarterly Report*, www.whitehouse.gov/administration/eop/cea/factsheets-reports/economic-impact-arra-4th-quarterly-report/summary/.

K. Crummy and A. Sherry (2009) 'Obama signs stimulus bill', *Denver Post*, 18 Feb.

E.J. Dionne (2006) 'Polarized by God? American politics and the religious divide', in P. Nivola and D. Brady (eds.), *Red and Blue Nation: Characteristics and Causes of America's Polarized Politics* (Washington, DC: Brookings Institution), pp. 175–205.

J.D. Foster (2009) 'Obama jobs deficit up again, real jobs strategy needed', Heritage Foundation webmemo, www.heritage.org/Research/Reports/2009/12/Obama-Jobs-Deficit-Up-Again-Real-Jobs-Strategy-Needed/.

A. Goldstein and D. Balz (2011) 'Governors differ on extent of flexibility for Medicaid', *Washington Post*, 27 Feb., www.washingtonpost.com/wp-dyn/content/article/2011/02/27/AR2011022703688.html?wpisrc=nl_politics/.

J. Hacker (1997) *The Road to Nowhere: The Genesis of President Clinton's Plan for Health Security* (Princeton, NJ: Princeton University Press).

J. Hacker and P. Pierson (2005) *Off Center: The Republican Revolution and the Erosion of American Democracy* (New Haven, CT: Yale University Press).

D. Herszenhorn (2009) 'A smaller, faster stimulus plan, but still with a lot of money', *The New York Times*, 13 Feb.

Huffington Post (2010) 'A big f---ing deal: Biden's health care F bomb on live TV', 23 March, www.huffingtonpost.com/2010/03/23/a-big-fucking-deal-bidens_n_509927.html.

L. Jacobs and T. Skocpol (2010) *Health Care Reform and American Politics: What Everyone Needs to Know* (New York: Oxford University Press).

H. Johnson and D. Broder (1997) *The System: The American Way of Politics at Breaking Point* (Boston, MA: Little, Brown).

J. Judis (2005) 'Movement interruptus', *American Prospect* 16 (1), pp. 23–7.

— (2009a) 'America the liberal?', 26 Sept., www.cbsnews.com/stories/2008/11/05/opinion/main4576776.shtml.

— (2009b) 'Fundamentally different', *New Republic*, 23 April, www.carnegieendowment.org/publications/index.cfm?fa=view&id=23034.

— (2010) 'The unnecessary fall: a counter history of the Obama presidency', *New Republic*, 12 Aug., www.tnr.com/article/politics/magazine/76972/obama-failure-polls-populism-recession-health-care.

J. Judis and R. Teixeira (2004) *The Emerging Democratic Majority* rev. edn. (New York: Lisa Drew/Scribner).

V.O. Key (1955) 'A theory of critical elections', *Journal of Politics* 17 (1), pp. 3–18.

J. Klein (2011) 'Misread mandates: how Obama and Ryan fooled themselves', Time.com, 2 June, www.time.com/time/nation/article/0,8599,2075194,00.html.

P. Krugman (2010) 'When zombies win', *The New York Times*, 19 Dec.

D.P. Kuhn (2007) *The Neglected Voter: White Men and the Democratic Dilemma* (New York: Palgrave).

R. Kuttner (2010) *A Presidency in Peril: The Inside Story of Obama's Promise, Wall Street's Power, and the Struggle to Control Our Economic Future* (White River Junction, VT: Chelsea Green Publishing).

D. Leonhardt (2010) 'Judging stimulus by job data reveals success', *The New York Times*, 16 Feb.

McKinsey Global Institute (2008) 'Accounting for the cost of US health care: a new look at why Americans spend more', Dec., www.mckinsey.com/Insights/MGI/Research/Americas/Accounting_for_the_cost_of_US_health_care/.

D. Mayhew (2002) *Electoral Realignments: A Critique of an American Genre* (New Haven, CT: Yale University Press).

G. Miller and N. Schofield (2008) 'The transformation of the Republican and Democratic party coalitions in the US', *Perspectives on Politics* 6 (3), pp. 433–52.

M. Moon (2006) *Medicare: A Policy Primer* (Washington, DC: Urban Institute Press).

C. Morris (2006) *Apart at the Seams: The Collapse of Private Pension and Health Care Protection* (New York: Century Foundation Press).

National Association of State Budget Officers (2011) *Summary: NASBO State Expenditure Report 2010*, www.nasbo.org/sites/default/files/Summary%20-%20State%20Expenditure%20Report.pdf.

D. Nather (2004) 'Social Conservatives propel Bush, Republicans to victory', *Congressional Quarterly Weekly*, pp. 2586–91, 6 Nov.

P. Nivola and D. Brady (eds.) *Red and Blue Nation: Characteristics and Causes of America's Polarized Politics* (Washington, DC: Brookings Institution).

OECD, Directorate for Employment, Labour and Social Affairs (2010) *OECD Health Data for 2010*, www.oecd.org/document/16/0,3343,en_2649_34631_2085200_1_1_1_1,00.html.

D. Peck (2010) 'How a new jobless era will transform America', *The Atlantic Online*, March, www.theatlantic.com/doc/print/201003/jobless-america-future/.

Pew Research Center (2008) 'Democrats hold party ID edge across political battleground', 30 Oct., http://pewresearch.org/pubs/1015/democratic-party-identification-swing-states/.

PBS Newshour (2009) 'Questions surface on impact of stimulus plan', transcript of PBS Newshour, 8 July, www.pbs.org/newshour/bb/business/july-dec09/stimulus_07-08.html.

Rasmussen Reports (2008) 'Trust and importance on issues', www.rasmussenreports.com/public_content/archive/mood_of_america_archive/trust_on_issues/trust_on_issues_tables/trust_importance_on_issues/.

C. Reinhart and K. Rogoff (2009) *This Time Is Different: Eight Centuries of Financial Folly* (Princeton, NJ: Princeton University Press).

C. Romer and J. Bernstein (2009) 'The job impact of the American Recovery and Reinvestment Act', 9 Jan., http://otrans.3cdn.net/45593e8ecbd339d074_l3m6bt1te.pdf.

L. Sabato (2009) *Marathon: Looking Back at the Historic US Election of 2008*, The Fourteenth Annual Douglas Bryant Lecture at the British Library (London: British Library).

R. Saldin (2010) 'Healthcare Reform: A Prescription for the 2010 Republican Landslide?', *The Forum*: Vol. 8 (4), Article 10, www.astrid-online.it/Elezioni-U/Studi--ric/Saldin_The-Forum_4_2010.pdf.

B. Sinclair (2006) *Party Wars: Polarization and the Politics of National Policy Making* (Norman, OK: Oklahoma University Press).

T. Skocpol (1997) *Boomerang: Health Care Reform and the Turn Against Government* (New York: Norton).

S. Skowronek (1993) *The Politics Presidents Make: Leadership from George Washington to George H. W. Bush* (Cambridge, MA: Harvard University Press).

S. Steinmo and J. Watts (1995) 'It's the institutions, stupid! Why the United States can't pass comprehensive national health insurance', *Journal of Health Politics Policy and Law* 20 (2), pp. 329–72.

J.L. Sundquist (1983) *The Dynamics of the Party System: Alignment and Realignment of Political Parties in the United States* (Washington, DC: Brookings Institution).

R. Teixera (2011) 'The white working class: the group that will likely determine Obama's fate', *New Republic*, 20 June, www.tnr.com/article/politics/90241/obama-election-2012-working-class-kerry?utm_source=The+New+Republic&utm_campaign=d4cb9da619-TNR_Pol_062011&utm_medium=email/.

The New York Times (2008) Exit Polls, http://elections.nytimes.com/2008/results/president/exit-polls.html.

Washington Post (2010) *Landmark: America's New Health-Care Law and What It Means for Us All* (New York: Public Affairs).

D. Thorne and E. Warren (2008) 'Get sick, go broke', in (ed.) J. Hacker, *Health at Risk: America's Ailing Health system and How to Heal It* (New York: Columbia University Press), pp. 66–87.

Tulsa Beacon (2009) 'Wasteful spending highlights the list of U.S. stimulus projects', 25 June, www.tulsabeacon.com/?p=2274/.

I. Urbina (2009) 'Beyond the beltway, health debate turns hostile', *The New York Times*, 7 Aug.

US Department of Labor (2010a) *Labor Force Statistics from the Current Population Survey*, http://data.bls.gov/PDQ/servlet/SurveyOutputServlet?data_tool=latest_numbers&series_id=LNS14000000/.

— (2010b) Bureau of Labor Statistics, *The Employment Situation March 2010*, www.bls.gov/news.release/pdf/empsit.pdf.

A. Waddan (2010) 'The US safety net, inequality and the great recession', *Journal of Poverty and Social Justice* 18 (3), pp. 243–54.

G. Wawro and E. Schickler (2006) *Filibuster: Obstruction and Lawmaking in the U.S. Senate* (Princeton, NJ: Princeton University Press).

J.K. White (2009) *Barack Obama's America: How New Conceptions of Race, Family, and Religion Ended the Reagan Era* (Ann Arbor, MI: University of Michigan Press).

8
The rise of the Tea Party movement and American governance

Edward Ashbee

The Tea Party protests of 2009 and 2010 and the part these seemingly played in stiffening the resolve of congressional Republicans to block White House legislative plans made headlines on both sides of the Atlantic. Some media analysts have represented the movement as part of a 'know-nothing' backlash against President Obama and congressional Democrats, while others have seen it as testimony to American exceptionalism, the resilience of what Hillary Clinton once termed the 'vast right-wing conspiracy', and a crisis of governance. In their own narrative, Tea Party activists saw themselves as disenfranchised outsiders and 'citizen patriots'.

This chapter examines the emergence and development of the Tea Party movement. It considers the ideas around which the movement has been constructed, the interests and constituencies from which it draws much of its support and the institutional arrangements that brought it into being. In doing so, it emphasises the process of interaction between ideas, interests and institutions.

Development

The election of Barack Obama as US president threw up different, although often interconnected, forms of opposition. 'Birthers' challenged the constitutionality and legitimacy of his presidency. Fox News, particularly after Glenn Beck joined it, focused on administration staffers and their characters. Christian right organisations such as the Family Research Council campaigned against the 'Obama agenda' on issues such as abortion, same-sex marriage and efforts to overturn the 'don't ask, don't tell' policy towards gays and lesbians serving in the armed forces. Nonetheless, while the Tea Party movement has overlaps and interconnections between these oppositional strands, it has a distinct identity, character and culture built around the principles of limited government, free markets and 'fiscal responsibility'.

The beginnings of the movement are usually dated back, at least in its own accounts, to Rick Santelli's 'rant' against expansionary economic policies from the floor of the Chicago Stock Exchange on CNBC less than a month after Obama's inauguration. The Tea Party's 'take-off into self-sustained growth', to use W.W. Rostow's[1] celebrated description of industrial development, came in the months that followed.

There had been opposition amongst Republicans within Congress and at grassroots level to the increases in federal government spending and the 'bank bailout' during the closing phases of George W. Bush's presidency. Such sentiments were compounded from January 2009 onwards by intense partisanship (which has been a defining feature of US politics in recent decades) and the succession of measures that seemed to enlarge dramatically the scope of government. The passage of the American Recovery and Reinvestment Act (ARRA) added an estimated $787 billion to the $700 billion already committed to the rescue of the financial sector. The Obama administration increased the funding for General Motors and Chrysler. On top of this, despite the concessions made to ensure passage, the Democrats' long-promised health care reform was finally enacted in March 2010.

Against this background, the protests that began in February 2009 quickly escalated. Even before ARRA had been signed, the 'Porkulus' protest, which denounced the 'generational theft' represented by its 'pork barrel' spending, took place in Seattle.[2] The protests that were organised two months later on 15 April 2009 (the last day on which tax returns can be sent) were said to have attracted at least 268,000 people at 207 different events (Murray 2009). The town hall meetings convened by many members of Congress during the summer of 2009 served as a focal point for further dissent.

House of Representatives Speaker Nancy Pelosi (D-California) dubbed the Tea Party as 'Astroturf' to signify her belief that it lacked popular authenticity as the creation of wealthy financial backers. In contrast, the movement's self-representations are structured around images of spontaneous, grassroots revolt.[3] Indeed, although the part played by established conservative elites and political entrepreneurs should not be disregarded, there is some legitimacy in these claims. A survey in October 2010 found that 86 per cent of local

---

[1] Walt Whitman Rostow (1916–2003) was a US economist and political theorist who served during Lyndon B. Johnson's presidency (1963–9) as Special Assistant for National Security Affairs.

[2] The term 'porkulus' is an adaptation of 'stimulus', suggesting that, in reality, ARRA was 'pork-barrel' spending undertaken so as to secure political advantage in particular districts or states.

[3] Although, writing in *The New Yorker*, Jane Mayer has pointed to the role of figures such as Charles and David Koch, who are among the richest individuals in the US, in funding Americans for Prosperity and other organisations that are tied to the Tea Party movement (Mayer 2010).

Tea Party leaders reported that most of their membership had not previously been involved in political activity. Most of the local groups had fewer than 50 members (Gardner 2010). According to another report, three-quarters of activists 'describe their groups as informal, with no governance structure, and only one in 10 act in coordination with a national organization' (Edwards 2010).

However, alongside these informal and unstructured associational forms that have done much to shape the movement's 'official' history, the Tea Party also incorporates more formal organisations, structures and networks. These include: the Tea Party Federation, a 'broad coalition' of local and regional groups (Tea Party Federation 2010); the Tea Party Nation that convened the first National Tea Party Convention in Nashville in February 2010, featuring speakers such as former Alaska Governor Sarah Palin; and the Atlanta-based Tea Party Patriots claim to provide 'logistical, educational, networking and other types of support to over 1.000 community based tea party groups around the country' (Tea Party Patriots 2010). Meanwhile, some long-established conservative organisations, most notably FreedomWorks, reorientated themselves as a bridge between the movement and mainstream conservatives. They also offered resources and tools enabling activists to build more effective forms of campaign organisation.

As the 2010 midterm elections approached, the Tea Party's visibility grew. While a large number of the Republican 'establishment' candidates secured re-nomination, the movement's endorsements, volunteering and funding inflicted casualties among some longstanding GOP office-holders. The most notable scalp was that of Senator Bob Bennett (Utah), a well-entrenched three-term conservative who had offended the Tea Party by voting for the Bush bank bailout of late 2008.

Ideas

The Tea Party movement can be understood, at least to some extent, by considering the ideas and grievances that have defined it. For the most part, movement organisations and groupings have focused on a limited range of economic issues. The policy questionnaires that they submitted to election candidates concentrated on concerns such as policy towards taxation rates, the federal budget and the overall role that government should play. The Tea Party Federation and the Tea Party Patriots restricted their goals to 'fiscal responsibility', constitutionally limited government' and 'free markets' (Tea Party Patriots 2010). Indeed, there was a turn away from the cultural and social issues that had defined much of the Republican right agenda since the late 1970s. A questionnaire submitted to candidates by The Independence Caucus (Utah), another movement organisation, asked their opinion of *Wickard v.*

Filburn (a 1942 Supreme Court ruling permitting a significant increase in the federal government's regulatory powers) rather than *Roe v. Wade*. As *The New York Times* concluded: 'God, life and family get little if any mention in statements or manifestos' (quoted in Zernike 2010).[4]

Nonetheless, these formal expressions of policy intent by movement organisations offer only a partial insight into Tea Party thinking. Opinion polls suggest that many activists are cultural as well as economic conservatives. In particular, there is evidence that the movement's stronger identifiers share many of the opinions and attitudes that have long defined the Christian right. The American Values Survey undertaken by the Public Religion Research Institute during the first half of September 2010 asked respondents if they considered themselves 'part of the Tea Party movement' and used a different form of phrasing to other surveys to capture the views of those who had relatively high levels of commitment. Whereas other polls recorded significantly higher levels of support, it found that only 11 per cent of the adult population considered themselves 'part' of the movement (Zernike and Thee-Brenan 2010). Within this group, there are pronounced connections and overlaps with the religious right, with 47 per cent of those surveyed saying they were 'part of the conservative Christian movement' (a more overtly political form of self-description than, for example, 'evangelical' or 'born again'). In addition, 63 per cent asserted that abortion should be illegal in all or most cases (Jones and Cox 2010, pp. 3, 28).

Moreover, it is important to look beyond policy statements and immediate expressions of opinion so as to consider the discourses that define the Tea Party and the norms, stories and framing processes on which these rest. Although some analysts suggest that the movement's thinking is structured around representations of the US as it appeared to be a half-century ago, or that it is an inchoate protest against the eclipse of American power by other nations, its emergence, development and growth are above all else testimony to the resilience and strength of classical liberalism and the founding creed of the US. Indeed, the movement not only celebrates the virtues of limited government but rejoices in a particular form of narrative structured around the American founding. As one analyst explained:

> Tea Party members devour books about George Washington, Thomas Jefferson, and Samuel Adams. They carry pocket copies of the Constitution and the Declaration of Independence. They believe strongly in the Bill of Rights, especially in the Tenth Amendment's admonition that all powers not delegated to the federal government are reserved for the states and

---

4   Furthermore, the Christian right and the Tea Party movement have different social bases. Whereas the Christian right and social conservatism have been largely rooted in the evangelical Protestant churches, the Tea Party movement owes more to movement organisations, social networking and the internet.

the people. Their rhetoric invokes the constitutional vision of a limited government with enumerated powers (Continetti 2010).

At the same time, there is a process of frame-bridging. The populism that underscores the movement's understanding of the American Revolution is tied together with a profound hostility towards contemporary political elites. As David Brooks of *The New York Times* has noted, the movement's thinking is, like earlier expressions of the populist mood, directed against liberal intellectualism, which it suggests is tied to other entrenched concentrations of power:

> The Tea Party movement is a large, fractious confederation of Americans who are defined by what they are against. They are against the concentrated power of the educated class. They believe big government, big business, big media and the affluent professionals are merging to form a self-serving oligarchy — with bloated government, unsustainable deficits, high taxes and intrusive regulation (Brooks 2010).

These suspicions are fused with a celebration of popular experience and a degree of disdain for the formal political process. Michael Gerson, formerly chief speechwriter for George W. Bush, commented on Christine O'Donnell's victory in the Delaware Republican senatorial primary and the criticisms Karl Rove, Bush's chief electoral strategist, made of her:

> In Tea Party theory, inexperience is itself seen as a kind of qualification ... People like O'Donnell are actually preferable to people like Rove, because they haven't been tainted by public trust or actual achievement (quoted in Luce 2010, p. 3)[5]

Indeed, the movement often celebrates misfortunes that might in other circumstances damage a candidate's political prospects because they convey authenticity. Arguably, O'Donnell gained political strength from her financial troubles while former Alaska Governor Sarah Palin solidified her backing within core Republican constituencies in 2008 once it became known that her teenage daughter was pregnant. In other words, the gap between the Tea Party movement and Republican Party elites is as much a cultural as well as a political phenomenon.

The Tea Party movement's populism gives its relationship with the Republican Party an ambivalent and ambiguous edge. In particular, there is a tension between criticisms of both the major parties for having allowed the expansion

---

5 Nonetheless, despite the charges that have often been made, Tea Party candidates were not as politically inexperienced as reports have sometimes suggested. Although the movement's candidates were less 'likely to have previously held elected office in more contested races, the differences are smaller than one might think — 48% of non-TP challengers in competitive districts ... versus 33% of TP challengers in competitive districts ... and 53% of non-TP open seat candidates ... versus 43% of TP open seat candidates' (Brendan Nyhan blog 2010).

of government and the bonds of affection that many of the movement's supporters have with Republicanism. If those who define themselves in polling as 'supporters' of the movement are considered, (about 18 per cent of the adult population), a significant minority (40 per cent) believed that a new political party should be formed. About the same proportion (43 per cent) also stated that they had a 'not favorable' opinion of the Republican Party (*The New York Times*/CBS News 2010, pp. 12, 17). Nonetheless, majority opinion opposed the formation of a new party and viewed the Republicans favourably. Furthermore, criticism of President George W. Bush was muted. Some conservative polemicists like Bruce Bartlett, author of *Impostor: How George W. Bush Bankrupted America and Betrayed the Reagan Legacy,* decry the increases in federal government spending, the rising deficit and the institutionalisation of Congressional 'earmarks' during the Bush years. In contrast, just six per cent of Tea Party supporters believe that the Bush administration was 'mostly to blame for most of the current federal budget deficit' compared to 39 per cent in the general population. Moreover, a clear majority (57 per cent) said that they had a favourable impression of Bush (compared with 27 per cent of the general population) (*The New York Times*/CBS News 2010, pp. 16, 21).

What explains the importance of ideas such as these for about 20 per cent of the US population? In part, they are a constant. Suspicion of government and faith in the market have, over a long time frame, secured the committed adherence of somewhere between a fifth and a third of Americans. The American National Election Studies (ANES) has over the years recorded the percentage of respondents agreeing, with different degrees of intensity, with the proposition that 'the government should provide fewer services, even in areas such as health and education, in order to reduce spending' (Table 1).

Alongside this constant, however, there are also variables that brought the ideas held by many Tea Party activists to the fore. The initial framing of the financial crisis in their eyes was important in structuring the evolution of attitudes. In its early stages, the crisis was defined in terms of mortgage delinquencies, defaults and foreclosures. The inability of many homeowners to maintain payments was widely represented by conservatives as individual failure. Government assistance, they believed, would compel those who had maintained their payments to subsidise those who were in default. All of this resonated with Tea Party activists, who regarded redistributive processes with suspicion and feared the moral hazard of collective provision.

Alongside framing, the political visibility of particular issues and events should be considered. The Tea Party movement was able to draw upon the widely shared belief that tax rates had either increased or remained at the same level during President Obama's period of office. The tax concessions enacted as a component of the American Recovery and Reinvestment Act (ARRA)

Table 1: Attitudes towards government services and spending — 'fewer services', 1982–2008 (%)

Year	1982	1990	1994	2000	2004	2008
%	32	22	36	18	20	24

Question text: 'Some people think the government should provide fewer services, even in areas such as health and education, in order to reduce spending. Other people feel that it is important for the government to provide many more services even if it means an increase in spending. Where would you place yourself on this scale, or haven't you thought much about this?' (seven-point scale) Source: adapted from American National Election Studies (2010) 'Government services and spending 1982–2008', The NES Guide to Public Opinion and Electoral Behavior (Ann Arbor: ANES), www.electionstudies.org/nesguide/toptable/tab4a_5.htm (1–3).

in February 2009 reduced income taxes by up to $400 a year for individuals and $800 for married couples. Nonetheless, they had a low level of visibility because they were introduced on a 'drip-feed' basis through wage packets so as to increase the chances that the additional funds reaching households would be spent rather than saved. According to a *New York Times*/CBS News poll taken in September 2010, less than a tenth of respondents knew that there had been tax cuts. Indeed, a third believed that their taxes had increased (Cooper 2010, p. A1).

At the same time, two further points should be considered. Ideas only acquire energy and momentum within particular contexts and, arguably, once an 'Other' has taken shape and been integrated into the narratives from which a movement draws strength and in-group identity. Although, as noted above, many activists had ambivalent attitudes towards the Republican Party and vigorously opposed the 'bailout' of the financial sector in 2008, President Bush and his administration could never serve as an Other. Despite a loss of faith by many conservatives, Bush's personal narrative, the personal ties between many in the Bush White House and the conservative movement, and the ways in which he framed the policies that his administration pursued prevented him playing such a role. It took the election of Barack Obama, together with the re-election of a Democratic Congress, for such an Other to emerge. Such 'Othering' may, in turn, be tied to other sentiments. Some analysts argue that the movement's thinking echoes that of earlier conservative movements insofar as it is structured around fear of generalised social change (a process symbolised by Obama's election victory) and resentment against the provision of federal 'handouts' to those represented as 'undeserving', many of whom are drawn from racial and ethnic minorities (Williamson et al. 2011, p. 26).

Furthermore, while ideas, issues and grievances contribute to the origin and growth of particular social movements, and simultaneously structure and shape their character, they cannot in themselves explain the process. Many of the grievances around which social movements are structured are, as power resource theory asserts, broadly constant in character. One scholar has noted that 'grievances are relatively constant, deriving from structural conflicts of interest built into social institutions ... [M]ovements form because of long-term changes in group resources, organization, and opportunities for collective action' (Jenkins 1983, p. 530). Given this, ideational variables have only limited explanatory value. It is important to consider the interests and constituencies within which particular concerns and grievances are embedded.

Interests and constituencies

The Tea Party movement is disproportionately rooted among whites, men and the older age cohort (see Table 2). It is also tilted towards some higher-income groupings including those with a family income of $100,000 or over.[6] Furthermore, 75 per cent of the movement's supporters were aged at least 45 and 29 per cent were over 64 (*The New York Times*/CBS News 2010, p. 41).[7]

These are constituencies that have either shifted to the right during recent years or have leant towards conservative issue positions and the Republican Party over a sustained period. If race and ethnicity are factored into the 2008 presidential election results, whites aged 65 and older voted for the Republican ticket by 58 to 40 per cent. In 2008, white men backed the Republicans by 57 per cent to 41 per cent. Amongst white evangelicals (those describing themselves as being 'born-again'), 74 per cent supported Senator McCain (CNN.com 2008).

Why do these constituencies and groupings lean towards conservative issue positions? Some institutional factors are significant. The porous character of the taxation system (and the American state more broadly) enables the highest-income groupings and corporate interests to secure substantial particularistic advantages. As John Plender noted in the *Financial Times*, '[T]he fiscal system is riddled with myriad concessions and exemptions won through lobbying and special pleading' (2011, p. 7). Those who are in the upper reaches of the middle class (rather than in higher economic cohorts) generally lack the resources and the ability to engage in significant tax minimisation and are thereby affected

---

6 Furthermore, the movement is not drawn from those who are downwardly mobile or face status anxiety. The proportion of Tea Party supporters who felt that they were '... at risk of falling out of your current social class' barely differed from that in the general population (*The New York Times*/CBS News 2010, p. 36). Indeed, it can be argued that higher income groupings are more likely to organise because the relative costs of mobilisation are lower for those with extensive networks and access to different modes of communication.

7 An acerbic report on a Tea Party rally held in Kentucky in *Rolling Stone* noted: 'Seemingly every third person in the place is sucking oxygen from a tank or propping their giant atrophied glutes on motorized wheelchair-scooters' (Taibbi 2010, p. 49).

Table 2: Tea Party movement supporters and the general population: selected demographic characteristics (April 2010) (%)

	Tea Party	General population
Male	59	49
Female	41	51
18–29	7	23
30–44	16	27
45–64	46	34
Over 64	29	16
White	89	77
Black	1	12
Asian	1	3
Other	6	7
Under $15,000	5	10
$15,000–$29,999	13	22
$30,000–$49,999	17	16
$50,000–$74,999	25	18
$75,000–$100,000	11	12
Over $100,000	20	14
Evangelical/'born again'	39	28

Source: adapted from *The New York Times*/CBS News (2010) National Survey of Tea Party Supporters (New York), 5 April, p.41, http://s3.amazonaws.com/nytdocs/docs/312/312.pdf (refusals to respond have not been included).

by taxation rates to a greater extent than those above them in socioeconomic terms.

Other long-term and short-term variables are also in play. Between the 1950s and the 1980s both men and women moved towards the Republican Party, but the trend among the former was disproportionately large (Kaufmann 2006, p. 447). This appears to have been tied to attitudes towards government provision. As Table 3 (which is based upon ANES polling) suggests, a significantly greater proportion of men moved towards the proposition that 'government should provide fewer services, even in areas such as health and education, in order to reduce spending' (see Table 3).

Table 3: Attitudes towards government spending and services — 'fewer services' (1–3 on a seven-point scale) (%), by gender, 1982–2008 (ANES)

	1982	1984	1986	1988	1990	1992	1994
Males	40	35	29	32	29	32	43
Females	26	23	20	21	17	20	28

	1996	1998	2000	2002	2004	2008
Males	37	32	26	**	25	26
Females	26	21	13	**	15	21

Question text and source: as for Table 1, www.electionstudies.org/nesguide/2ndtable/t4a_5_1.htm.

Karen Kaufmann concludes that there is a particularly close relationship between conservative attitudes towards social welfare issues and Republican identification: 'opinion regarding the desirable level of government services and prospects for government-provided health insurance and jobs are the most robust predictors of male party identification' (2002, p. 295). Kaufmann's findings can be applied to the unfolding economic crisis in 2008–09. Once the initial shock had subsided, the policies pursued by both the Bush and Obama administrations brought 'social welfare' issues, on which many white men hold highly conservative attitudes, to the forefront of political discourse. With each successive step — the 'bailout' of the banks, support for the automobile industry, the passage of the ARRA and, at a later stage, health care reform — the federal government seemed to assume greater powers. The spiralling projections for the national debt symbolised government profligacy.

Seniors, another constituent grouping within which the Tea Party movement is embedded, also had pronounced fears about government interventionism. In part, this may be a long-term process. The Republican share of the vote amongst those aged 65 or more rose from 47 per cent in 2000 to 52 per cent in 2004 to 53 per cent in 2008.[8] Indeed, seniors were one of the very few demographic groupings to swing from the Democrats to the Republicans between 2004 and 2008 (Observationalism n.d.).

Once President Obama assumed the presidency, this long-term shift appears to have been compounded by concerns about the Democrats' proposals for health care reform. Polling data suggest that for many seniors, it seemed that government authority would intrude into their lives and at the same time the health care provision offered to seniors through Medicare would be diluted

---

[8] The figure for 1996 was 48 per cent, although this was a race in which a minor party candidate (Ross Perot) made a significant electoral impact.

through the extension of coverage to other groupings. A Kaiser Family Foundation tracking poll reported in July 2010 that 50 per cent of seniors believed that reform would reduce Medicare benefits and 36 per cent said it would 'allow a government panel to make decisions about end-of-life care for people on Medicare' (Kaiser Family Foundation 2010). Some have suggested that fears health care would be extended to those regarded as less deserving are pivotal:

> The harsh reality is many voters consider the health care bill a multibillion-dollar transfer of taxpayer money to the uninsured, a population disproportionately, although by no means exclusively, made up of the poor, African Americans, Latinos, single parents, and the long-term unemployed (Edsall 2010).[9]

John Judis suggests that the Republicans' victory in the January 2010 US Senate special election in Massachusetts was a consequence of these sentiments. He cites a pre-election poll indicating that senior citizens aged 65 to 74 'opposed national health insurance by 48 per cent to 28 per cent and thought the federal government couldn't afford such a plan by 66 per cent to 33 per cent'. They backed Scott Brown, the Republican candidate, by 58 to 38 per cent (Judis 2010).

A further constituency should be considered. Although the Tea Party movement draws upon disproportionate numbers of white men in the older age-cohorts, it is also rooted in independent or 'freewheeling' conservatives, whom Jonathan Rauch termed 'debranded Republicans'. In his assessment, there has been a growth in the proportion of conservatives in the electorate and a corresponding fall in the proportion of self-defined moderates. At the same time, however, he notes that Republican partisanship has remained stagnant at about a quarter of the electorate. In other words, there are, as he emphasises, significant numbers of conservatives who either do not identify as Republicans or define themselves as Republican 'leaners' rather than giving more committed forms of support (2010).

Such 'debranded Republicans' appear to constitute the backbone of the Tea Party movement. The poll run by *The New York Times*/CBS News found that although almost three quarters of the movement's supporters define themselves as conservative, their loyalty to the Republican Party is less than solid or secure. Although over half (54 per cent) identify as Republicans, only 18 per cent state that they always vote Republican and 36 per cent

---

9   Some see support for assertions such as this in the conclusions drawn by Robert Putnam in a 2007 paper. In this, Putnam suggests that social and cultural differences provoke anxiety and distrust. In other words, the process of long-term demographic change and increasing multiculturalism is leading individuals and groups, in Putnam's phrase, to 'hunker down' (Putnam 2007, p. 37).

define themselves as independents (*The New York Times*/CBS News 2010, pp. 35, 40).

Institutional arrangements

Ideas and constituencies only come to the fore within particular institutional contexts. As Say's Law (or at least Keynes's interpretation of it) suggests, supply brings forth its own demand. In other words, particular forms of institutional architecture or 'supply' offer opportunities, facilitate collective action and invite initiatives by political actors.

There is much in the institutional structures of the US political process that enhance access to a far greater degree than is the case in many European political systems. The multiplicity of 'entry points' not only allows but promotes campaigning and lobbying by interest groups and movements. The structural weaknesses of the principal parties, particularly in terms of their organisational structures at state, local and precinct levels, have created a vacuum that groups and movements can fill. The gap between 'Beltway' politics in Washington DC and the country at large has grown as the powers of the federal government have expanded, thereby fuelling the passions of those seeking to curb 'big government'. Alongside this, as Lawrence Jacobs and Desmond King argue, the limited capacity of the American state has brought disappointment and resentment to those who place their faith in the rallying cries of particular election candidates or incumbent office-holders (2009, pp. 6–7).

Furthermore, the primary process, which was established to rein in the powers of party 'bosses', offers opportunities for mass participation and allows 'outsiders' as well as 'insiders' to seek public office at both federal and state level. At the same time, the advent of new technology, social networking sites and highly partisan forms of broadcasting have changed the opportunity-cost ratios associated with participation as well as campaigning and mobilisation processes, thereby opening up possibilities for organisations with initially limited resources.

During the 2010 primary season, when the nominees for the congressional elections were chosen, the Tea Party movement took advantage of these openings and mounted frontal assaults on some incumbents and other candidates with long-established political credentials. At Senate level, Tea Party candidates defeated more mainstream contenders in Kentucky, Alaska, Nevada, Wisconsin, Colorado, Utah, Pennsylvania, Florida and Delaware (where Christine O'Donnell defeated Mike Castle, a relative moderate and a former state governor). The evidence suggests that the movement drew many into the primary process who were relatively new to party politics. Indeed, in 2010 four million more people voted in Republican primaries than the Democratic primaries. In every other election since 1930, more had participated in the Democrats' nominating process (Will 2010, p. A23).

Nevertheless, the emergence of the Tea Party was not a simple case of popular mobilisation. Although it benefited from the institutional openings offered by the US party and electoral systems, there are always processes of contestation. To use the terms and concepts developed by Wolfgang Streeck and Kathleen Thelen, 'Rule takers do not just implement the rules made for them, but also try to revise them in the process of implementation, making use of their inherent openness and under-definition' (2010, p. 15). Indeed, structures and rules can be regarded as an invitation to struggle. There is, as James Mahoney and Thelen assert, 'a degree of openness in the interpretation and implementation of these rules. Even when institutions are formally codified, their guiding expectations often remain ambiguous and always are subject to interpretation, debate, and contestation' (2010, pp. 10–11).

That process of contestation is evident if the Tea Party movement's relationship with the Republican 'establishment', comprising the interlocking party elites tied to the Republican National Committee (RNC), the National Republican Senatorial Committee (NRSC), the National Republican Congressional Committee (NRCC) and state, local and precinct organisations. Although much can be made of the Tea Party movement's successes, the GOP 'establishment' sought to curtail the inroads that it made. Although the elites that collectively constitute the 'establishment' share much of the movement's hostility to the Obama administration, they are also compelled by electoral considerations to accommodate and include, at least in presidential and many senatorial contests, different and diverse geographical and demographic constituencies.

The attitudes of Republican elites have therefore been more accommodative and nuanced than those of many grassroots activists. A February 2010 survey of 75 party leaders (current and former members of Congress, former Cabinet officials, state elected officials, county party chairmen and other senior officials) provides some further evidence of a gap between elites and mass within Republican ranks. A clear majority (57 per cent) of party leaders wanted to see more moderates in Congress so as to create a larger but more ideologically diverse Republican caucus. Just 12 per cent hoped that Sarah Palin would be the party's 2012 presidential candidate whereas 31 per cent backed former Massachusetts governor Mitt Romney (*Esquire* 2010). In contrast, Romney is regarded with considerable suspicion by many Tea Party supporters.

The distance between the movement and the Republican 'establishment' is evident in other ways. During George W. Bush's presidency, congressional Republicans repeatedly endorsed the increases in federal expenditure that the White House proposed. And, although there was a rebellion against the $700 billion 'bank bailout' and the creation of TARP, it was backed by the party's leadership on Capitol Hill. According to John Boehner (Ohio), then the House Minority Leader, 'These are the votes that separate the men from the boys and the girls from the women' (Viser 2010, p. A1).

The process of contestation between party elites and Tea Party activists took different forms. Party rules were a particular battleground because these, for the most part, deterred challenges to incumbents. For example, some states require the payment of sizeable fees and impose filing requirements. According to Nathan Mitchell and Nelson Dometrius, 'structural barriers to competition can have real consequences for who decides to run for political office', and states with particularly high requirements 'tend to see high degrees of uncontested seats at the Congressional level' (2009). The rules of others were open to contestation and exploitation by Tea Party activists. Under Utah law, candidates must receive 35 per cent at the party's state convention if their name is to be placed on the primary ballot (Ballot Access News 2008). Tea Party supporters organised at the state's Republican caucuses and the subsequent party convention so as to prevent the incumbent, Senator Bob Bennett, contesting the primary.

Alongside formal rules and arrangements, there were other battlegrounds. Firstly, state party endorsements for primary candidates can be pivotal. In Wisconsin, for example, the state party provoked discontent by backing candidates for both governor and US senator about whom Tea Party activists had profound misgivings. Those pre-primary endorsements provided staffing along with state and national voter lists (Vogel 2011). Secondly, there was a process of contestation around finance. Party elites, particularly the NRSC, the NRCC and the state parties can draw upon large-scale financial resources. In Wisconsin, the state party's pre-primary endorsements also allowed the channelling of funds to preferred candidates. 'Establishment' 527s such as American Crossroads (set up by Karl Rove and Ed Gillespie, former top-level senior advisers in the Bush White House) and the American Action Network (founded by former Senator Norm Coleman of Minnesota and Douglas Holtz-Eakin, a policy adviser to Senator John McCain's 2008 presidential campaign) also used their resources strategically.

The process of contestation led political actors to adopt different approaches and tactics at different times. There were moments, particularly in the run-up to the Republican senatorial primary in Delaware, when the tensions took a highly visible form. In comments that attracted widespread attention, Karl Rove, President George W. Bush's principal electoral strategist, called some of Christine O'Donnell's past statements 'nutty' and suggested very publicly that the selection of Tea Party-backed candidates such as O'Donnell had frustrated hopes of the party winning back the Senate in the November midterm elections. There were also clashes at meetings of the Republican National Committee. As *Politico* reported, calls for Republican candidates to commit themselves to Tea Party demands for limited government, and for the party organisations to deny funding and backing to those who did not do so, were easily defeated. Indeed, at the beginning of February 2010, state party chairmen unanimously passed a resolution expressing their opposition to such an idea. The defeat of a proposed 'purity test' for candidates in the Republican National Committee meeting confirmed that party officials 'are no more willing to turn over the keys to right-wing activists now than they were during the Bush years' (Martin 2010).

At other times, however, there was greater accommodation of the Tea Party. In Wisconsin, the state party may have thrown its weight behind preferred candidates through pre-primary endorsements, but it reportedly assisted movement activists in organising protests at the state capitol in Madison (Vogel 2011). Furthermore, as the November 2010 midterm elections approached, 'establishment' 527s donated significant sums to Tea Party-backed Republican candidates. Crossroads GPS spent $2,253,258 in its efforts to unseat Senate Majority Harry Reid in Nevada, thereby aiding Sharon Angle's campaign (OpenSecrets.org 2010).

The Tea Party movement and the 2010 midterm elections

As the November 2010 elections approached, the political culture that defined the movement (in particular, the populist representations of the disenfranchised outsider) increasingly informed and structured the forms of discourse adopted by the Republican leadership. In September 2010, the House Republicans issued the *Pledge to America*, a platform modelled on the 1994 *Contract with America*. Although it incorporated a commitment to honour 'traditional marriage' and 'life', it emphasised the economic and constitutional issues promoted by the Tea Party movement. These included calls to stop 'job-killing tax hikes', repeal health care reform, establish 'strict budget caps' (although there were assurances regarding defence expenditure) and provide specific constitutional authority for all legislation (GOP.gov 2010). Instead of being announced in Washington DC, the *Pledge to America* was unveiled at a news conference held at a hardware store and lumber yard in Sterling, Virginia.

Although the movement shaped some of the cultural forms and the modes of discourse that were adopted by the Republican 'establishment', its impact on the Republican primaries and the November contest was more limited than the scope and scale of press commentaries might suggest. The process of contestation between Tea Party activists and the party elites showed the weaknesses of the movement and the scale of the resources upon which elites could draw. Indeed, as the 2010 primary season progressed, the movement's impact became more limited. Despite the political noise that the Tea Party created and the success of some of its candidates in securing the Republican nomination, notably in states such as Delaware and Nevada, relatively few incumbent members of Congress faced a significant challenge. The revolt against Bob Bennett in Utah has already been noted. Alaska Senator Lisa Murkowski failed to secure re-nomination in the state primary but then stood successfully as a write-in candidate. Of the 12 incumbent Republican senators who sought re-election, however, ten won their primaries or were unopposed (The Green Papers 2010).

Having made only limited inroads during the primaries, the Tea Party's impact on the November elections was necessarily restricted. *The New York Times*' estimates suggest that the overwhelming majority of its 129 candidates seeking election to the House of Representatives were running in districts that were solidly Democratic (67) or were leaning towards the Democrats (29). Only seven Tea Party candidates ran in solidly Republican Congressional districts (see Table 4).

Table 4: Estimates of Tea Party/Republican candidates and the character of districts/states, November 2010

	House	Senate
All races	129	9
Solid Democratic	67	0
Leaning Democratic	29	1
Toss-up	19	4
Leaning Republican	7	3
Solid Republican	7	1

Source: adapted from *The New York Times* (2010) 'Where the Tea Party candidates are running', 14 Oct., www.nytimes.com/interactive/2010/10/15/us/politics/tea-party-graphic.html?ref=politics.

The results in the seats that were winnable, or potentially winnable for the Republicans where Tea Party candidates were standing, had a mixed character. Although Rand Paul, Pat Toomey and Marco Rubio won their Senate races in Kentucky, Pennsylvania and Florida respectively, there were also noteworthy losses. Christine O'Donnell's defeat in Delaware had been predicted. Much of the American right had expected, however, that Ken Buck would take Colorado and Sharron Angle would topple Senate Majority Leader Harry Reid in Nevada. These defeats cost the Republicans their majority in the Senate.

Consequences

What should be said about the long-term impact of the Tea Party movement? Firstly, the emergence and growth of the movement compounded a shift in issue priorities and a change in the character of the American right that had begun with the financial crisis and the recession. Although, as has been noted, many activists had ties or at least an affinity with the Christian right, the cultural issues which defined religious conservatism were relegated to a lower place on the political agenda as the Tea Party movement's demands for limited government and its focus on economic policy came to the fore. There was a consequent shift in the balance of power within the Republican Party as the Tea Party movement displaced the Christian right and secured the ability to act as 'kingmaker' in Congressional and presidential nominating contests. As Tiffany Stanley has noted:

> Who can blame the Christian Right for needing a little reassurance that it isn't obsolete? Tea Party activists are the new go-to agitators of the conservative base. The 2004 election, when 'values voters' helped push George W. Bush to victory, and the 1994 Republican revolution, when Newt Gingrich and Dick Armey, bolstered by the Christian Coalition, ushered in the first GOP-controlled Congress in over 40 years, seem like distant memories (2010).

Secondly, the movement has created space for a new generation of political entrepreneurs who can draw upon its resources (both human and financial capital) to advance themselves within the Republican orbit. Senator Jim DeMint of South Carolina, Glenn Beck of Fox News, Congresswoman Michele Bachmann (of Minnesota's Sixth District) and former Alaska Governor Sarah Palin are amongst the most commonly cited names. However, in the straw poll organised at the Virginia Tea Party Patriots Convention in October 2010, the winner (albeit in a vote spread between a large number of candidates) was Governor Chris Christie of New Jersey. For the most part, such entrepreneurs have sought to maintain relations with the Tea Party movement and the Republican leadership. As Jonathan Bernstein suggests, '[T]he trick is to be as far to the right as possible without actually sounding crazy to those outside the faction (and thus perhaps drawing vetoes from more pragmatic conservatives, and possibly some GOP-aligned interest groups)' (2010). In the wake of the midterm elections and the defeat of the movement's most prominent Senate candidates, the degree of space for those who can to some extent identify with the movement, but at the same time remain tied to mainstream Republicanism, will almost certainly grow.

Prospects

The early history of the 112th Congress offered testimony to the Tea Party's political strengths. Although some legislators who were aligned with the movement sought to go further than John Boehner, the new Speaker of the House of Representatives, the House Republican Conference repeatedly stood its ground against the White House. The prospect of a federal government shutdown loomed in April 2011 and was only averted hours ahead of the deadline through a formula that initially seemed to promise budget cuts of $38.5 billion in addition to the $10 billion that had already been agreed. There was a further crisis just over three months later when Congressional Republicans successfully demanded that the increase in the federal government debt ceiling sought by the administration be tied to further expenditure cuts. There was also evidence of the Tea Party inroads among grassroots Republicans as movement supporters rallied around Texas Governor Rick Perry during the intra-Republican debates that preceded the 2012 presidential nominating season.[10]

Nonetheless, the Tea Party may in the longer term have a relatively limited life expectancy, at least in its present form. Fragmented and decentralised movements rarely have long histories.[11] Insofar as generalisations can be made, public opinion may be broadly sympathetic to the movement's proclaimed goals, but in the wake of the 2011 federal government debt-ceiling crisis, there was significantly less backing for the movement itself. A *New York Times* poll taken at the beginning of August 2011 suggested that the movement was regarded unfavourably by 40 per cent of respondents and favourably by just 20 per cent. Meanwhile 82 per cent of the sample said they disapproved of the way Congress was handling its job, the highest figure since this particular survey first began asking the question in 1977 (Cooper and Thee-Brenan 2011). Furthermore, despite the attention that the movement has garnered, and the ways in which it compelled some Republican figures, most notably Senator John McCain, to shift rightwards, there are other constituencies within the Republican orbit that may limit and constrain the further advances that it may seek to make. The ways in which party elites checked the movement's advances have already been noted.

---

10 On the other hand, some movement activists, particularly those in Texas, had doubts about Perry's Tea Party credentials (Adler 2011).

11 Resource mobilisation theory generally suggests that decentralised movements are at a disadvantage when compared with those that have a more centralised character. According to one analyst, 'centralized, formally structured movement organizations are more typical of modern social movements and more effective at mobilizing resources and mounting sustained challenges than decentralized, informal movement structures' (Jenkins 1983, p. 528).

Amongst the different Republican constituencies, business interests may also play a role in curbing the Tea Party, even though at times they appeared to have interconnections and overlaps with the movement. There was cautious corporate backing for ARRA at the beginning of 2009, but this gave way to a suspicion that the Obama administration was business-unfriendly. There were, in particular, fears that health care reform would add significantly to employer costs. Corporate interests and peak business organisations, such as the US Chamber of Commerce, rallied to the Republicans as the 2010 elections approached. Nonetheless, there are significant ideological cleavages between business and the Tea Party. Some movement activists have sought policies that provoked concern among corporate interests. They have called, for example, for the removal of illegal immigrants, the imposition of restrictions on legal as well as illegal immigration and the abolition of the Federal Reserve. Others have urged the adoption of protectionist measures and fears of world government have led them to regard organisations such as the G-20 with suspicion. There have been attacks on 'corporate welfare', including farm subsidies and aid for overseas business. According to Lisa Lerer and John McCormick, 'The Tea Party's brand of political nitroglycerin, in short, is too unstable for businesses that look to government for predictability, moderation, and the creation of a stable economic environment' (2010). Significantly, US Chamber of Commerce funding during much of the 2010 election cycle was channelled to candidates such as Carly Fiorina in California and Rob Portman in Ohio (former US Trade representative and Director of Bush's Office of Management and Budget), while its first endorsement was for Senator John McCain's re-election bid in Arizona.

Should the Tea Party survive as a movement, activists face dilemmas. There are likely to be strains if legislators seek to implement the austerity measures that flow from a commitment to more limited forms of government. As has been noted, the movement draws disproportionately upon the older age cohorts who benefit to a greater degree than many other groups from government social provision. Indeed, polling already suggests that, although there is strong support for deficit reduction, there is also an ambivalence rather than hostility towards the principal government programmes for senior citizens. A large majority (62 per cent) of Tea Party supporters surveyed in *The New York Times/CBS News* poll felt that Social Security and Medicare were worth the cost to taxpayers (2010, p. 26).

Conclusion

The chapter has argued that studies of the Tea Party movement should go beyond ideational variables and also consider the constituencies from which it draws (which lean disproportionately towards white men in the older age cohorts, many of whom can be considered independent or 'freewheeling' conservatives) and the institutional arrangements and rules that govern both the Republican Party and electoral processes. These have a Janus-like character. They incite collective mobilisation at grassroots level (through, for example, the primary process) but at the same time incorporate structures and relationships that allow elite interests to maintain and sometimes bolster their position.

The political friction that such institutional arrangements create contributes to the formation and growth of movements on the edges of the formal party system and thereby compounds broader problems of governance. Prior to the emergence of the Tea Party movement, it laid a basis for networks and organisations such as the 'new right', the Moral Majority, the Christian Coalition and militia groupings. Whatever the short-term future of the Tea Party movement, independent conservatives are likely to remain a significant and potent constituency. Within the institutional contexts that shape US political processes, their anxieties will almost certainly give rise to further movements and protests on the edges of those processes and the party system.

References

B. Adler (2011) 'The nation: is Rick Perry the Tea Party favorite?', National Public Radio, 7 Sept., www.npr.org/2011/09/07/140244748/the-nation-is-rick-perry-the-tea-party-favorite/.

American National Election Studies (2010) *The ANES Guide to Public Opinion and Electoral Behavior — Liberal-Conservative Self-Identification 1972–2008* (Ann Arbor, MI: American National Election Studies), www.electionstudies.org/nesguide/toptable/tab3_1.htm.

Ballot Access News (2010) 'Senator Bennett barred from Utah Republican primary', Ballot Access News, www.ballot-access.org/2010/05/08/senator-bennett-barred-from-utah-republican-primary/.

J. Bernstein (2010) 'Two types of candidates who could challenge Sarah Palin in 2012', *New Republic*, 28 Sept., www.tnr.com/blog/jonathan-cohn/78020/two-types-candidates-who-could-challenge-sarah-palin-in-2012/.

Brendan Nyhan blog (2010) *How much are Tea Party candidates hurting the GOP?*, www.brendan-nyhan.com/blog/2010/10/did-the-tea-party-weaken-gop-candidate-quality.html.

D. Brooks (2010) 'The Tea Party teens', *The New York Times*, 4 Jan., www.nytimes.com/2010/01/05/opinion/05brooks.html.

CBS News (2010) '"Pledge to America" unveiled by Republicans', 22 Sept., www.cbsnews.com/8301-503544_162-20017335-503544.html.

CNN.com (2008) *Election Center 2008 — Exit Polls*, http://edition.cnn.com/ELECTION/2008/results/polls/#USP00p1/.

M. Continetti (2010) 'The two faces of the Tea Party', *The Weekly Standard*, 28 June, www.weeklystandard.com/articles/two-faces-tea-party/.

M. Cooper (2010) 'From Obama, the tax cut nobody heard of', *The New York Times*, 19 Oct., pp. A1, A18.

M. Cooper and M. Thee-Brenan (2011) 'Disapproval rate for Congress at record 82% after debt talks', *The New York Times*, 4 August, www.nytimes.com/2011/08/05/us/politics/05poll.html?ref=us/.

T.B. Edsall (2010) 'Ghost story', *New Republic*, 20 Jan., www.tnr.com/article/politics/he-doesnt-feel-your-pain/.

M. Edwards (2010) 'Don't blame the Tea Party', *The Atlantic*, 25 Oct., www.theatlantic.com/politics/archive/2010/10/dont-blame-the-tea-party/65106/.

Esquire (2010) 'The *Esquire* survey of America's Republican elite', 11 Feb., www.esquire.com/features/republican-party-survey-0310/.

A. Gardner (2010) 'Gauging the scope of the tea party movement in America', *Washington Post*, 24 Oct., www.washingtonpost.com/wp-dyn/content/article/2010/10/23/AR2010102304000.html?hpid=topnews/.

GOP.gov (2010) *A Pledge to America: The 2010 Republican Agenda* (Washington DC: House Republican Conference, http://pledge.gop.gov).

J.C. Jenkins (1983) 'Resource mobilization theory and the study of social movements', *Annual Review of Sociology* 9, pp. 527–53.

R.P. Jones and D. Cox (2010) *Old Alignments, Emerging Fault Lines: Religion in the 2010 Election and Beyond*, Findings from the 2010 Post-Election American Values Survey, http://publicreligion.org/site/wp-content/uploads/2011/06/2010-Post-election-American-Values-Survey-Report.pdf.

J.B. Judis (2010) 'Does he feel your pain?', *The New Republic*, 20 Jan., www.tnr.com/article/politics/he-doesnt-feel-your-pain/.

Kaiser Family Foundation (2010) *Kaiser Health Tracking Poll — July 2010* (Menlo Park: Kaiser Family Foundation), www.kff.org/kaiserpolls/8084.cfm.

K. M. Kaufmann (2002) 'Culture wars, secular realignment, and the gender gap in party identification', *Political Behavior* 24 (Sept.), pp. 283–307.

— (2006) 'The gender gap', *PS: Political Science & Politics* 39 (July), pp. 447–53.

L. Jacobs and D. King (eds.) (2009) *The Unsustainable American State* (Oxford: Oxford University Press).

L. Lerer and J. McCormick (2010) 'The devil you don't know', *Bloomberg Businessweek*, Oct. 18–24, pp. 66–74.

E. Luce (2010) 'Tea Party draws on tradition of activism', *Financial Times*, Sept. 18–19.

J. Mahoney and K. Thelen (eds.) (2010) *Explaining Institutional Change: Ambiguity, Agency and Power* (Cambridge: Cambridge University Press).

J. Martin (2010) 'Tea leaves: Republican establishment still rules', *Politico*, 3 Feb., www.politico.com/news/stories/0210/32502.html.

J. Mayer (2010) 'Covert operations: the billionaire brothers who are waging a war against Obama', *The New Yorker*, 30 Aug., www.newyorker.com/reporting/2010/08/30/100830fa_fact_mayer/.

N.K. Mitchell and N.C. Dometrius (2008) 'Ballot access rules and candidate entry into state legislative primaries', paper presented at the Southern Political Science Association's annual meeting, http://citation.allacademic.com/meta/p_mla_apa_research_citation/2/0/8/5/6/p208569_index.html.

M. Murray (2009) 'Tea party attendance: 268,000-plus?', *NBC News - First Read*, 16 April, http://firstread.msnbc.msn.com/_news/2009/04/16/4426422-tea-party-attendance-268000-plus/.

Observationalism (not dated) 'Selected exit poll comparisons, 2000-2004-2008', http://observationalism.com/2008/11/09/selected-exit-poll-comparisons-2000-2004-2008/.

OpenSecrets.org (2010) Crossroads Grassroots Policy Strategies, www.opensecrets.org/outsidespending/detail.php?cmte=Crossroads+Grassroots+Policy+Strategies/.

J. Plender (2011) 'Discount the revolting rich at your peril', *Financial Times*, 9 Sept., www.ft.com.

R. Putnam (2007) '*E pluribus unum*: diversity and community in the twenty-first century', *Scandinavian Political Studies* 30 (2), pp.137–74.

J. Rauch (2010) 'The Tea Party paradox', *National Journal*, 31 July, http://services.nationaljournal.com/njmagazine/cs_20100731_1026.php.

T. Stanley (2010) 'Will the Tea Parties revive the Christian right?' *New Republic*, 20 Sept., www.tnr.com/blog/jonathan-cohn/77824/will-the-tea-parties-revive-the-christian-right/.

W. Streeck and K. Thelen (2010) *Beyond Continuity: Institutional Change in Advanced Political Economies* (Oxford: Oxford University Press).

M. Taibbi (2010) 'Tea and crackers', *Rolling Stone* 1115, 14 Oct., pp. 49–55.

Tea Party Patriots (2010), www.teapartypatriots.org/about/.

The Green Papers (2010) '2010 senatorial primaries at a glance', www.thegreenpapers.com/G10/spaag.phtml.

The New York Times/CBS News (2010) *National Survey of Tea Party Supporters*, 5–12 April, http://s3.amazonaws.com/nytdocs/docs/312/312.pdf.

The Tea Party Federation (2010), www.thenationalteapartyfederation.com (home page).

M. Viser (2010) 'Defense and denunciation of TARP', *Boston Globe*, 18 Oct.

K.P. Vogel (2011) 'Reince Priebus's tea party tightrope', *Politico*, 17 Jan., www.politico.com/news/stories/0111/47676.html.

G.F. Will (2010) 'A historic shift in the making?', *Washington Post*, 14 Oct., p. A23.

V. Williamson, T. Skocpol and J. Coggin (2011) 'The Tea Party and the remaking of Republican conservatism', *Perspectives on Politics* 9 (1), pp. 25–43.

K. Zernike (2010) 'Tea Party avoids divisive social issues', *The New York Times*, 12 March, www.nytimes.com/2010/03/13/us/politics/13tea.html.

K. Zernike and M. Thee-Brenan (2010) 'Poll finds Tea Party backers wealthier and more educated', *The New York Times*, 14 April, www.nytimes.com/2010/04/15/us/politics/15poll.html.

INSTITUTE FOR THE STUDY OF THE AMERICAS

UNIVERSITY OF LONDON · SCHOOL OF ADVANCED STUDY

The Institute for the Study of the Americas (ISA) promotes, coordinates and provides a focus for research and postgraduate teaching on the Americas – Canada, the USA, Latin America and the Caribbean – in the University of London.

The Institute was officially established in August 2004 as a result of a merger between the Institute of Latin American Studies and the Institute of United States Studies, both of which were formed in 1965.

The Institute publishes in the disciplines of history, politics, economics, sociology, anthropology, geography and environment, development, culture and literature, and on the countries and regions of Latin America, the United States, Canada and the Caribbean.

ISA runs an active programme of events – conferences, seminars, lectures and workshops – in order to facilitate national research on the Americas in the humanities and social sciences. It also offers a range of taught master's and research degrees, allowing wide-ranging multi-disciplinary, multi-country study or a focus on disciplines such as politics or globalisation and development for specific countries or regions.

Full details about the Institute's publications, events, postgraduate courses and other activities are available on the web at www.americas.sas.ac.uk.

Institute for the Study of the Americas
School of Advanced Study, University of London
Senate House, Malet Street, London WC1E 7HU

Tel 020 7862 8870, Fax 020 7862 8886, Email americas@sas.ac.uk
Web www.americas.sas.ac.uk

Recent and forthcoming titles in the ISA series:

Joaquim Nabuco, British Abolitionists and the End of Slavery in Brazil: Correspondence 1880–1905 (2009)
edited with an introduction by Leslie Bethell & José Murilo de Carvalho

Contesting Clio's Craft: New Directions and Debates in Canadian History (2009)
edited by Christopher Dummitt & Michael Dawson

World Crisis Effects on Social Security in Latin America and the Caribbean: Lessons and Policies (2010)
Carmelo Meso-Lago

Caamaño in London: The Exile of a Latin American Revolutionary (2010)
edited by Fred Halliday

Evo Morales and the Moviemento Al Socialismo in Bolivia. The First Term in Context, 2006–2010 (2011)
edited by Adrian J. Pearce

Fractured Politics. Peruvian Democracy Past and Present (2011)
edited by John Crabtree

Organized Labour and Politics in Mexico: Changes, Continuities and Contradictions (2012)
Graciela Bensusán & Kevin J. Middlebrook

Traslados/Translations: Essays on Latin America in Honour of Jason Wilson (2012)
edited by Claire Lindsay

Democracy in Mexico: Attitudes and Perceptions of Citizens at National and Local Level (forthcoming 2012)
edited by Salvador Martí i Puig, Reynaldo Yunuen Ortega Ortiz & Mª Fernanda Somuano Ventura